POLICING DIGITAL CRIME

Policing Digital Crime

Edited by

ROBIN BRYANT
Canterbury Christ Church University, UK

SARAH BRYANT

Routledge
Taylor & Francis Group

LONDON AND NEW YORK

First published 2014 by Ashgate Publishing

Published 2016 by Routledge
2 Park Square, Milton Park, Abingdon, Oxfordshire OX14 4RN
711 Third Avenue, New York, NY 10017, USA

First issued in paperback 2016

Routledge is an imprint of the Taylor & Francis Group, an informa business

British Library Cataloguing in Publication Data
A catalogue record for this book is available from the British Library

The Library of Congress has cataloged the printed edition as follows:
Policing digital crime / [edited by] by Robin Bryant and Sarah Bryant.
      pages cm
   Includes bibliographical references and index.
   ISBN 978-1-4094-2343-0 (hardback : alk. paper)
1. Computer crimes. 2. Computer crimes—Prevention. 3. Computer crimes—Investigation.
4. Computer crimes—Case studies. 5. Computer crimes—Prevention—Case studies.
6. Computer crimes—Investigation—Case studies.
I. Bryant, Robin, 1958– II. Bryant, Sarah, 1959–
   HV6773.P647 2014
   363.25'968—dc23

2013020848

ISBN 13: 978-1-138-25744-3 (pbk)
ISBN 13: 978-1-4094-2343-0 (hbk)

Contents

Contents

List of Figures

List of Tables

Notes on Contributors

David Bennett

Dr David J. Bennett is a Senior Lecturer at Canterbury Christ Church University. He has taught aspects of cryptography on postgraduate degrees to serving law enforcement officers and undergraduate programmes to students of Computing, Forensic Computing and Forensics. His interests in the field of policing digital crime are in human aspects of forensic tools.

Robin Bryant

Professor Robin Bryant is the Department Director of Research and Knowledge Exchange at Canterbury Christ Church University. He has published widely in the fields of policing, criminal investigation and digital crime. Robin is also a Special Advisor to the Board of the European Cybercrime Training and Education Group (ECTEG) convened and hosted by Europol. ECTEG is responsible for implementing a European-wide programme of training in digital crime investigation.

Sarah Bryant

Sarah Bryant specialises in editing technical, academic material for a wider readership. Her background is in science education and the development of learning material for adults.

Ed Day

Ed Day is a Senior Lecturer in Forensic Investigation at Canterbury Christ Church University. He specialises in computer forensics and mathematical methods and is currently involved in research to implement grid computing for mobile device investigation.

Ian Kennedy

Ian Kennedy is practicing Digital Forensic Investigator with over a decade of experience investigating fraud, paedophilia, malware, murder, theft and other crimes all involving digital devices. Ian has received extensive training from the Royal Military College, Guidance Software Incorporated, the National Police Improvement Agency, AccessData and BlackBag amongst others. Initially a C++ programmer, Ian is a Chartered Engineer (CEng), a member of the British Computer Society (MBCS), and a Chartered Information Technology Professional (CITP). He is also lectures on a number of MSc Forensics courses and is an Associate Lecturer for the Open University on their post-graduate Computer Forensics course. Ian is currently undertaking his PhD in malware analysis.

Paul Stephens

Dr Paul Stephens is a Principal Lecturer and the Programme Director for the BSc (Hons) Forensic Computing at Canterbury Christ Church University. He has worked with, and taught, police officers across Europe, including representatives from Interpol, Europol, and the UN ODC.

Foreword

Nicola Dileone

Cybercrime National Expert, CEPOL, the European Police College

We live in a digital world where the boundaries between our physical and our virtual identities are becoming increasingly blurred. Many of us have become completely accustomed to making payments using computer networks and associated technologies, and to using social media for keeping in contact with our friends and families. And compare the ways we went about meeting new people in pre-digital times with how we can now do so via the internet – we can search for a new partner using 'profiling' on online dating sites, and before meeting up we can even (if we so choose!) scour the internet for information on our prospective date, using social networks and open source information available to anyone.

The evolution in digital technology and systems has been particularly rapid over the past ten years, especially with the advent of new communication protocols and the increasing use of mobile devices. We embrace this new technology without a second thought, and eagerly look forward to yet more streamlined and interconnected systems – the fruits of new technological developments. Digital systems allow us to reach out and communicate on a global scale, to ask questions and find answers, or maybe just exchange a few ideas with other people all around the world who happen to share our particular interests.

At the same time however we must be mindful that the vast freedom provided by this new digital world imposes new responsibilities on us. We need to keep our new digital domains secure, and protect ourselves and our fellow citizens from criminality. After all, as human beings, we each employ technology for our own chosen ends, so age-old human behaviours (both the good and bad) are often transposed onto the digital networks. However, many people are unaware of the reality of the darker side of the internet. We are of course shocked and upset when we hear about a bomb attack, particularly if people are injured or killed, and our reaction to such an event is immediate because of the tangibility of the crime. But for cybercrime our reaction is different because it does not come to our attention until we are affected by the consequences, for instance our bank account being hacked into, or our children being targeted by cyber-bullies. In this sense it is unfortunate that the evolution of digital technologies has been so rapid, because the regulations and our ideas about what constitutes anti-social behaviour have simply been unable to keep pace. Some parts of the internet are still subject to very little regulation, and in this regard there is still much to be done. We need to develop new strategies for policing the cyber-world, with respect to data retention and protection, users' privacy, and crime prevention and detection. Adequate regulations must be put in place because the digital world will undoubtedly continue to develop in a myriad of ways, including the unexpected. Digital technological and industrial R&D will continue apace, and it is simply neither possible nor desirable to try to prevent people from using new technologies. However, the down-side to this is the absolute certainty that some (if not many) people will find ways of using these bright new technologies for illicit and undesirable purposes, and this is very unlikely to change.

New forms of digital crime appear every day, and this is especially true of hacking. Over the past 20 years or so, malware has evolved enormously. The first generation of viruses were designed for disrupting computer systems, but the Trojans in use today are far more complex and can also be used to extract data and use it for illegal purposes. In fact, stolen personal and financial data has become a new and valuable commodity for criminals: large volumes of such data are channelled between countries and continents to be used for criminal purposes. Criminal organisations quickly adopt and adapt new technologies for making money or simply facilitating secure channels of communication. We know that digital communication networks can be, and are, used by people and organisations for spreading radicalising propaganda and perpetrating cyber-attacks. The term 'asymmetric war' is most certainly pertinent here; it would take just one lone criminal with sufficient knowledge and skill to undermine the entire network system of a nuclear plant through hacking. The design of the Stuxnet 'worm' is a clear example of just how powerful and dangerous the new generation of malware can be. Computer systems are vulnerable because of their interconnectedness, and clearly need to be made more resilient, but this is only one of a number of requirements for securing critical infrastructure such as nuclear and military facilities.

Victims and especially young people also need to be protected, and this presents a major challenge, particularly in the face of rapidly developing technologies. Considerable efforts have already been made to counter internet-linked abuse of children, but the problem is far from being solved. When a child abuse image is posted and circulated via the internet, it can never be removed and remains permanently in circulation, and the child in the image will continue to be affected into adulthood. Unfortunately little progress has been made in addressing these issues so far.

Providing an appropriate response to cyber-incidents is inherently difficult and problematic. Many will not even be reported to the police, if for example a private company is targeted it might want to avoid a consequent loss of reputation, fearing the case could be reported in the media. When attending a reported incident the police first responder bears the major responsibility for ensuring that forensically sound evidence is preserved and collected. It is well-known that the first few hours at a crime scene are the most critical for evidence recovery for many criminal investigations, for both traditional and digital crimes. But this applies particularly for digital evidence as much of it is both transitory and ephemeral. The first responder must be sufficiently trained and follow the correct procedures, but unfortunately this is not always the case. Worldwide, the availability of quality training must be improved so that investigators at all levels possess the appropriate level of knowledge and skills. However, the investigators only carry out the first stage of the process of bringing criminals to justice: prosecutors and judges also need training and education to meet the new challenges. Law enforcement and the private sectors should cooperate to develop and establish a common taxonomy for cyber-crime, and work towards a joint approach for preventing, detecting and investigating digital crime.

Governments and industry should invest more resources in education and training for the future, as digital crime has the potential to cause significant harm. Considering for example that nearly two billion people belong to social networks across the world, there are still remarkably few central government initiatives. How can we protect our online communities from the exposure to crime, and how could a proper code of conduct be applied to help provide enhanced security?

Moreover, law enforcement agencies face particular challenges when investigating digital crime, for example its international dimension. It is not uncommon for an investigation to start in one country, and for the trail to become ensnared in several other states before leading back to the first. The organisation under investigation could be a multi-national company with partner companies in other countries, all interconnected through a virtual private network (a VPN). Thus the investigation has to be conducted on, and through the organisation's network. How and where will the investigation be carried out, and who will be in overall charge? It may be difficult to pinpoint the geographical location of the crime, so under which jurisdiction would the crime be prosecuted, and who would be responsible for retaining the data needed for the investigation? There are no easy answers to such questions, but they are indicative of the pertinent issues that must be addressed. In particular, clear procedures are required concerning the exchange of electronic evidence. Currently there is no clear international agreement on the standards for the presentation of electronic evidence to a court; each country still tends to focus on their own domestic issues instead of taking a broader and more international perspective.

The need is urgent. Now is the time to consider the issues and take more action against cybercrime. Many of these questions present challenges to internet stakeholders in particular, but it is clear that the private and public sectors need to work together. The sharing of responsibility is the key to success, and to making our societies richer and safer. The book that follows is one such attempt to develop a greater understanding, to enhance skills and to stimulate a renewed debate on the issues that surround digital crime. I recommend it to you.

Preface and Acknowledgements

This book will be of interest to members of the law enforcement community (particularly those engaged in the policing of digital crime), and students of criminology, policing, police studies and forensic computing. However, we have attempted to keep the technical language to a minimum and hence make the book accessible to a wider readership.

Digital crime is a wide-ranging subject with its own fair share of controversy (even how to refer to these new forms of criminality is the subject of debate), and this book reflects this breadth of interest and discourse. Hence we examine not only the theoretical basis to understanding digital crime but also aspects of its prevention, investigation, and the recovery and analysis of digital evidence (including in its most transient forms). Our emphasis throughout is primarily on digital crime within a 'civilian' rather than 'military' context: although we do not ignore so-called cyber-warfare, we focus much more on the digital crime that affects the security and well-being of people on a day-to-day basis.

The authors of the book live and work in the UK and this has obviously influenced many parts of the text. However, we have written the book also to be of interest and value to readers from other parts of the world and have drawn on examples to reflect this.

Each of the chapters is written so that it can read in isolation from the others although there is occasional cross-referencing to other chapters for further explanation. However, the book is structured so that the more generally applicable material is near the beginning, followed by more specialist forms of policing digital crime in the main body of the book. We conclude with a look at some of the possible opportunities and challenges for the future. Inevitably, given the subject matter, by the time you read this book some of the content will be out-of-date or superseded by more recent developments. We have attempted to minimise this shortcoming by concentrating on what we perceive as the more enduring concepts involved in policing digital crime, but regrettably this will not always be possible.

The author(s) of each chapter are listed at the outset and we have employed the system of using 'and' or 'with' where appropriate – in the first case 'and' means roughly equal contributions whereas 'with' means that the first named author contributed the bulk of the material. Note that a few short sections of the book first appeared in our 2008 publication 'Investigating Digital Crime' but have been re-written and updated.

All trademarks referenced within this book are the property of their respective owners.

The editors wish to thank Emily Wilkins for her painstaking and highly skilful proofreading and correction of the text, John Morgan for his helpful contribution to Chapter 1, and Liam Tallis for his advice on cybercrime. Paul Stephens wishes to thank Lee Taylor from Essex Police and Mark Roberts from the PCeU.

Robin Bryant
Sarah Bryant

Chapter 1
Digital Crime

Robin Bryant

Introduction

In this chapter we discuss the theoretical background, nature and extent of digital crime; how it might differ from traditional forms of criminality, and conclude with an example of the novel way that some digital crimes are enacted.

Digital technology and digital forms of communication are increasingly important to individuals, to communities and to most sectors of society, including business, health and education. Our electricity supplies, transport logistics and infrastructures and even the defence of our national states depend on the effectiveness and security of our digital networks. It is no longer hyperbole to claim that the digital world touches all of our lives, and for much of our time, in profound ways. The digital economy grows in size and in importance year by year. For example, practically the only growth recorded by retail and supermarket businesses in the UK in the run up to Christmas 2012 was through their online sales divisions, in marked contrast to more traditional forms of retailing. Digital devices are now found in unexpected locations, such as cars, cookers and washing machines. We send fewer letters and more emails, we receive our news courtesy of Twitter and we maintain our relationships with family and friends through Facebook.

However, with the advent any form of new technology, 'digital' or 'analogue', there will be unexpected and unwanted consequences in terms of criminal exploitation and endeavour. For example, 800 years ago in the 1300s, the metal working techniques used for making genuine currency were rapidly adopted by criminals for making imitation coins for criminal use and financial gain. In the 19th Century the invention of typewriters provided increased anonymity for those writing blackmail letters (and by the 1920s the FBI had developed the forensic examination of typewriters and text). When motor cars became available for public use, bank robbers soon began to use them, as later portrayed in Hollywood movies such as *Bonnie and Clyde*. More recently, criminals employ digital technology and fast digital networks in their attempts to access internet-based banking systems in order to launder the proceeds of criminal enterprises. But it is argued by many that we are not simply witnessing a familiar story of criminal exploitation of new opportunity, but instead distinctively new forms of criminality. It might even be the case that traditional forms of volume crime (such as shoplifting) will soon be overtaken by cybercrime as the new 'typical' crime (Anderson et al., 2012, p. 26).

When crime rates unexpectedly fell in England and Wales in 2012 one academic commentator even suggested that this might be as the result of conventional property crime developing into new digital forms that are less likely to be reported (Fitzgerald, cited by the Guardian, 2013), such as the use of eBay to sell stolen goods (Treadwell, 2012). More organised forms of criminality would also appear to be exploiting the opportunities provided by increasing digitalisation. The conclusion of a recent report (Detica with the John Grieve Centre for Policing and Security, 2012) claimed that 'we are entering a "fourth great era" of organized crime – the "age of digital crime" – as online and offline worlds converge' and that '80% of digital crime may now originate in some form of organised activity' (although it has to be said that details of the methodology used to establish this estimate were unclear). Digital crime is also considered a threat to the further deployment of e-government and e-business services (ITU, 2012, p. 1).

There is a strong case therefore, for the need to 'Police Digital Crime'. This book is an exploration of the preventing, detecting and investigating of digital crime together with the attendant recovery and analysing of digital intelligence and evidence. All these aspects are covered in detail in the remaining chapters.

Digital Crime and the 'Network Society'

The concept of the 'Network Society' (sometimes 'Networked Society') became widespread in the mid-1990s, and is most closely associated with the work of the sociologist Manuel Castells (Castells, 1996) and his three volume opus (*The Rise of the Network Society, The Power of Identity* and *The End of Millennium*). Castells argues that 'technology is a necessary, albeit not sufficient condition for the emergence of a new form of social organization based on networking, that is on the diffusion of networking in all realms of activity on the basis of digital communication networks' (Castells and Cardoso, 2005, p. 3). This technology is now largely in place in the developed world and is rapidly spreading, albeit in a patchy manner, across the globe. According to Castells, society is 'morphing' from the industrial age to the information age as a consequence of the new technologies. However, by 'Network Society' Castells doesn't mean the 'information' or 'knowledge society' (he argues that knowledge and information have always been central to society). His is more a reference to the social and economic 'connectedness' of society, which has profound impacts on the way we communicate and do business, our politics and the way that culture, power and knowledge are appropriated and shared. Power for example, is no longer centralised within tangible institutions and organisations, but is instead diffused through global networks in virtual spaces. The Network Society is a consequence not only of technological change but also the economic changes brought about by the demise of modern capitalism and state communism, and by the rise of phenomena such as the 'green movement'. Nor is Castells simply referring to the 'internet' when he writes of this connectedness: he notes for example that the beginnings of the Network Society predate the internet (Castells, 2000). As we shall see in the remainder of this book, the Network Society is also having a profound effect on the way that the 'business' of crime is conducted. In this sense 'digital crime' is less about technology and more about the way in which we relate to each other.

Castells also introduced the concept of a 'culture of real virtuality' (an apparent oxymoron as 'reality' and 'virtuality' are often seen as opposites) by which he meant the new culture arising as a consequence of the Network Society, and which employs electronic communication. This culture is diverse and reactive, with individuals continually defining themselves in different ways in different contexts: as consumer, as gender, as part of a collective. Facebook, Twitter and similar online social networks for example, mean that many people live for at least part of their day in a 'real virtuality' because the interactions we engage in when online, and the identities that we present and explore are very much part of our reality. We discuss how notions of identity influence behaviour later in this chapter and in Chapter 2.

Castells also comments on the relationship between organised crime and the Network Society. In the second and third volumes of his opus he described the 'Global Criminal Economy' as one part of the Network Society, noting that although 'Crime is as old as humankind [...] global crime, the networking of powerful criminal organizations, and their associates, in shared activities throughout the planet, is a new phenomenon that profoundly affects international and national economies, politics, security and ultimately societies at large' (Castells 1998, p. 166). Although Castells' emphasis here is on the way networks have affected 'conventional' crime (particularly illegal drug cartels), we shall see that digital technology has also impacted on the very nature of crime itself.

Digital Crime and the 'Information Society'

Allied to the concept of the 'Network Society' (see above) is the 'Information Society' (or 'Information Age'), first espoused as such by Daniel Bell in the 1970s (Bell, 1974 and 1979), but with earlier origins in the 1930s. It is often couched in terms of a paradigm shift from the 'Industrial Society'. The 'Information Society' (or 'Societies') is a reference to the various developments and changes arising from the increased production, collection, dissemination and processing of information, and the creation of knowledge, and the impact these have had on society. That there has been a major increase in stored in information is irrefutable, most notably as a result of digital forms of storage and distribution (particularly through the internet). It is also clear that an increasing number of people and organisations are able to share in both the consumption and generation of this information (see below). In many national economies there has been a shift from producing tangible material objects to providing information-based services and products, and information is now a major commodity not only in the economically advanced nations, and is often more highly valued than labour itself. Just as the industrial revolution was much more than simply applying steam power to the means of production, so will our new ways of generating knowledge and sharing information profoundly change the way that we earn our living, spend our leisure time and relate to each other. A visible manifestation of the 'Information Society' is the phenomenon of the 'wisdom of the crowd' on the internet where the best answer to a question or problem is found by aggregating the collected responses of the many (by 'crowd sourcing'), and in effect filtering out the 'noise' of any one individual.

If the 'Information Society' is, or is becoming, a reality then security is likely to be a fundamental issue, and the 'policing' of this society a necessary requirement for confidence to be maintained.

Digital Crime and the 'Risk Society'

Deibert and Rohozinski (2010, pp. 15–16) argue that cyberspace presents a special category of risk, and for a number of reasons: it is a transnational communication network, outside the control of states, organisations and individuals; its governance is distributed between the public and the private; it is unlike traditional physical domains (such as the sea, land, air or space) in that it is human-made and based on the ingenuity of the users and hence in a state of constant change and flux; it is both material and virtual (a space of both 'things' and 'ideas').

Published before the web existed, Ulrick Beck's *Risk Society* (1992, the original German published in 1986) is often described as one of the most influential works of social analysis in the twentieth century. The influence of Beck's ideas continues to this day, particularly with respect to the ways we view the risk presented by digital crime. As Guinchard notes 'Twenty-odd years later, the risks and patterns of reactions he described in a world without the Internet are surprisingly apt for analyzing security issues in cyberspace' (Guinchard, 2011, p. 76).

Beck describes three chronological phases in the development of society: the age of traditional societies, early modernity and the current late modernity (the latter consisting of simple and reflexive modernity consecutively). In the past we might have feared the dangers around us; starvation, wild animals, other people, but these dangers had a recognisable place and role within our lives. Now the dangers that confront us are less immediate and tangible, but we remain uneasily aware of the risks that surround us. Beck suggests that these late modern risks are both often invisible and also open to interpretation (for example, of a 'scientific' nature, or requiring specialist knowledge, and hence contestable by the media and others). Beck's early examples of risk were often drawn from controversies about the environment (including the effects of pollution such as depletion of the ozone layer), nuclear technology and genetic engineering. More recently he has argued that the global financial crisis and our fears about international terrorism provide further telling examples of his concept of risk. In terms of the policing of digital crime, distinct echoes of Risk Society concerns can be heard in current discourses, for example in relation to the uncertainties posed by the 'freedom' offered to the users of cyberspace. Interestingly, an analogy with the 'Wild West' was often drawn in the early days of the public internet (and continues to be used, for example see Mattice, 2012) in terms of its lawlessness and pioneering (risk-laden) nature. As Hudson (2003) noted, Beck's concept of the Risk Society helps explain how our supposed expectation of security can never be realised in practice – and this is perhaps particularly true of cyberspace. The unpredictable nature of risk in cyberspace is also partly due to some of the unintended consequences of technological innovation: the extent to which the inadequacies of online security could facilitate cybercrime is often the subject of disagreement and controversy. The media play an important role in this, with regular 'moral panics' over paedophile use of the internet, the dangers inherent in social network sites, the phenomenon of 'sexting' and so on.

Alongside risk in late modern society we have the notions of responsibilisation, prudentialism, and actuarialism (concepts arising from the work of Michel Foucault and others). For example, we have witnessed a move away from relying on governments and the state towards the individual being more responsible for the management of risk (responsibilisation). Therefore individuals need to exercise a more 'calculating' approach (actuarialism) to the management of that risk (prudentialism).

Digital Crime, the Principles of Economics and Game Theory

There are a number of economic principles of potential relevance to understanding the policing of digital crime (Walker, 2012). For example, in the 1960s Garett Hardin (in the context of ecology), drew on an historical example 'The Tragedy of the Commons' (Hardin, 1968) to explain and illustrate one such principle. The Commons were (and in some parts of the world, still are) agricultural land with no private owner, which any grazer can use for their animals. As no additional direct financial cost was involved, the herders all had an interest in increasing the number of cows they each grazed there - an apparently rational decision they were likely to make. However, if most herders adopted the same decision then the land would become over-grazed and suffer long-term damage, reducing its yield. (By 'tragedy' Hardin is referring to the apparent inevitability of this process as much as to the actual outcome). In general terms Hardin had identified an economic principle that refers to the tendency for any resource which appears to have no financial cost to become overused until its marginal utility (the benefit that accrues from its use) decreases to almost zero. In the case of online digital crime the 'common land' is the 'internet' and the 'herders' are 'cyber-criminals'. Further, the online digital crime 'market' (attempts at phishing, extortion through DDoS attacks, theft using credit card details) is completely 'unregulated': anybody can enter the market, there is little in the way of preliminary training, specialist knowledge or equipment required (and this would in any case be supplied by the market itself, for example hardware skimmers and software rootkits), and no significant initial financial investment is required. In economic terms common-access unregulated markets soon become exhausted, with lower and lower average returns for the individual, but as we shall see later in this chapter, many claim that the cybercrime market is in fact highly profitable and expanding. However, there is not necessarily a contradiction here; the 'Tragedy of the Commons' occurred because the amount of common land was restricted (for example, in England and Wales as a consequence of the 'Enclosures Acts' in the 18th Century), but for online digital crime the common land (the internet) has expanded both in terms of capacity (the spread of broadband around the world) and in terms of variegation (new opportunities such as social networks and new devices such as tablet computers).

Economic principles are also relevant to the prevention of digital crime. In the 'Market for Lemons' (Akerlof, 1970), bad products drive out the good ones (a 'lemon' is American slang for a poor quality car, for example one with faults discovered after purchase (ibid., p. 489)). This type of market can occur when the quality of a product is not readily observable by potential buyers, and as a consequence the seller knows much more about its quality than the potential customer. The buyers will then expect sellers to 'skimp' on quality (even though they know less about the quality than the seller) and will accordingly be less willing to pay a higher price. This will lead to a reduction of the average market price, and to sellers lowering the quality in order to maintain profit, thereby creating a non-virtuous cycle of reducing quality. In the end only 'lemons' will be left for sale. From the perspective of a customer, an inherently insecure software or hardware product is barely distinguishable from a secure one (this is even the case of products explicitly designed for security purposes, such as encryption software, or hardware such as 'secure' USB pen drives). Insecure software is normally cheaper to produce than more secure versions (for example, the development costs are likely to be lower), and thus the market for software and digital hardware can become dominated by lemons with the obvious implications for cyber-security. However, the 'Market for Lemons' may be counteracted by intervention (such as regulatory bodies), or by sending a 'signal' that enables customers to distinguish between the 'lemons' and more secure products. For example, a contrast is sometimes made between the more expensive but more reliable 'apps' from the Apple 'App Store' and the more freely available Android apps. The Apple apps are apparently 'certificated' to the effect that they do not contain malicious code, giving customers 'confidence in the quality of the apps they buy' (Apple, 2012, p. 5). Cheaper apps are available via the Android marketplace, but these occasionally have to be removed by Google because of malicious code (Google, 2011).

Yip and Webber (2103) have also applied the 'Market for Lemons' economic theory to online markets for stolen data (specifically the market in the illegal trading of credit card details and the methods of card crime conducted by 'carders'). Much of the trading takes place by means of internet relay chat (IRC) or other types of discussion forum. Would-be carders encounter two main issues when attempting to trade within the illegal online market: the likely quality of the goods and services on offer, and the identities of possible trading partner, that is whether the partner is a 'genuine' fellow cyber-criminal, or a dishonest trader (a 'ripper'), or even an undercover law enforcement official (Yip and Webber, 2013, p. 13). There appears to be good evidence to suggest that rippers are indeed a real problem for 'genuine' illegal traders in credit card information and methods, making the goods and services traded over the IRC or through online forums worth very little. They conclude that '[i]n essence, the underground economy as that observed on the IRC do exhibit all the characteristics associated with that of a market for "lemons"' (ibid., p. 14).

The 'Prisoners' Dilemma' is a well-known example of a non-zero-sum game from mathematical game theory, and has relevance to the behaviour of some internet stakeholders such as ISPs. It was first formally set out in the 1950s (Axelrod, 1984) but the idea almost certainly pre-dates this. The 'game' involves the hypothetical situation of two suspects ('A' and 'B') who are arrested and imprisoned on suspicion of having jointly committed a serious offence. The two prisoners occupy separate cells and cannot communicate with each other. They are both separately offered a deal by the authorities: to confess and provide evidence against his or her accomplice, and to then receive consideration through a reduced punishment. The 'dilemma' for each of them is that if, for example, A confesses and gives evidence against B, but B remains silent, then A achieves the maximum benefit from the deal. However, B is almost certainly reasoning in the same way and arriving at a similar conclusion. Further, the prisoners both also know that if they are found guilty after keeping silent ('no comment') then they are likely to receive a more severe punishment as a result, but not as bad as the outcome that would arise if both confessed. The various outcomes are illustrated in Table 1.1, with some notional severities of punishment suggested by the author.

Table 1.1   The Prisoners' Dilemma – Possible Outcomes

		Prisoner B	
		Remain silent	*Confess and testify*
Prisoner A	*Remain silent*	Prisoner A: 1 year Prisoner B: 1 year (Total 2 years)	Prisoner A: 4 years Prisoner B: 2 months (Total 4 years, 2 months)
	Confess and testify	Prisoner A: 2 months Prisoner B: 4 years (Total 4 years, 2 months)	Prisoner A: 3 years Prisoner B: 3 years (Total 6 years)

It is likely that the final outcome is that both prisoners will confess and testify against each other – in terms of the total punishment meted out to the pair of prisoners this the worst outcome (an example of a 'sub-optimal outcome to the game). It has to be acknowledged that in its original formulation, the Prisoner's

Dilemma is somewhat contrived and unrealistic (few if any justice systems work in quite this way) but can be summarised with the observation that although cooperation is normally in the interests of the many, individuals often choose to act in ways that they erroneously believe maximise their own personal interests. The Prisoner's Dilemma has been observed at work in practice in some real-life situations including competition between the companies Coca Cola and Pepsi Cola, international relations (particularly the 'Cold War') and most recently in the 'fiscal cliff' negotiations in the US in 2012. In terms of the prevention of digital crime, particularly online cybercrime, each individual 'node' of the internet (websites, ISPs) is prepared to pay to put preventive security measures in place to prevent attacks against themselves, but are not prepared to pay to prevent their own systems being used to attack others.

Digital Crime, Psychology and Identity

In the next two sections we examine three features of digital online environments which are relevant to the policing of digital crime, namely anonymity, disinhibition and impulsivity. Although described separately, in practice these facets of online communication and behaviour often overlap and inter-relate.

Anonymity

There are two main issues surrounding anonymity and online crime: the deliberate attempt by some motivated offenders to hide or fake their identity and remain anonymous, and a more general sense of unreality which may facilitate illegal acts by otherwise law-abiding individuals. In terms of the former, digital crime (particularly if conducted over the internet) provides a much greater scope for anonymity, through either secrecy or by presenting a false identity (DiMarco, 2003). Baggili and Rogers go so far as to claim that the '[l]iterature suggests that one of the major reasons people are attracted to cybercrime is the anonymity they encounter in computer mediated environments' (2009, p. 551, citing Lipson, 2002; Williams, 2002). A sex offender may carefully assume a faked identity (perhaps as another young person) in an attempt to groom a potential victim in an online chatroom. In comparison, in the pre-internet era a paedophile often had to gain the child and family's trust face-to-face, which is usually slower and more risky. This deliberate form of the adoption of anonymity perhaps requires little in the way of further explanation, in terms of the psychology of motivation.

In terms of a general sense of anonymity however, Cooper (2002) observed that the vastness of the World Wide Web combined with its home-based use often induce a strong sense of anonymity in many users, and not only for people who set out with the explicit intention to commit crime. Most people who participate in, or simply read and follow online forums, will be aware on the phenomenon of the internet 'troll' – a person posting deliberately inflammatory messages, almost always under the anonymity provided by a pseudonym, in order to provoke other users of the forum. (The phenomenon is probably almost as old as the internet itself). It is not just that anonymity simply enables people to act in ways that they might not otherwise; it might in fact actually encourage them to do so, and the online world is an (apparently) conducive environment for assuming anonymity. The drummer of The Who, Pete Townsend, describes in his autobiography, that a few years after illegally accessing a site offering child sexual abuse imagery (he claims that this was intended to help him start an awareness campaign against the problem) he saw that there were now plans 'to change the law retrospectively to ensnare anyone who had ever searched for child pornography on the internet' (Townsend, 2012, p. 483). He goes on to note that 'I guessed that might include me, but several years had passed [...] Even so, I wasn't concerned, not at first' (ibid.).

Disinhibition

Danet (1998, cited in Elliott and Beech, 2009) observed that the apparent anonymity of the internet, coupled with the 'playful' nature of online communication can have a disinhibiting effect on users, and lower their self-control of 'impulsive' behaviour. A number of academics (notably, Suler, 2004) have developed this idea to embrace the existence of a claimed 'online disinhibition effect' and suggested (ibid., p. 321) there are two main effects:

- 'benign disinhibition', for example, people sharing intimate facts about themselves or displaying unusual acts of openness and kindness to others, including strangers ; and
- 'toxic disinhibition', where the online environment means that some individuals are more likely to express hatred, issue threats and visit 'the dark underworld of the internet'.

The latter is undoubtedly of greater relevance to policing digital crime. He went on to suggest that there were at least six factors are involved in the cause of the online disinhibition (some of which *overlap*). These are shown in Table 1.2.

We could perhaps add a further factor to Suler's list which might increase the likelihood of increased disinhibition within some individuals: most people access online environments whilst alone or otherwise not under some form of surveillance; in everyday terms, 'I'm alone'.

It is certainly the case that at least some people are prepared to behave differently online and do sometimes pretend to be a person that they are not. Certainly many more people seem prepared to commit an IPR offence online (such as downloading copyrighted music and video) than would commit a 'real theft' in the 'real world' (such as shoplifting). Online disinhibition may be part of the explanation for this, although it is unlikely to be the only or even primary reason. Similarly, we may be more likely to read an email meant for another person than we would a letter. However, the empirical evidence to support the detail of

Table 1.2   Factors Causing Disinhibition

Factor	Explanation	Everyday explanation	Notes
Dissociative anonymity	The anonymity provided by online environments lends itself to feelings of 'dissociation' from usual self	'You don't know me'	Suler considers this to be a 'primary' factor
Invisibility	Users are not physically visible to others (unless they choose so)	'You can't see me'	Invisibility 'overlaps' with anonymity
Asynchronicity	Delayed reaction; interaction with others does not have to happen in 'real time'	'See you later'	Sometimes manifests itself as an emotional 'hit and run'
Solipsistic introjection	The impression that an individual's mind has 'merged' with that of an online correspondent: a form of talking to oneself	'It's all in my head'	Particularly the case with text communication e.g. through email
Dissociative imagination	The online world is seen as part of a 'game' with different rules compared with everyday life	'It's just a game'	A combination of solipsistic introjection with the 'escapability' of the online world
Minimizing status and authority	The absence of traditional cues to status and authority	'We're equals'	Status in cyberspace is determined by communication skills etc.

(Based on Suler, 2004 and Suler, 2012, but author's interpretation)

Suler's model is also somewhat equivocal, for example although Lapidot-Lefler and Barak (2012, p. 435) cite six studies that confirmed anonymity as a factor in online toxic disinhibition, another study by Fullwood found little evidence for it (Fullwood et al. 2012).

Impulsivity and Risk-taking

Linked with both anonymity and disinhibition is the online phenomenon of impulsive and risk-taking behaviour. In general terms impulsive behaviour often consists of 'risky' spontaneous actions where the consequences of the action have not been thought through. Patton and Stanford (2012, p. 262) claim that with respect to impulsivity '[w]ith the possible exception of intelligence, no other personality dimension or trait so broadly influences various areas of human endeavor: interpersonal relationships, education, fiscal responsibility, personal moral behavior, business ethics and entrepreneurship, aggression, and criminality'. Consequently, there are many studies of impulsive behaviour to be found in the literature, including research into the psychology of 'kleptomania', a supposed impulsive condition where the individual feels an overwhelming and uncontrollable urge to steal. That some people are 'naturally' more impulsive seems irrefutable, and a number of studies have found evidence for a neurobiological basis for this (as an example see Goldstein and Volkow, 2002). One new line of research is investigating whether the online environment might be a place that facilitates greater risk-taking and other forms of impulsive behaviour when compared with 'real' environments, or whether in fact individuals with 'impulsive' personality traits might simply be more attracted to online environments than others who are less impulsive.

However, the potential effects of online impulsivity apply to victims as much as to offenders, with increased impulsivity leading to an increase in the vulnerability of users. This is of particular concern with children and young people whose risky online behaviour might expose them to grooming or other forms of harm. Livingstone and Haddon (2009) examined 400 research studies that analysed young people's use of the internet in Europe. They found that the revealing of personal information online was the most common risky behaviour (around half of teenagers online) and that meeting an online contact in person was the least common risk, although around 9 per cent of online teenagers go to such meetings, rising to 20 per cent in Poland, Sweden and the Czech Republic, (ibid., p. 16).

Identity

The notion of 'identity' is a particularly ambiguous and multifaceted concept but normally refers to an individual's sense of being a unique individual, including what defines him or her as being different from others, but also what is shared in common. It is clear that no-one has a single identity, but rather we each have a number of overlapping identities which coexist at the same time: we are (variously) employees, parents, sports fans, a homeless person, a Facebook user. However we may identify three broad facets of identity: individual identity, social identity and official identity (based in part on Finch, 2003, p. 87, who in turn references Goffman 1963). We summarise these in Table 1.3 (our interpretation and examples).

Each category overlaps interacts with the other and there are symbiotic reinforcing relationships between individual and social identities in particular. For example, our ethnicity can be variously an aspect of our individual, social and official identities. (Note however, there are many other ways of 'cutting the identity cake' for example, in terms of typologies which include cultural, national identities). Figure 1.1 shows one way of representing how identity varies according

Table 1.3   Three Facets of Identity

Form of identity	Meaning	Examples
Individual	A subjective construction of what the self is, based in part on interactions with others	A 'good sister' Our personal likes and dislikes
Social	Identity as part of a group, assigned in part by the group itself	Being a member of a gym Supporting a pressure group
Official	Unique characteristics of the person, relatively fixed and immutable and assigned to them	Name, address, date of birth Nationality

to the context with 10 sectors representing various aspects of a person's life (such as hobbies) and four continuous lines, each representing the profile of a particular identity (such as 'identity at home'). The further the line is from the centre the more important the particular aspect is.

Our identities are somewhat fluid, both on the level of the individual (during a person's lifetime), and at the level of society (for example, during the historical move from agrarian to industrial forms of social organisation). More recently the use of online environments has stimulated further significant change, but there is

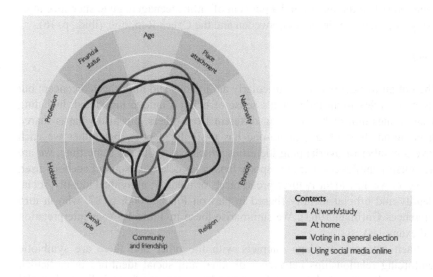

Figure 1.1   Mapping Identity Profiles (Source: Foresight Future Identities, Final Project Report, 2013, p12. The Government Office for Science. © Crown copyright. URN 13/523)

some debate over whether the advent of online environments (particularly social network sites) has led to users inventing 'new' forms of identity distinct from their non-virtual lives, or whether the internet has merely provided a means of extending and exploring their existing identities. Certainly, during the early years of widespread internet use research interest focused very much on how some of a person's online identities were markedly different from (and even in opposition to) their real world identities. However the emphasis has now changed, and research is more likely to start with a presumption that online identities effectively complement and extend those offline. Of course, this change in emphasis might also reflect the blurring of distinctions between online and offline identities made possible through the increasing maturity of Web 2.0. That said however, although online environments probably do allow an individual's various identities to differ and even drift, cognitive dissonance may arise when apparent contradictions emerge between, say, our Facebook and our LinkedIn identity. In this sense, with its increasing sophistication and accessability, the online environment will perhaps become more like the offline environment; omni-present and pervasive.

However, even if the internet does not lead to 'new' identities it does without doubt permit the blurring of personal, social and official identities, and this has major implications for the policing of digital crime. For example, users place increasing amounts of their personal information on online, and details of our official identity are revealed alongside our personal and social identities. There has been a dramatic growth in the use of social networks (for example, see Dutton and Blank, 2012, p. 34 for a discussion of the 'striking' rise in social networking in the UK). Facebook users (for example) post news and comment about their 'personal', 'work' and 'social' identities in a seamless fashion, as well as revealing information concerning their geographical location. The 'richness' of information provides opportunies for more targeted cybercrimes such as spear-phishing.

The Nature of Digital Data

In this section we examine the nature of digital data and the bearing this has on the policing of digital crime. In particular we examine how digital and analogue differ, the malleability and reproducible nature of digital data, and finally how data is a commodity with value.

The term 'digital' probably arose from the word digit, referring to the fingers when used for counting (*digitus* is latin for a finger or toe). Increasingly, digital has come to mean the representation of information (in its most fundamental form) as a number of states, usually two, but sometimes three or more. Dual-state systems are sometimes referred to as 'binary', with representations such as '1' and '0', or 'on' and 'off'. This is not a new idea; the reliability of such systems is exploited in Morse code which uses a two state representation of dots and dashes, (although intervals of four different lengths are used to help decode messages). According to the Oxford English Dictionary the more modern sense of the word 'digital' first came into use in 1945 with Eckert's description of the ENIAC (OED, 2012), the 'Electronic Numerical Integrator And Computer', often referred to as the first electronic general purpose computer. However, it was not until the mid 1980s that the term digital began to assume its more general association with digital data, technologies and the like.

Analogue and Digital Representations

Digital representation is often contrasted with precursor analogue (or analog) forms of representation. In analogue representations the information is conveyed in a form that is analogous in some way to the quantity or quality itself. Perhaps the classic example of this is the difference between analogue watches (using the movement of hands to represent the passage of time), and digital watches which use only numbers. We can draw an analogy between position and time for the hands of an analogue watch; the hands move through space at a rate proportional to the lapse of time. In this way, an analogue watch attempts to replicate the phenomenon of time itself by a direct copying; the smooth movement of the hands representing time as a continuous variable. Digital watches use a more abstract representation instead, identifying points in time such as 10:23, with the passage of time itself not represented visually. The time will then appear to suddenly move on, to 10:24, 10:25 and so on; time is represented as if it is a discrete variable.

Music and other sounds may also be stored using analogue or digital means. A comparison of the earliest analogue methods (using a wax cylinder) and later digital approaches (for example, using an mp3 algorithm) provides a further illustration of some key differences between analogue and digital representations. Whichever means we choose (analogue or digital) there is the unchangeable fact that in a physical form (as perceived by the human brain) music is simply 'sound':

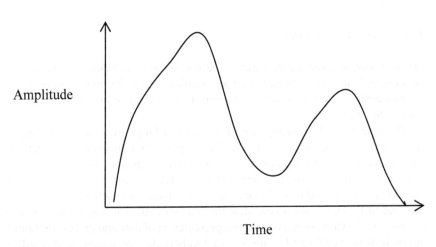

Figure 1.2   Analogue Representation of Sound

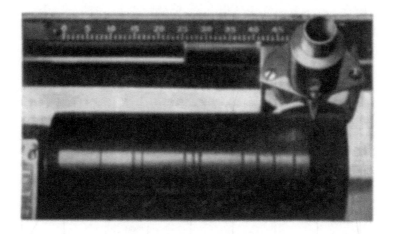

Figure 1.3   A Wax Cylinder for Recording Sound (Columbia Phonograph Co. 1922; Reproduced under the GNU Free Documentation License)

that is a stream of sound waves of varying frequencies and amplitudes, sensed by the ear as variations of air pressure.

The changes in air pressure were first recorded using analogue means. This involved creating a spiral groove with variable peaks, troughs and gradients in the soft wax on a cylinder (Figure 1.3). The complex shapes were analogous to the sound pressure variations produced when the music was performed for the recording. After hardening, the wax cylinder would be played back and the sound amplified using a phonograph. The same principle (albeit with significant technical innovation in the interim) is employed in the manufacture of vinyl records.

On the other hand, an mp3 track is represented as digital data; it consists of only a series of digits. In effect the peaks and troughs of the sound waves in this case are approximated (the degree of approximation is called the sampling rate) by rectangular bars: the continuous variable becomes discrete.

In Figure 1.4 the analogue sound wave is represented by the digital denary representation [3][5][6][2][1][3][4][1]. In digital binary this would be [011][101] [110][010][001][011][100][001]).

The Advantages of Digital Data

Due to their inherent simplicity, digital data representations have significant advantages over analogue for data transmission and replication. As a digital signal is composed of just two or more states (for example 0 and 1), each relatively easily distinguishable from the other, it will remain clear and readable, almost regardless of the amount of distortion inadvertently introduced. For the same

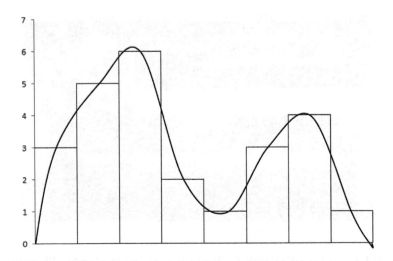

Figure 1.4   Comparing Digital and Analogue Representations of Sound

underlying reason, messages in Morse code remain clear even when transmitted over thousands of miles; it comprises only six elements which are relatively easy to distinguish. Crucially, because of the way that information is represented in a digital signal, there is no loss of quality when copying or sharing: the 10,000th copy sounds exactly the same as the original.

The differences between analogue and digital means of representation, storage and reproduction may appear to be largely technical in nature but they are important when attempting to understand the nature of digital crime. For example, the means to illegally share or sell copied commercial DVDs on a vast scale is made possible by the fact that the medium of storage is digital rather than analogue. Video tape uses an analogue system for storing the information, and a VHS tape copied 'serially' (that is, making copies of copies) is virtually unwatchable after at most three or four such copies, due to compounded errors in reproduction. However, digital formats can be serially copied without any loss of information, so reproduction of such material is far easier.

A further advantage of digital storage is that the physical systems used for storing digital forms of representation tend to occupy far less volume than their analogue equivalents. For example, a novel of 125,000 words would probably cover about 500 paper pages, but could be stored digitally in a volume much smaller than a pinhead, occupying about 1.25 Mb in digital terms. Similarly, 128,000 such novels could be stored on a single 160Gb hard disc drive on a typical PC. The digital storage 'space' required can be reduced still further through the use of encoding and compression techniques. An average CD audio track occupies between 50 to 60Mb but can be compressed to about four Mb when encoded in mp3 format, and for most listeners there will be no noticeable loss of quality.

This makes data inherently 'concealable' and 'removable'; both qualities that normally feature relatively highly in how 'CRAVED' an object is by thieves (that is 'Concealable, Removable, Available, Valuable, Enjoyable and Disposable', Clarke 1999). Further, digital data, despite its virtual and intangible nature, can also be an inherently valuable commodity. It is perfectly possible for one person to give a 'present' of an Amazon gift voucher (a digital object) to another person via the internet (digital transmission), and for the recipient to use it to download music in a digital form to her ipod. In criminal terms, sets of stolen login names and passwords, financial details and warez software (copyright protection removed) are often illegally traded on the internet. More organised forms of criminal activity are sometimes directed towards stealing potentially valuable commercial data, including so-called 'big data'.

Finally, given its essential simplicity of representation, digital data is 'malleable'; it is easily re-shaped, transmuted and manipulated. This means it can both be re-configured (for example, the function a software program performs, or the 'loudness' of mp3 encoded music can be changed) and also restored to a previous form. The latter feature is particularly useful when countering the effects of digital crime employing viruses and worms: a network or PC can returned to its previous state relatively easily and quickly (when compared to the 'up to 18 months' it will take to repair the Rothko painting deliberately damaged in 2012 (BBC, 2012d)). Digital data can also physically move quickly (at the speed of light when in transit), which has a pronounced effect on the epidemiology of digital crime: for example malware can spread very quickly and infect hundreds of thousands of PCs within days. Indeed, the number of Slammer worm infections was found to have doubled every 8.5 seconds (Caida, 2003)), and in 2013, within hours of the news emerging that over 250,000 Twitter users had had their accounts hacked, fraudsters had launched phishing attacks to take advantage of Twitter's decision to contact affected individuals by email (the phishing attacks masquerading as a genuine email from Twitter). Further, when data is altered, the changes are invisible to the eye. If a house has been burgled the victim will normally be able to see this clearly but a PC that has been 'taken over' by a botnet is unlikely to appear to function any differently in an immediately obvious way.

Steganography: concealment within digital data

There is a vast array of methods open to those who wish to commit digital crimes. These include the hardware and software necessary for theft, fraud and hacking. There are forums for sharing criminal methods, and forums offering bespoke hacking and malware kits for sale, with lists of emails for phishing attacks and so on. Offenders will also employ techniques to attempt to hide their identities and evidence, including techniques such as using proxies, DNS spoofing, end-to-end tunnelling, and cryptography. To illustrate some of the issues involved within offender methodology we examine here in detail the use of steganography for criminal purposes, and how the digital nature of data has facilitated this ancient craft.

Steganography is the process of concealing information (data, text, images), and also hiding its very presence; the documents or images containing the concealed information appear to be normal documents or images. The hidden information may be completely recovered at a later time using the appropriate method and keys. (The term is assumed to come via Latin from two Greek words meaning literally 'covered writing'. It is sometimes shortened to 'steg' or 'stego'). The 'craft' of steganography has a long history, ranging from its use in Ancient Greece to convey secret tattooed military dispatches on the scalps of messengers, via Second World War PoWs sending hidden messages back to their home country, to its use in Eastern Europe during the Cold War as a form of covert resistance to Soviet domination. The methods used were usually physical or written in nature. However, with the advent of computing and the digital representation of data, steganography has become less of a specialised craft and is now a technique that is available to anybody who can download and run software from the internet. There are a number of legitimate uses of steganography, for example the digital watermarking of files (such as music and video) to indicate intellectual property ownership. However, steganography also has distinct advantages for offenders wishing to send and share illegal material, or to communicate secretly. For example whereas cryptography is obvious in its use (the plain text message 'Share pictures on the IRC channel AnonNet' is converted to '$34RtYu^67kMM?5') and hence might give rise to suspicion, in steganography data is concealed in an apparently 'innocent' file (the 'carrier file'). Laskar and Hemachandran argue that 'steganography could be considered as the dark cousin of cryptography' (2012, p. 58), explaining that 'Cryptography assures privacy whereas Steganography assures secrecy' (ibid.).

There are a variety of types of steganography, such as least significant bit (LSB), EOF and DCT. In the case of a digital image, LSB steganography works by utilising the fact that an image consists of a finite number of pixels. The number of bits per pixel determines the number of possible colours for that pixel; 24 bits provides a choice of about 16.8 million colours. The 24 bits of the coding for each pixel are split into three octets, 8 each for red, green, and blue – RGB. The final bit for each octet is the 'least significant bit' (an LSB), and it can be changed without the colour looking any different to the human eye.

As an example, consider that a certain grey colour (as shown selected in Figure 1.5) has RGB values as follows:

    R=180 (denary) = 10110100 (binary)
    G=190 (denary) = 10111110 (binary)
    B=185 (denary) = 10111001 (binary)

The coding for a pixel of this colour will therefore be 101101001011111010111001 (binary, with the LSBs underlined).

In LSB steganography the software often used (such as Steghide) will select certain pixels, and these will be used to carry the data to be concealed. The coding for each pixel has three least significant bits (one for each of the red, blue and

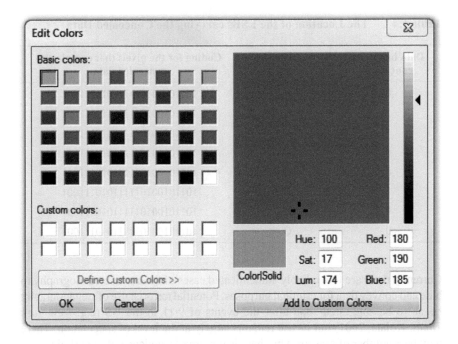

Figure 1.5 Selecting a Shade of Grey

green coding components) but only one LSB will be employed for each selected pixel. In this way the data is carried by the pixel coding, but the consequent colour changes will be too slight to be detected by a person looking at the image.

Let's say we want to hide the letter 'd'. In ASCII the letter 'd' is 100 in denary ('base 10'), and this is written as 1100100 in binary ('base 2'). The data to be concealed therefore consists of 8 bits (01100100), so we require eight target pixels. For some the LSB for the red octet coding will be changed (R), for others only the green (G) and for others only the blue (B), all predetermined by the software (using an algorithm).

Once the data has been concealed, the code for the selected pixels (coding for the shade of grey in this example) will read as shown in Table 1.4. The LSBs carrying the concealed data are in bold.

This part of the image will look the same as it did before to the human eye, but the data for it now contains the hidden character 'd'. By using the same software, but in 'reverse', a recipient can extract the hidden data (in this case a single letter) from the file (this process is sometimes referred to as 'steg-extracting'). The same principle applies to hiding and recovering text, whole images and other data. Steganography can also be combined with cryptography so that a passphrase is required as part of the process of recovering the hidden data, increasing the level of security for the user.

Table 1.4   The Location of the LSBs carrying the Concealed Data

Data bits to be concealed	Octet selected	Coding for the pixels that contain the concealed data
0	R	1011010010111110101110111001
1	G	1011010010111111110111001
1	B	1011010010111110101110111001
0	R	1011010010111110101110111001
0	G	1011010010111110101110111001
1	B	1011010010111110101110111001
0	R	1011010010111110101110111001
0	G	1011010010111110101110111001

Currently there are few reliably authenticated cases of the use of steganography to hide and convey data for criminal purposes. Potential terrorist use of steganography began to be suggested soon after the events of 9/11 in the US (e.g. *New York Times*, Kolata, 2001) but its use remains largely at the level of speculation. There may be a number of reasons why there is not greater evidence of the criminal use of steganography: the technique is not widely used, its use is evading detection, or law enforcement agencies are finding signs of the use of steganography but are unable to extract evidence. However, steganography software has certainly been downloaded from the internet hundreds of thousands of times and it does not appear unreasonably to presume that it has been used, and is likely to be used further in the future.

In terms of law enforcement there are at least two issues with regard to steganography: first to identify that steganography is being utilised for criminal purposes (often called 'steganalysis' or 'passive steganalysis') and, if it is, to extract the suspect file to recover the hidden data ('steg-extracting' or 'active steganalysis'). Steganalysis can be problematic but a number of techniques are open to LEAs and others. Identification of the software that has been used for performing the steganography is important because this can provide clues as to the file type being hidden, as certain software and the underlying algorithms employed are sometimes specific to certain types of file. When LSB steganography is used with images there is sometimes (and otherwise unexpected) repetition of identical colours in the colour palette, and this can raise suspicion. Software is also available that claims to identify when steganography has being used, although some tests have shown that some software produces many false positives when looking for steganography (El-Guindy, nd). The process of steganalysis is made easier if the *a priori* (original, unaltered) file is available for comparison purposes, but this is often not the case in a criminal enquiry. If the software is known (and hence the underlying algorithms employed) then extracting data from a steganogram is relatively straightforward, as long as a passphrase is either not relevant, not used, or not known (in the latter case for example, brute-force methods can be used). In the case of added encryption or unknown steganographic techniques then statistical methods of 'de-stegging' are being developed but have still not reached maturity.

Smartness, Hyper-connectivity and Digital Crime

As is obvious to us all, in recent decades there has been an exponential growth in both the number of digital devices in circulation and the number of digital services available for us to use. The processing power of digital devices has also increased dramatically. Moore's Law, originally formulated in the mid 1960s, observed that the number of transistors in an integrated circuit doubled every two years, but that the real cost remained constant year after year. In popular use Moore's Law has now assumed a more general meaning, and is often used (perhaps erroneously) to make the case that the processing power of a device doubles on average every 18 months to two years. However, the speed and power of processing is no longer the defining factor of 'new technology' that it once was: there is now an abundance of speed and processing power (for example, as is often observed, the average smartphone today harnesses more computing power than that required for Apollo 11 to travel to the moon and back). Instead the current wave of new development is more concerned with enhancing the general 'smartness' of technology, and if anything this provides more of challenge to policing digital crime. Smartness is an ill-defined concept but usually includes some of the following qualities:

- *Ubiquity*: always available, for example switching from a desktop PC, to a smartphone, to a tablet device in order to continue reading an e-book;
- *Hyper-connectivity*: always connected, using wireless technology (people to people, people to machines, machine to machine) - for example the availability of public wifi, paid wifi, 3G, 4G services, and also washing machines with IP addresses and RFID enabled devices;
- *Flexibility*: a multitude of functions in one device such as in a smartphone: GPS, digital camera, motion sensor, music player;
- *Portability*: easily transported, for example smartphones that fit in a coat pocket, tablet devices that fit in a handbag;
- *Sociability*: sharing and merging of public and personal identities (see above), for example hardware and software for accessing social networking sites at any time and in any place, and online photo-sharing; and
- *Capacity*: in effect limitless storage, capacious information, for example using a smartphone in-store to check reviews of a product.

Estimates vary widely, but globally there are at least two billion people with the ability to connect to the internet, and approximately five billion devices have been sold which can be used to access the internet (World Economic Forum, 2013). The developing 'Internet of Things' (IoT) means that human intervention might not even be needed in the future for device to device communication. This growing smartness of technology, and in particular its ubiquity and its facilitation of ever-increasing hyper-connectivity, will undoubtedly produce significant challenges to the policing of digital crime in particular, and cyber-security in general. For example, the near-field communication (NFC) form of connectivity now being incorporated into smartphones (primarily to enable seamless payments) might well give rise to new criminal opportunities and present new policing challenges. The number of Android apps available for smartphones containing malicious code has increased rapidly to over 20,000 (TrendMicro, 2012), and coupled with the frequent use of personal smartphones for business use, the threat becomes clear.

Horizontal Networks

In 2004 Dupont noted that the advent of the internet was precipitating a decline in vertical hierarchical social structures and a concomitant rise in horizontal networks. In the past, the flow of some forms of information, if it occurred at all, tended to be 'top down', and hence under the control of people higher up the hierarchy. Since the early 2000s, the advent of Web 2.0 and increasing hyper-connectivity (see above) has accelerated the changes Dupont originally observed. For example, the role that social media played (particularly the use of Twitter, Facebook and YouTube) during the early stages of the 'Arab Spring' in 2011 in countries such as Tunisia and Egypt has been widely noted and debated (e.g. Howard et al., 2011).

However, if we accept that the internet has led to an increase in horizontal communication; that is amongst peers with little or no control exercised by authorities, there will also be new opportunities for those interested or intent upon criminal activities (including terrorism) to share information and techniques. Afuah and Tucci describe this as a reduction in the traditional 'information asymmetry' (Afuah and Tucci, 2003). Forms of communication and access to information are no longer so constrained by authorities, time or space. It is now far more difficult, largely as a result of the internet, for groups, organisations, authorities and official bodies to control access to certain forms of information, many of which may be considered to be sensitive or even dangerous. For example, high resolution satellite imagery of most parts of the world (previously only available to the military) is now available to all. Once a Pandora's digital Box has been opened it is almost impossible to track down and remove any information released, and on reflection, this should not be surprising, given the origins of the internet as a network designed to withstand attack. The notorious 'Anarchist's Cookbook' is still circulating on the internet and provides details, inter alia, on how to manufacture improvised explosive devices (IEDs). A number of people (working independently) have since developed and expanded the Anarchist's Cookbook and similar documents, for example the 'Terrorist's Handbook', the 'Mujahedeen Poisons Handbook', and the 'Encyclopaedia of Jihad'. These are all potentially available to anyone through the dark web (see Chapter 10). In 1999 David Copeland (not believed to be a member of any terrorist organisation) used information from the Terrorist's Handbook to construct nail bombs that he used to attack people in a gay bar in Soho in London, and passers-by in Brick Lane and Brixton, both multi-cultural areas of London (BBC, 2000).

Just as information of all kinds flows relatively easily with the increase in horizontal networks, so do other forms of communication. There are obviously major positive benefits to this but it also means that extremist groups are more able to propagate their message, organise themselves, and attempt to recruit others. And more generally, those who are intent upon harming themselves and/or others are able to exploit the untrammelled horizontal communication pathways. In 2002 a person known as 'RC' (thought to be Petri Gerdt) participated in the 'Forum for home chemistry', a Finnish chatroom that discussed bomb-making amongst other topics. He learnt how to construct a lethal IED that subsequently killed seven people (including himself) in a shopping centre in Vantaa, Finland. Likewise, methods for committing crime can be easily spread with readily available 'crimeware' such as customisable phishing kits. And for the aspiring car thief in 2012, the hardware, software, and information needed to create a dummy electronic key for an expensive BMW car were all easily available on the internet (BBC, 2012b), whereas in the past information about how to break into cars was more likely to have spread relatively slowly by word of mouth.

The Definition of Digital Crime

In popular discourse, in law enforcement and within the academic community, a number of terms are used when describing the criminality associated with the growth of digital technologies and means of communication. These terms include 'computer crime', 'online crime', 'internet crime', 'new technology crime', 'cybercrime' and (less frequently now) 'high (or 'hi') tech crime'. We have 'cyber-criminals', 'cyber-bullies', digital pirates', 'digital thieves', 'hackers' and 'crackers', In addition, the prefix 'e' tends to be attached to existing labels to indicate a new and 'digitised' version of a pre-existing crime phenomenon. There is also a further tendency in the literature to append the prefix 'cyber' to conventional crimes to signify their online variants – hence cyber-harassment, cyber-trespass and cyber-pornography. This confusion over definition might well be why some commentators such as Wall suggest that the term cybercrime tends to be used 'metaphorically and emotionally rather than scientifically or legally' (Wall, 2007, p. 10). Hunton goes further and suggests that '[...] the concept of cyber criminality is often clouded by the interchangeable, inaccurate and even contradictory terms commonly used to describe the vast array of illicit activities and behaviours associated with cybercrime and cyber security' (Hunton, 2012, p. 202). It is perhaps understandable that the definition of digital crime is enveloped in a fog of confusion. As we discussed above, we are only just beginning to understand the implications of the Network Society on crime, and any definitions will attempt might inevitably be confounded as digital crime itself morphs into different and probably unexpected forms. There is also the problem (common to much criminology) that we aspire to create definitions with some form of universality, but we are then faced with the reality that certain actions considered as cybercrimes in some countries are not considered as such in others. There are also vested interests at play: for example, the novelty of the 'threat' posed by certain digital crimes can be used to support the case for a larger share of inevitably limited financial resources.

However, 'digital crime' is normally a broad term which embraces more than the usual definitions of computer crime and cybercrime. It includes other forms of crime such as IPR music and video piracy which have grown and developed largely as a consequence of the growth of digital forms of representation, and the use of online environments to facilitate traditional crimes such as drug dealing. As Kshetri (2005) notes: 'Crimes target sources of value, and for this reason, digitization of value is tightly linked with digitization of crime'. Likewise, the term 'policing digital crime' also includes digital forensics, as well as the prevention and detection of digital crimes. Figure 1.6 illustrates some of the crimes often classified as 'digital crimes'.

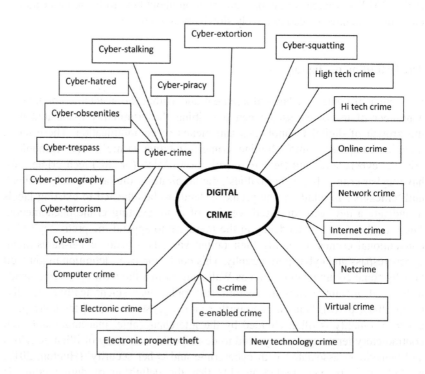

Figure 1.6   Digital Crime Terminologies

Table 1.5   Digitality and Novelty for Digital Crimes

	Increasing digitality	
	————————————————————————————⟶	
Increasing novelty	Traditional crimes, few digital crime features, other than digital forensics e.g. burglary of a dwelling	Traditional crimes with some digital crime features e.g. credit card fraud
∨	Digital crimes with some traditional crime features e.g. hacking using social engineering to gain a password	Digital crimes, few traditional features e.g. DDoS attacks

Alternatively, we might classify 'digital crimes' in terms of the degrees of 'novelty' and 'digitality' as illustrated in Table 1.5.

However, we acknowledge that such a wide and all-embracing conception of digital crime results in a somewhat tautological or 'catch all' definition. In this sense we are closer to Grabosky (2007) and Clough (2012). Grabosky uses the term 'electronic crime' to describe 'a wide range of crimes committed with the aid of digital technology' (p. 2), but, like ourselves also acknowledges that this is a 'label of convenience'. Clough defines 'cybercrime' as '[t]he use of digital technology in the commission or facilitation of crime' (Clough, 2012, p. 363).

Digital Forensics

The meanings of 'digital forensics' and 'digital forensic investigation' perhaps require less in the way of discussion as there is less theoretical and discursive baggage to unpack. Often seen as a branch of forensic investigation (or 'forensic science'), digital forensics is concerned with the recovery, capture and analysis of data and other information to be found within devices that have the capacity to store and manipulate digital data (see Chapter 8). The process of digital forensic investigation is applied to many types of crime (including 'traditional' interpersonal crimes such as homicide) and is not exclusive to digital crime. Put simply, many digital crimes will require a digital forensic investigation but so will many other 'non-digital' crimes. Hence it is somewhat of a misnomer to treat 'digital crime' and 'digital forensics' as if the latter was simply the application of scientific methods of investigation to the former. In this book we examine the policing of digital crime in both the sense of 'digital crime' and 'digital forensics'. Consider an analogy with, for example, a subject such as equine studies: the subject is the 'horse' but the content ranges from the biological sciences, nutrition and safety, physical and emotional care, skills of horsemanship, the history of the horse and so on. Our wide and imprecise interpretation of 'policing digital crime' might perhaps lack academic coherence of other subjects (such as pure mathematics) but it reflects the reality of professional work.

'Cybercrime' as a form of digital crime is steadily acquiring a more defined meaning. It is normally used with reference to crimes occurring in a networked environment (such as the internet), but which are more than simply facilitated by that environment. In 2007 the European Commission's definition of cybercrime (Commission of the European Communities, 2007, p. 2) included:

- traditional forms of crime such as fraud or forgery committed over electronic communication networks;
- illegal content transmitted over electronic media (for example child sexual abuse material or incitement to racial hatred); and
- crimes unique to electronic networks, such as attacks against information systems, denial of service and hacking.

The term cybercrime therefore usually embraces the following criminal or anti-social activities: computer hacking and cracking; developing and/or spreading malicious code (such as viruses and Trojans); spamming; network intrusion; software piracy; network-based or network-enabled crimes (such as phishing and identity theft), IPR crimes (for example illegal file-sharing) and distribution of child sexual abuse imagery.

The Distinguishing Features of Digital Crime

Underlying the debate concerning the meaning of 'digital crime' (and specifically cybercrime) is a deeper debate concerning the 'newness' or otherwise of these forms of criminality, and whether it is the case that *'plus ça change, plus c'est la même chose'* – the more things change, the more they stay the same (see for example, Brenner, 2004). But if cybercrime really does present a new set of challenges, then what should be the response of law enforcement agencies and others? We argue that a claim for the 'distinctiveness' (and hence 'newness') of digital crime, when compared with more traditional crimes, could perhaps be based on the former's virtuality, secrecy, proximity, scalability, malleability and portability, accessibility and de-localisation. Table 1.6 compares and contrasts the pertinence of each of these characteristics for digital and traditional crime.

However, it is acknowledged that the information in Table 1.6 represents a somewhat 'caricatured' description of both traditional and digital crime, suggesting a clear dichotomy which in fact rarely exists. In reality, crimes tend to be situated somewhere along a continuum between the two extremes for each characteristic, and many crimes exhibit both traditional and digital qualities. For example, a thief might attempt to fence the haul from a conventional (real world, physical) burglary in a digital environment such as eBay.

Digital crime also often exploits the fact that online environments provide the means to disseminate information widely, repeatedly and cheaply. As a result, what we might term the 'sucker quotient' for digital crime can be much lower than for conventional crime; the investment of time and effort for digital crime may be low,

Table 1.6   A Comparison of Digital and Traditional Crimes

Characteristic	Traditional crime	Digital crime	Notes
Virtuality	Takes place in a physical environment, here and now	Often takes place in a virtual (e.g. online) environment, less bounded by space and time	Note however a conflation between digital forensics (which increasingly occurs as part of the investigation of traditional crime) and 'pure' digital crime (such as DDoS attacks) – see above
Secrecy	Although offenders often attempt to hide their identity, their physical presence at a crime scene	Offenders can electronically hide their identities, their actions	Closely allied to the concepts of anonymity (see above) and proximity (see below)
Proximity	Offender and target/victim normally have to be physically close. Criminal conspirators will converge in the same place at the same time.	Offender and target/victim can be physically far apart. Criminal conspirators might never need to meet in person.	Locard's Principle applies in forensic investigation of traditional crime, as a consequence of proximity
Scalability	Most offences are committed singularly or in series	Offences can be committed in parallel and target many potential victims simultaneously at low cost– 'de minimis'	For example, the cost of sending email compared with conventional post. See below for a fuller description.
Malleability, portability and manipulability	The targets of traditional crime are often physical objects (such as cash) that occupy space and require physical concealment	Digital property occupies no space, can be easily stored and transmitted and converted into different forms	See above for a discussion of malleability
Accessibility	Offenders tend to target people and property that can be easily accessed; offenders remain relatively isolated and criminal methods spread slowly	The online world provides access to a myriad of targets and criminal possibilities and knowledge (e.g smartcard piracy, fake escrow scams)	One implication is that traditional crimes are easier to commit
De-localisation	The distances between offender and offence location tend to be physically constrained	The internet means that there are effectively no limits to the reach of the criminal; a hacker physically based in the Netherlands who hacks a PC in Germany but realises the gains in Belgium.	For example, in traditional domestic burglary crimes in the UK the average (mean) distance travelled from offender location to target is less than two miles (Wiles and Costello, 2000)

(Based in part on Clough, 2010, pp. 5–8, Yar 2005b, p. 5 and p.42, Sandywell 2010, p. 44, but definitions and explanations are the author's).

but the activity may still nonetheless provide high returns for the criminal. The 'traditional' con artist will only have access to a few hundred passers-by, and is dependent on quite a high proportion of them being gullible enough to fall victim to the con; the sucker quotient has to be relatively high for the con to yield results. On the other hand, a phisher can send tens of thousands of fake emails relatively easily, and even if only one victim responds and provides information, it could be subsequently used to commit identity theft, a potentially very lucrative crime. The pattern of rewards from other digital crimes follows a somewhat related principle of many victims incurring small losses. As Wall (2004, p. 30) suggests:

> Where once a robber might have had to put together a team of individuals ... in order to steal £1 million from a bank, new technologies are powerful enough (in principle at least) to enable one individual to rob one million people of £1 each.

Further, individual victims are also less likely to report the theft of small amounts and hence the authorities are less likely to be able to link these crimes together.

In many online crimes a combination of two or more of the seven characteristics above may be encountered. In terms of 'proximity' and 'reachability', in 2012 the Las Vegas Metro Police Department broke up what prosecutors in the US claimed was an illegal sports betting ring with alleged ties to organised crime, seizing more than $2.8 million in cash and casino chips, and arresting 25 people (Las Vegas Sun, 2012). The alleged conspirators lived in Las Vegas, California, New York, New Jersey and Pennsylvania, and the prosecutors claimed that they used an apparently legal gambling website physically based in Curacao, a Caribbean island off the coast of Venezuela, to electronically hide their proceeds. In the UK organised criminals are beginning to exploit the 'anonymity' and 'portability' of pre-paid gift cards (such as those available through iTunes) to launder money made from illegal activities – for example, in 2011 five men from Rochdale in the UK were jailed for using stolen credit card details to buy £750,000 worth of vouchers which they then re-sold through eBay (The Herald, 2011).

The History and Development of Digital Crime

In this section we examine the history of digital crime, and the much more vexed issue of the growth and development of digital crime. We provide an overview of some of the major events in the history of digital crime, although by necessity it is somewhat limited in scope and mainly from a UK and US perspective. (In terms of the latter, reference here is to only to Federal rather than State legislation, constitutional law or US Code. For example, Florida passed a Computer Crimes Act in 1978, and every US state outlaws hacking but the dates of such legislation are not provided here).

Table 1.7   A Brief History of Digital Crime

Year(s)	Event
Late 1950s and early 1960s	The origins of hacking in the MIT labs using PDP-1 mainframes
1957	In the US the 8 year old Joe Engressia discovers that the 2600 Hz tone allows control of a telephone trunk line and subsequently develops phone phreaking
1963	First use of the prefix 'cyber', but the association with digital technologies was not made until the 1970s
1969	The beginning of ARPANET (Advanced Research Projects Agency Network), a network built by the US Defence Agency to withstand nuclear attack. ARPANET was wound down in 1990.
Early 1970s	Beginning of widespread phone phreaking; for example John Draper (aka Cap'n Crunch) discovers that the a toy whistle generates the same 2600 hertz signal used by the US AT&T telephone switching network
1970–73	The US Union Dime Savings Bank loses $1.5 million when a chief teller uses a computer to commit fraud.
Mid 1970s	First examples of video piracy emerge using VCR tape machines
1975	John Walker inadvertently created the first ever virus (to distribute the game 'Animal'), which infected mainframes through executables run on magnetic tape.
1976	Bill Gates, in an open letter to the Homebrew Computer Club, alleged that its hobbyists had 'stolen' most of the software they were using.
1978	First electronic Bulletin Board Services (BBS) established
1979	Start of Usenet, quickly used by some to distribute copyright music, software and offensive sexual abuse imagery.
Early 1980s	A range of Bulletin Board Services (BBSs) were widely used. By 1990 the first arrests were made of individuals using BBSs to trade stolen credit card details and techniques to commit phreaking crimes (see below)
1981	The establishment of BITNET, a university-based network connected by modems; 'Captain Zap' (Ian Murphy) convicted of breaking into AT&T's computers and changing the computer time clock
1982	First use of the word 'cyberspace', subsequently popularised in William Gibson's 1984 book *Neuromancer*.
1983	The Hollywood film 'War Games' introduces the public to the concept of hacking, and the hacker as a hero or villain
1983	Arrest of the '414' gang, a group of teenagers accused of hacking around 60 computers, including at the Los Alamos National Laboratory (their exploits were earlier featured in 1982 as a cover story in the *Newsweek* magazine).
Mid 1980s	Advent of public key encryption; trading of 'warez' (illegally cracked and copied software) using BBSs.
1984	The 'Legion of Doom' hacking group formed.
1985	The '2600 BBS Seizure' in the US.

continued ...

Year(s)	Event
1986	The US Congress passes the Computer Fraud and Abuse Act; in many European countries stored-value phone chip cards are hacked; the first IBM-PC virus is seen (the 'Brain' virus), rapidly followed by other viruses; Robert Schifreen and Stephen Gold are prosecuted for illegally accessing the Duke of Edinburgh's electronic mail but their conviction is overturned on appeal.
1987	A Trojan horse virus that replicated itself (although not technically a worm) affected BITNET and other networks
1988	Robert Morris from Cornell University launched a self-replicating work that adversely affected thousands of networked computers; the UK's Copyright, Designs and Patent Act was passed.
Mid 1980s	First definition of 'computer virus', probably by Cohen at DEC
Mid 1980s	Attitudes to hacking began to change. More examples came to light of hackers using their skills and knowledge for personal criminal gain.
1989	Hackers in West Germany are found selling information obtained by breaking into US government networks to the KGB; publication of Clifford Stoll's book *The Cuckoo's Egg* which describes the tracking down of a hacker.
1989	Stealth viruses appear (such as 'dark avenger')
Late 1980s/ early 1990s	Probably the first use of the term 'cybercrime' as currently understood (origins unclear, but possibly linked with the 'cyberpunk' cultural era of 'cyber' books, film, TV, anime and gaming)
Early to mid 1990s	Growing use and popularity of the internet, particularly after the introduction of the Netscape Navigator browser in 1994; decline of BBSs; significant increase in computer crime in the West.
1990	First Botnet programs developed; in the US Operation Sundevil is launched against users of BBSs sharing illegal methods; the Computer Misuse Act 1990 (CMA) is passed in the UK
1991	PGP ('Pretty Good privacy') developed by Philip Zimmerman
1992	The 'Don't copy that Floppy' campaign in the US.
1993	Kevin Poulson convicted of computer and telephone fraud
1994	The UK's Sky TV smartcard is hacked with the source code distributed on BBSs and the internet; AOL (America Online) user's mailboxes congested by email bombs
1995	The Russian Vladimir Levin is found 'cracking' Citibank of around $10 million and transferring the funds to Finland and Israel; Kevin Mitnick arrested.
1996	First mention of phishing scams, although the scams (including 'advanced fee' such as the 419 scams) do not begin to surface in number until 2003–4; hackers deface the websites of the US Department of Justice, the US Air Force and the CIA; the US Congress adopts the Child Pornography Protection Act (the CPPA)
1997	First description of the concept of 'cyber-terrorism' (Pollitt); RIAA lawsuits against some of those involved in illegal file-sharing
1998	Release of the Trojan Horse program 'Back Orifice'; the US Digital Millennium Copyright Act is signed into law; UK-based and other police forces arrest over 100 men as part of 'Operation Cathedral' against a child sexual abuse imagery ring ('*The Wonderland Club*').

Year(s)	Event
1999	Napster music file-sharing site established (closed in 2001); Melissa (macro) virus, masquerading as an email attachment, causes hundreds of millions of dollars damage; an international criminal group ('Phonemaster') hacks the systems of MCI, Sprint, AT&T and others selling on calling-card numbers to Italian organised crime groups
Late 1990s	Emergence of DDoS tools such as 'Tribal Flood Network'
1999	The FBI launch a major investigation into 'Landslide Productions', an internet-based service offering, inter alia, sexual child abuse imagery. It led to hundreds of arrests and then to Operation Avalanche (US), Operation Ore (UK), Operation Snowball (Canada), Operation Amethyst (Ireland) and other LEA operations around the world.
2000	Major DDoS attack against eBay and Amazon. The 'I Love You' (or 'ILOVEYOU') virus causes significant damage to data across the world; peer-to-peer networks begin to emerge.
2001	Passing of the US Patriot Act; the EU's Convention on Cybercrime is adopted; 'Code Red' distributed and used in attempts to access Microsoft webservers; first illegal 'mods' of the Xbox console appear; the UK's National Hi-Tech Crime Unit (NHTCU) is formed, later subsumed within a larger organisation.
2002	Large DDoS attack on internet servers; the UK's Mobile Telephones (Re-programming) Act is passed; the FBI's Cyber Division is formed
2003	'Slammer' malware infects thousands of computers; formation of the hacker group 'Anonymous'
2004	US 'CAN SPAM' Act passed and first prosecutions under the Act; evidence against US serial killer Dennis Rader (the 'BTK killer') is found by examining the metadata left on a floppy disc
2006	Turkish hacker defaces over 20,000 websites; UK's Fraud Act is passed; Russian Business Network (RBN) registered as a website: RBN later becomes notorious for identify theft; cyber-attacks against over 70 organisations including the IOC
2007	Large-scale cyber-attack on Estonia; Austrian LEAs break an organised online child sexual abuse imagery ring, involving over 2000 people from over 70 different countries; spear-phishing attack against the office of the US Defence Secretary; the 'Storm' botnet is uncovered affecting at least a million computers, and considered a major risk by the FBI and other authorities
2008	Electrical supplies interrupted by hackers in the US; the group Anonymous hacks and distributes documents belonging to Scientologists; cyber-attacks against Georgian websites in the run up to the conflict in South Ossetia; the US Identity Theft and Restitution Act comes into effect; creation of the UK's Police Central e-Crime Unit (the PCeU).
2009	Conficker worm causes damage; Pirate Bay found guilty of copyright infringement; DDoS attack by Anonymous against the IFPI; US action (part of 'Operation Delego') closes the 'Dreamboard' website involved in the distribution of child abuse imagery, making over 50 arrests; cyber-attack allegedly originating in China on Google, Adobe and a number of other companies
2010	Stuxnet worm found and analysed: believed to be part of a cyber-attack against Iran's nuclear programme; concerted DDoS attacks against Burma

continued ...

Year(s)	Event
2011	'Lulz security' hacker group formed; Sony PlayStation network compromised and put off line, and details concerning millions of its users released; the FBI's 'Operation Ghost Click' targets a botnet consisting of more than 4 million infected computers in over 100 countries; 'Operation Swiper' directed against an organised theft ring in the US uncovers evidence of digital theft on a large scale
2012	Several UK government websites are brought down by 'Anonymous'; the European Cybercrime Centre (EC3) is established; in the US the proposed Cyber Intelligence Sharing and Protection Act (CISPA) is passed by the House of Representatives but is not yet law
2013	A number of newspapers (e.g. the *New York Times*) claim to be victims of organised Chinese hacking and theft of journalists' emails, contacts and files

David Wall (2007, p. 47) characterises the 'first generation' of cybercrime (pre 1970s) to be largely traditional crimes where computers were simply a tool to commit the crime. For 'second generation' cybercrime (post 1970s), new technology and networks meant that traditional crimes gradually became more distributed and globalised. The 'third generation' he suggests are *sui generis* cyber-crimes' (literally 'of its own kind', or unique), crimes that could and would not have existed without the internet.

In somewhat more specific terms we can also outline the historical development of digital crime. It first arose in the 1970s with the fraudulent use of mainframe computers. Then by the 1980s various forms of digital piracy, network crimes and malicious software were added to the mix. By the 1990s with the development of the internet and broadband there was a growing problem with hacking, online child sexual abuse crimes and IPR crimes, and post-2000, phishing, botnets and more sophisticated cybercrimes had become everyday players on the digital crime scene.

It is clear that from the outset, individuals have always exploited the new opportunities afforded by digital forms of representation, technologies and communication structures. For example, an early type of digital fraud exploited a particular aspect of the automated accounting systems employed on mainframe computers in a bank (Whiteside, 1978). The interest on customers' accounts would be automatically calculated to several decimal places, and this would inevitably often result in fractions of a cent. The figure would be rounded down before payment to the customer (for example, the program would calculate that interest payable that month as $12.2465 but only $12.24 could actually be paid to the customer). The usual routine was for the fractional differences (in this example 0.65 of one cent) to be temporarily added to a computer memory store, and when one cent had accumulated this would be arbitrarily added to the customer's next interest calculation, and the memory reset to zero. This was soon spotted by unscrupulous bank employees who would modify the program to 'siphon off' the fractions to an account that they controlled which would soon accrue substantial amounts of money. The technique was known as the 'salami' fraud; each stolen slice was very thin. Compare this with pre-digital automated forms of calculation – such a fraud would be almost inconceivable before the advent of digital forms of calculation.

Extent and Economic Cost of Digital Crime

There is debate about the current extent of digital crime around the world. However it is clear that in parallel with the increasing rapid adoption of digital technologies and the number of organisations and individuals accessing the internet, there has also been a rapid increase in the volume and variety of digital crimes committed. Whereas 20 years ago it was still just possible to view cybercrime as 'a highly sophisticated activity that the technologically unsophisticated and uninitiated find difficult to grasp' (Treadwell, 2012, p. 176) it is now undoubtedly much more 'mainstream'. In 2012, approximately four out of five households in Britain (21 million) had internet access (Office of National Statistics, 2012), presenting vast opportunities for the criminally minded, and as is often observed within criminology, 'crime always follows opportunity'.

Without doubt, digital crime carries both significant economic and human costs. However, estimates for the precise financial cost of digital crime (to economies, organisations and individuals) vary wildly, and many such studies are statistically suspect and unreliable. In the majority of countries most of the reliable data, where it exists, is derived from reported and police recorded crime statistics. Additional data may be available from victim surveys (such as the Crime Survey for England and Wales; the Information Security Breaches Survey; the Oxford Internet Surveys; and the Internet Watch Foundation). Even so, there are problems with using recorded data; as Wall notes, cybercrimes often 'fall outside the normal police routine business, which means that unless they are substantial (over £500– £1000, sometimes even more) they are often not investigated even when reported, and most importantly not recorded' (Wall, 2013, p. 6). Using data on prosecutions as a proxy for the extent of digital crime is also problematic because some digital crimes may be prosecuted using laws not specifically intended for computer or other electronic crime (probably because the crimes involved acts that did not necessarily have to be committed by using a computer or through a network). This makes the tracking of the incidence, reporting and recording of digital crime all the more difficult. Moreover, it could be argued that many present-day crimes are likely to include some element of electronic evidence because mobile phones and the internet are now so widely used.

As we saw earlier, defining digital crime is often difficult and this compounds the problem of estimating the extent of digital crimes. The UK's Institute for Engineering and Technology and others argue that:

> … any reported statistics that purport to state the extent of, growth in, or damage caused by cybercrime or e-crime, should be regarded with considerable caution

> unless they are accompanied by full definitions of these terms, a breakdown of the incidents that fall into each sub-category and full details of how any losses have been calculated. (Engineering the Future, 2012)

Further problems in estimating the extent of cybercrime include: the inherent difficulty in economically quantifying certain types of cybercrime (for example DDoS attacks); the fact that companies that fall victim to cybercrimes may prefer to keep this information confidential because a public report might compromise their reputation; victims simply not reporting digital crime because of the small loss incurred or through embarrassment (for example, being subject to a drive-by attack after visiting an adult content website).

One widely cited estimate from the UK ('The Cost of Cyber Crime' produced by Detica in February 2011 and endorsed by the Cabinet Office; Detica, 2011), estimates the cost of cybercrime to the UK to be around £27 billion per year, or approximately 2 per cent of GDP. However, the research conducted for the report did not take into account some digital crimes, for example cyber-stalking and child sexual abuse imagery, because indirect costs were not considered. It focused instead on digital economic crimes such as fraud, identity theft, intellectual property rights theft, extortion and industrial espionage (although the latter is not even technically a crime in the UK).

The security company Symantec regularly publishes estimates of the cost of cybercrime, not only for the US and the UK but also in global terms. For example, in 2012, Symantec estimated that globally there were 556 million victims of consumer cybercrime a year, with a global financial cost of $110 billion (Symantec, 2012). Other estimates from industry include those produced by the Ponemon Institute (sponsored by HP Enterprise Security), the Motion Picture Association of America (MPAA), and the Recording Industry Association of America (RIAA). Such estimates are often accused of being over-inflated, sometimes to comic effect (see for example Reid (2012)).

In 2012 Anderson et al. published what they claimed to be 'the first systematic study of the costs of cybercrime' (Anderson et al., 2012, p. 1) in a report prepared for the UK's Ministry of Defence, following the sceptical response to the Detica report described above. For many of the reasons we have already explored, the authors of the new report were reluctant to put any kind of definitive figure on the cost of cybercrime to any one country. However, it states in relation to cyber-fraud (such as the use of fake anti-virus software) that one cyber-crook's earnings 'might amount to a couple of dollars per citizen per year (ibid., p. 25). The report also argued, based upon the available figures with the inherent data limitations, that we are spending too much on security defence solutions such as firewalls, anti-phishing toolbars and anti-virus software, and significantly, that a relatively small number of criminal gangs are responsible for a large proportion of cybercrimes. They suggest it would therefore be better if more resources were deployed on law enforcement measures so these groups are caught, prosecuted and imprisoned.

As David Wall (2010) and others have noted, our perception of the seriousness of digital crime (and cybercrime in particular) is almost certainly also influenced by dystopic science fiction (including hacker narratives), 'haxploitation' movies (from *War Games* in 1983, via *Hackers* in 1995 to *The Matrix* in 1999), TV and video games as well as sensationalist reporting in the press. In many of these accounts there are distinct echoes of the process that Edward Said referred to as 'othering' (Said, 1979): a casting of groups as different 'others' to better affirm our own 'self', but also the superiority of the group we belong to (for example, a 'westerner'). Between 2007 and 2010 Karatgozianni surveyed the 'mainstream' media (such as national newspapers) and found Russia to be regularly portrayed as the top national producer of viruses (Karatgozianni, 2010, p. 130) and as a nation of 'super-hackers' responsible for sophisticated cyber-attacks (ibid.), with Russian hackers presented as talented highly educated individuals forced to turn to cybercrime to make a living. Interestingly, attitudes to hacking have changed; the contemporaneous meaning of the term 'hacker' has slipped from being a reference to person who can coax an unsuccessful program into some kind of life or devise an innovative solution, to being an archetypal 'cybercriminal' (Wade et al., 2011).

Finally, note that there are theoretical arguments against attempting to quantify digital crime as a separate and distinct form of criminal activity. In his book *Hypercrime: The New Geometry of Harm*, McGuire (2007) argues that the cybercrime paradigm is intrinsically problematic, and that our level of concern about cybercrime is not matched by the real risks. According to McGuire, in many key respects cyberspace is no different to 'ordinary' space, albeit it in a more extended and complicated form. This 'hyperspatialisation' does not lead to new crime per se but rather an expansion of already existing forms of deviancy into an extended environment, an echo perhaps of Grabosky's reference to 'old wine in new bottles' (in Brenner 2004).

Categorisation of Digital Crime

As discussed earlier in this chapter, digital crime is often defined by delineating the broad sweep into distinct typologies. Here we provide an overview of the different examples of digital crime and anti-social behaviour. The emphasis before the 1980s in terms of the categorisation of digital crime tended to be on computer crime. An early (and particularly influential) way of distinguishing between different forms of 'computer crime' was set out by Donn Parker in the 1970s and 80s. The typology (Parker, 1976, 1983 and 1998 cited by Casey 2011, p. 40) differentiates between:

- the computer as object of crime (e.g. a PC that is stolen or maliciously physically damaged);
- the computer as the subject of a crime (e.g. a tablet PC infected by a virus); and

- the computer as a tool in committing a crime (e.g. in order to share obscene images).

There are clear advantages to this approach, and it still has its adherents as it provides clear demarcation between crimes which are genuinely novel and those which are simply 're-tooled', and as Casey notes (ibid., p. 40) it can provide useful guidance to investigator on the likely motivation of an offender. However, the inclusion of 'computer as object' in particular will strike many readers as rather dated.

More latterly, David Wall's approach to classification (set out in detail in Wall, 2001, pp.3–9) has been more pervasive. He drew a broad distinction between 'computer assisted' and 'computer oriented' crimes and proposed the existence of four groups of behaviours:

- cyber-trespass (unauthorised entry into computer systems, for example, hacking);
- (cyber)-deceptions/thefts (online acquisitive harm such as cyber-piracy);
- (cyber)-pornography/obscenity (online publication or trading of sexual materials); and
- (cyber)-violence (online violence enacted on individuals or groups, such as cyber-stalking).

Note that Wall describes the four areas as 'types of behaviour' (Wall, 2001, p. 3) rather than a typology, and explains that they illustrate a range of activities and themes in public debates rather than specific criminal offences.

These 'cyber-behaviours' are often sub-divided into typologies, as illustrated in Table 1.8. (Note the categories below are not mutually exclusive e.g. cyber-harassment could well also include cyber-violence and that, for example, Wall includes 'cyber-terrorist' under the general heading of 'cyber-trespasser', (Wall, 2001, p. 4). The reader will also encounter many other forms of cybercrime described in the literature, such as 'cyber-hatred', 'cyber-rape' and so on).

The Council of Europe's Convention on Cybercrime (2001), also signed by the US and several other non-European countries, adopts a definition of cybercrime which focusses primarily on the offences that should be included and the measures that should be taken by signatories to the Convention. We summarise these measures in Table 1.9 (we have omitted Articles 11 and 12 which address attempts, aiding or abetting and corporate liability):

The Convention itself has received wide international support (for example, from the Organisation of American States). However, given that the offences were first defined in 2001 there are now inevitably some omissions. There have been attempts to add to the list above, for example to include 'acts of a racist or xenophobic nature committed through computer networks' (Council of Europe, 2006). These are categorised as 'Additional Protocols' to the main Convention, and the process of agreement is slow; only a few countries are signatories.

Table 1.8   Typologies of Cyber-behaviours

Type of cybercrime	Explanation	Example
Cyber-violence	Using digital means in an attempt to inflict (usually psychological) harm on others	Homophobic and racist abuse via social network sites
Cyber-theft	Use of cyberspace to commit, or attempt, crimes of theft of data	Phishing for payment card details, stealing IPR digital property
Cyber-trespass	Unauthorised accessing of computer systems belonging to another	Hacking and cracking
Cyber-damage (or 'cyber-vandalism')	Deliberate damage against digital structures	Website defacement, sometimes as part of a political demonstration ('hactivism'); damage to an operating system caused by a virus
Cyber-obscenity	Use of the internet to view, distribute and trade obscene and offensive materials	Electronic trading in child sexual abuse imagery; 'sexting'
Cyber-harassment	The use of online environments to facilitate harassment activities	Stalking and bullying activities via email and social networks
Cyber-terrorism	Use of online environments to promote or enact acts of terrorism	Widespread DDoS attack against the internet in Estonia, 2007

(Based in part on Wall, 2001 although the explanations and examples are the author's).

Table 1.9   The Categorisation of Offences in the Convention on Cybercrime

Offence		Meaning
Offences against the confidentiality, integrity and availability of computer data and systems	Illegal access	'the access to the whole or any part of a computer system without right'
	Illegal interception	'interception without right, made by technical means, of non-public transmissions of computer data to, from or within a computer system'
	Data interference	'the [intentional] damaging, deletion, deterioration, alteration or suppression of computer data without right'
	System interference	'the serious hindering without right of the functioning of a computer system by inputting, transmitting, damaging, deleting, deteriorating, altering or suppressing computer data'

continued ...

Offence		Meaning
Computer-related offences	Computer-related forgery	'[commit intentionally] and without right, the input, alteration, deletion, or suppression of computer data, resulting in inauthentic data with the intent that it be considered or acted upon for legal purposes as if it were authentic, regardless whether or not the data is directly readable and intelligible'
	Computer-related fraud	'[intentionally causing] the of a loss of property to another person by any input, alteration, deletion [or] suppression of computer data [or] any interference with the functioning of a computer system, with fraudulent or dishonest intent of procuring, without right, an economic benefit'
Content-related offences	Offences related to child pornography	'[producing, offering, making available, distributing, transmitting, procuring (for oneself or for another) child pornography through a computer system]' or 'possessing child pornography in a computer system or on a computer-data storage medium'
Offences related to infringements of copyright and related rights	Offences related to infringements of copyright and related rights	'[infringement of copyright] where such acts are committed wilfully, on a commercial scale and by means of a computer system'

The FBI defines a number of categories of cybercrime, for example, 'computer intrusion' is listed as 'Bots, Worms, Viruses, Spyware, Malware, Hacking' (FBI, 2013). However, as Finklea and Theohary observe, 'Federal law enforcement agencies often define cybercrime based on their jurisdiction and the crimes they are charged with investigating' (Finklea and Theohary, 2013, p. 2). There is no overarching official definition of cybercrime in the US (ibid.).

As noted earlier, digital crime normally includes not only crimes usually categorised as 'computer crimes' or 'cybercrimes' but also other crimes where a digital opportunity is exploited. In Table 1.10 we provide our own detailed differentiation between digital crimes, based on previous work in this field, and with the proviso that digital crime rarely fits neatly into defined typologies; the categories described are not mutually exclusive (for example 'copyright infringement' is usually consider a form of 'intellectual property theft'), nor is the list exhaustive. Note also that we have not provided the legal definitions (where these exist) as they vary from jurisdiction to jurisdiction. The very existence of some of the 'crimes' is also contested (for example, cyber-warfare).

Table 1.10   A Detailed Categorisation of Digital Crimes

Type of digital crime	Digital crime	Explanation	Examples
Piracy and IPR crimes	Intellectual property theft	Stealing intellectual property, such as inventions, images and designs	Hacking the computer systems of a commercial company to steal software for chip design (often facilitated by an 'insider')
	Copyright infringement	Making unauthorised copies of digital or other content and products	Torrents used to share music and video, 'warez' software, commercial DVD copying
	Trademark infringement	Unauthorised using of the same or similar registered trademark	Online selling of goods using another's trademark and logo
	Counterfeiting	Producing an imitation version	Using digital means to counterfeit currency
	Circumvention of conditional access systems	Bypassing or 'fooling' systems which control access to paid products or services	Smartcard emulation using PIC chips, satellite TV card-sharing
Abuse of Network	DDoS attacks	Distributed Denial of Service: Attempting to overwhelm and disable a computer system by repeatedly requesting information	ICMP flood, peer-to-peer forms of attack
	PBX hacking (phreaking)	Hacking telephone system and exchanges to enable free and untraceable calls	Criminals trading CBX/PBX maintenance port numbers and passwords
	Spamming	Unsolicited, bulk electronic communication, either to sell a product or pass on malware	SpamSoldier sending out SMS messages from Android OS phones
	Botnets	A connected net of computers, controlled without the knowledge of the users	Rustock botnet sending spam
Trespass, illegal access or interception	Hacking and Cracking	Accessing a computer without the user's knowledge or permission	Includes illegally accessing corporate and personal data for commercial purposes, for selling on to organised crime groups
	VoIP interception/ interruption	Intercepting or breaking into VoIP calls	Launching a DDoS attack to deprive a company of its VoIP service

continued ...

Type of digital crime	Digital crime	Explanation	Examples
Malware	Virus, worms, trojans etc.	Malicious programmes or code that replicate themselves. Malicious software affecting PCs, smartphones etc. but may also be installed via 'pop-up' windows, initiated via a phone (e.g. purporting to be from Microsoft)	Drive-by websites ransomware (for example, as delivered by Citadel malware) Loozfon malware (Android operating system) 'Boy in the Browser' (BitB) trojans
Offensive material	Child sexual abuse imagery	Obscene sexual imagery of pre-pubescent and pubescent children	Use of 'deep web' resources to sell images
	Internet hate crime	Electronically making and distributing material with the intent to stir up hatred on the grounds of race, religion, sexual orientation or disability	'Far right' webpages glorifying violence against ethnic minority groups
	Cyber-sex	Sharing sexual content with others without the permission of the person concerned	Sexting via smartphones
Inter-personal aggression	Cyber-harassment	Using digital means to cause alarm and distress to others	Repeated personal comments made on Facebook
	Cyber-bullying	Harassing, threatening or un-reasonably embarrassing another person using digital means	Repeated sending of bullying SMS texts
	Cyber-stalking	Restricting a person's freedom by constant monitoring, contacting and spying	Stalking an ex-girlfriend using the GPS tracking device on a smartphone
	Libel	Online libelling of a person	Allegations made through a Twitter account
Conflict and Espionage	Cyber-warfare	'Authorised' attacks on the computer systems and networks of one or more nation states conducted by another	The 2009 attacks on official organisations in the US and South Korea allegedly emanating from North Korea; the Stuxnet worm
	Cyber-terrorism	The use of terrorist methods over networks	Few, if any, documented cases
	Cyber-attack	A general term for any concerted and organised attack on a computer system or network	The 2013 attacks on the computer systems of the New York Times

Type of digital crime	Digital crime	Explanation	Examples
Illegal services	Unregulated Gambling	Unlicensed betting using online means or other digital technologies	Illegal website poker games
	Pharmaceuticals, controlled substances and alcohol	Selling of prescription-only or otherwise restricted drugs or alcohol through the internet	Illegal online pharmacies
	Weapons and firearms	Selling over the internet of weapons and firearms to individuals with no legal right to ownership	Alleged market in weapons through 'dark web'
Theft, Fraud and Forgery	Card cloning	Copying some or all of information contained on a credit, debit or other form of payment card	Using a skimmer secretly fitted to an ATM to collect personal account and other details; intercepting and capturing PIN during payment
	Re-chipping, unblocking tele-communication devices	Changing a SIM card; re-programming a mobile telephone	Using software and hardware to offer an 'unblocking' service
	Advanced fee fraud	Using digital means to request upfront payment for goods or services that are non-existent	The so called Nigerian '419' fraud and variants
	Identity theft/ Identity fraud	General term for obtaining online personal and/or official information about a person normally with the intent to commit an offence	Creating a fake profile on a social networking site using somebody else's name and details
	Online auction fraud	Offering for auction items which are then not delivered, or misrepresented in some way	Using digital images to fake the existence of an item for auction; offering what appears to be an expensive item but is simply a description
	User account theft	Using various means to collect information about a person's computer or network account	User-accounts are hacked from a variety of sources: websites, forums, Xbox live accounts etc.
	Digital forgery	Using digital technology and software to illegal alter a document or other object	Altering passports and other identity documents

continued ...

Type of digital crime	Digital crime	Explanation	Examples
	Phishing	Attempting to steal identity information such as login, password and personal identification numbers using electronic means	Email masquerading as from the recipient's tax office requesting that they complete details online
	Spear-phishing	Personalised and individualised and often more credible version of phishing	An email that purports to be from a person's employer with authentic details harvested from a social network site but carrying malware
	Phone-based scams	Attempt to elicit information to conduct theft or to gain access to SIM card or mobile or to make unauthorised calls	Phone call purporting to be from recipient's bank. Text message claiming recipient has won a prize
Extortion	Cyber-extortion	Using electronic means to obtain money or other property of value by issuing threats or using force	Mounting a DDoS attack against an online casino and then threatening more if payment is not received
	Cyber-squatting, domain name piracy	Registering domain names with the intent to gain or profit	Registering a domain name confusingly similar to a well-known company with the intention of profiting from the confusion

Chapter 2

Criminological and Psychological Perspectives

Robin Bryant

Introduction

In this chapter we examine a number of criminological and psychological perspectives and discuss how these might help with the policing of cyber and other network-related crimes. For a variety of reasons, for example the inevitable difficulties encountered when researching online illegal activity, this is not a widely researched or discussed subject. However, there is perhaps a deeper reason why criminological theory emanating from the study of digital crime is relatively sparse; the 'newness' or otherwise of many crimes encountered in networked digital environments, as discussed in Chapter 1. However, some might argue that theft, whether it occurs from a shop in a local high street or after a successful phishing event is simply theft, and its occurrence requires no new theory, nor even the shoehorning of traditional theory into the postmodern world. There would appear to be some substance to this argument, particularly where genuine cybercrime (for example, hacking) is conflated with digital forensics evidence recovery (for example, the recovery of location data from a satnav device). After all, it is people who commit crimes, not technology, and presumably people will continue to commit crime for the same time-honoured reasons; addiction, greed, revenge, jealousy, poverty (amongst a myriad of others). However, as we discussed in Chapter 1, the virtual nature of much cybercrime in particular does provide what Segel calls a 'compelling challenge' to criminologists (Segel, 2008, p. 33). With this in mind we look primarily in this chapter at how some traditional and psychological criminological theory (for example, routine activities theory) might apply within the novel contexts provided by a digital network environment. This inevitably begs the question of what possible relevance could psychology and criminology have for the policing of digital crime? We propose two main responses here. Firstly, theory might provide the basis of preventative strategies for countering the further development of certain particular digital crimes, and could therefore reduce the occurrence of some criminal activities. Secondly, grounded criminological and psychological theory, carefully applied, can provide additional leads for police investigation of digital crime, for example a better understanding of the personality of an online child groomers might help investigators predict the means by which the suspect would collect, collate and store digital imagery.

Although we will consider criminological and psychological perspectives separately here, there is in practice often no such clear distinction, not only in terms of arbitrary discipline division but also in terms of the application of the theory. For example, a number of psychological perspectives have clear links with the positivist school of criminology (see below), and some criminological and psychological theories clearly articulate or overlap, both between and within, the two disciplines. The US criminologist Akers argued, for example, that rational choice theory is a consequence of social learning theory, and not separate from it (Akers, 1990, cited in Blackburn, 1993, p. 109). Nor (as would also be the case with other, more conventional 'non-digital' crime), have we attempted to identify an all-embracing and explicative theory from within the canon of criminological theory; it is very unlikely that 'one size' will fit all. Instead we have identified below the criminological and psychological perspectives which appear to offer the greatest value to law enforcement. The chapter concludes with an examination of a number of specific digital crimes. We seek to identify how theory and research each illuminate the motives and methods for committing these crimes, and also suggest some ways in which theory and research inform (or might inform) their policing.

Criminological Perspectives

Criminology draws upon a wide range of disciplines, for example, sociology, psychology and history. Broadly, criminological theory can be conceptualised as falling under one of three main headings or 'Schools':

- classical/neo-classical theory (rational choice theory, routine activity theory);
- positivist theory (biosocial and psychological theories, the Chicago school, social learning/differential association theory); and
- sociological theory (strain/anomie theory, social control theory, labelling).

However, these categories are far from being mutually exclusive, nor are they exhaustive. For example, labelling theory has its basis in sociological theory but an application of labelling theory at the level of the individual is also likely to invoke a psychological mechanism as an explanatory factor. Similarly, differential association theory (as part of social learning theory) is often associated with the behaviourist tradition in psychology (see below).

Table 2.1 provides a summary of the main theories, and includes examples to illustrate some of the ways in which each theory could apply within the context of digital crime. Some of the theories are developed further in the sections that follow.

All of the theories listed in Table 2.1 pre-date most forms of digital crime and certainly pre-date the internet, but this does not in itself invalidate the theories in

Table 2.1   Criminological Theories and Digital Crime

School	Example of theory	Brief description of the theory	Possible application to understanding digital crime
Classical or neo-classical	Rational Choice	Crime is a rational act, that needs no special explanation, other than that it is a consequence of a 'cost-benefits' analysis	Phishing; the potential benefits (economic) far outweigh the possible costs (detection and punishment)
	Routine Activity	Crime occurs when motivated offenders and attractive targets intersect in time and space, with no or ineffective capable guardianship	Online IPR crimes – for example, illegal downloading of copyright-protected content
	Control/General Theory of Crime	The absence of effective control (external or within the individual) leads to crime	Hacker groups coalescing and expanding
Sociological	Social Disorganisation	The breakdown of informal social controls allow the progressive dominance of criminal cultures (see also 'Broken Windows' theory)	Innovations in digital crime often originate from countries and populations experiencing rapid social change
	Social Learning/ Differential Association/ Subcultures	Crime is a form of behaviour learned through association with others: those involved in crime itself, or tolerant of its existence	Assimilation of attitudes and learning of criminal methods (for example, payment card crime) through online forums and/or social networks
Positivist	Strain (anomie)	Individuals lack legitimate opportunities to achieve their goals (for example, wealth, status, authority) and use illegal means instead	Illegal online 'pharmacies' offering prescription drugs
	Labelling	Individuals 'labelled' as being criminal or anti-social unwittingly adopt the label (a form of self-fulfilling prophecy)	'Hacktivists' who turn to non-political internet fraud after criminalisation

the context of digital crime. However, as Prichard et al. (2011, p. 585) note, there has been a hesitancy amongst criminologists to apply criminological theory to digital crime, and for a number of reasons: the rapid changes in communications technology, the distributed and nefarious nature of the internet, problems around 'cyber-law' and how it applies to victims and offenders, and not least the scarcity of reliable data surrounding digital crime.

Despite these reservations, there are nonetheless some notable applications of criminological theory to digital crime, some of which we discuss below. There is also the growing field of 'cyber-criminology' (see, for example, Moore, 2011, Chapter 13) which either seeks to 're-tool' existing theories for the digital era, or to even develop distinctly different theories (e.g. Jaishankar's 'Space Transition Theory', see Jaishankar, 2008).

Social Learning Theory and Differential Association

A major criminological theory is 'social learning theory'. It was developed from Edwin Sutherland's differential association theory, and subsequently revised, for example by Akers, (1985). According to social learning theory, crime is a learned behaviour and in this sense is essentially no different from other more socially acceptable examples of learned behaviours. Individuals, particularly young people, learn through communicating and participating in groups, and in the early years this takes place within the immediate group surrounding the child, normally the family. The child assimilates a general sense of what is 'normal' from what they experience and see in day-to day events. From adolescence onwards, other social groups become more influential, including peer groups. (However, it is important to note that social learning theory is not the same as 'peer group pressure' but is instead a more subtle form of social learning). If a person associates mainly with groups that consider crime as normal and acceptable behaviour and less frequently with those that consider criminal acts as unacceptable, the person is more likely to adopt the stance of the former than the latter. Hence 'differential association' underpins the rationale for the theory. Some parts of the internet, particularly Web 2.0, are very much comprised of 'groups', such as usenet, Google groups, blogs, forums and FaceBook, and these all provide new opportunities for differential association with no geographical limitations. Many of the groups are based on special interests, most of which are entirely legal in outlook. However some social groups operating on the internet are undoubtedly used by their members for communicating and sharing information relating to digital crimes, including practical details on how to perpetrate such activities.

Early accounts of hacking (during the late1980s) fit easily within the social learning theory and differential association frames of reference. The hacker is portrayed as a loner with poor traditional social skills, associating almost only with other like-minded individuals to the exclusion of 'normal' people (e.g. Sterling, 1992). The accounts describe how hackers learn their behaviour from others, sometimes through membership of quasi-secret hacking groups such as 'Cult of the Dead Cow' and 'Legion of Doom'. The hackers were also perceived as needing the approval and respect of their hacking peers, their behaviour being reinforced due to the prestige they acquired by demonstrating hacking knowledge and skills. Quite possibly reinforcement also occurred through the romanticised versions of hacking that appeared at the time in the popular press and media (such as the 1995 fictional Hollywood film 'Hackers', featuring two teenagers who used their hacking skills to thwart a plot to unleash a damaging virus). In the early 1990s it was still just about possible to view hacking as largely a harmless activity, undertaken primarily for its intellectual and technical challenge, and with its own form of ethical code. (This was despite the fact there was abundant evidence of malicious hacking activity pre-dating this period, and that hacking, per se, was illegal in many countries of the world). Since then however, hacking has moved away from its more idealistic and free-thinking origins to embrace a wide typology of behaviour, including hacking undertaken for criminal purposes. These changes have been so significant that some commentators now prefer the term 'cracker' to describe criminally-motivated hacking (see Yar, 2005a). Disappointingly, little research has been conducted on whether social learning theory can provide a successful basis for the analysis of the more criminally-intent forms of hacking.

Social learning theory would therefore seem to provide a persuasive explanation for at least some forms of behaviour associated with digital crime. However, there are some general limitations for such theories, for example, differential association in particular offers no explanation for why people in superficially similar circumstances behave differently – why do some choose to 'learn' deviant behaviour whilst others do not (Newburn, 2007, p. 152)? We would suggest that part of the explanation might be that a person is not merely a passive recipient of his or her environment; most people play an active role in creating and shaping their immediate environment, for instance when choosing friends and leisure activities.

Routine Activities Theory

Routine activities theory (RAT, and also known as routine activity theory) was developed by the criminologists Ron Clarke and Marcus Felson in the 1980s and 1990s (Clarke and Felson, 1993), although it has its roots in much earlier classical and neo-classical theories. They proposed that crime (and in particular acquisitive crime) was modelled as a consequence of three variables ranging over space and time:

1. the existence of a suitable target;
2. the presence of a motivated offender; and
3. the absence of a suitable guardian (which includes non-human guardians, such as alarm systems).

Crime at a certain location and time would be more or less likely to occur depending on how these variables combined. There is some empirical evidence supporting this idea when considering traditional forms of crime or anti-social behaviour (for example, Goff, 2008). As an example of 'three variable RAT' applied to a conventional crime, consider a public car park with a growing number of thefts of satnavs. Some of the local residents from the adjacent housing estate are recidivist volume crime offenders, the car park is poorly lit and largely unsupervised, and there are no CCTV cameras nearby. In terms of the RAT variables we have:

- suitable targets in the form of cars with valuables;
- motivated offenders from the neighbouring estate; and
- few capable guardians; poor security and monitoring.

Felson and Clarke (1998, cited in Burke, 2005), later added a specific form of guardianship to the routine activities mix, namely the 'intimate handler', a person who would normally exercise some restraining control over the potential offender. Examples of an intimate handler would include a parent or significant other. With respect to digital crime, sitting and using a tablet or laptop tends to be a solitary activity, and it is far less obvious to an intimate handler that a person may be engaged in a form of online criminal activity.

Routine activities theory has been particularly influential in terms of approaches to crime reduction and is almost an orthodoxy (certainly in the UK) in terms of 'official' ways of conceptualising high volume acquisitive crime. A crime reduction strategy for the car park scenario above would involve an analysis of each of the three components. In terms of motivated offenders little could be done, at least in the short term, but steps could be taken to encourage users of the car park to remove valuables from sight and there are some reasonably obvious ways in which we could increase the guardianship, including installing CCTV or monitoring the car park in some other way.

However, now consider the illegal downloader of copyrighted media from the internet, probably using peer-to-peer software or accessing usenet. This activity requires minimal technical knowledge on the part of the downloader, and there is no shortage of suitable targets. For example, a search using the BitTorrent isohunt. com site in May 2012 for the DVD rip of the film 'Contagion' showed over 55,000 IP addresses 'seeding' and over 34,000 'leeching'. The forms of motivation here are likely to include:

- relatively instant gratification;
- low financial cost (which is in any case difficult to disaggregate from the broadband costs the user might be paying);
- a greater range of product 'on offer', including unauthorised or unissued recordings, foreign language albums and 'bootlegs'; and
- libertarian beliefs in the 'freedom' of intellectual property (Wall, 2007, p. 97).

At any one time there are likely to be millions of people around the world using peer-to- peer software to share copyrighted media and software. Although there are occasional highly publicised reports of filesharers (particularly uploaders) being pursued for costs, people who are sharing relatively low-volumes are likely to be aware that the probability of detection is small, that the consequences normally involve no more than paying costs, and that they might only face civil action (rather than criminal proceedings). There is the distinct lack of any sense of a capable guardian. It would seem therefore that RAT provides a reasonably sound explanation for the phenomenon of illegal file-sharing, or 'digital piracy' (Higgins, 2007).

However, when applied more generally to digital crime (and particularly cybercrime) RAT may begin to show its limitations. As Yar (2005b) argues, these limitations become most acute where crimes are enacted in virtual environments. For example, much of RAT is based on the reasonable assumption that the motivated offender and suitable victim must be present at the same time at the same place for a crime to occur. However, for a range of cybercrimes this seems not to be the case as many can be committed at distance and can even (in the example of Trojan viruses) be displaced in time.

Maimon et al. (2013) argue that Yar's point might well be correct in the broad context of cyberspace but a distinction needs to be drawn between a motivated offender's and victim's presence on a computer network and hence Yar's assumption of temporal convergence might be 'misleading' (ibid., p. 337). In 2011 van Wilsem attempted an integrated approach to comparing both 'traditional' and 'digital' risk factors for victimisation but found that 'routine activity theory needs to be tested in new ways in contemporary digitalised societies' (van Wilsem, p. 115).

In conclusion, perhaps 'classic' RAT can be reconciled with the digital era through extending the definitions of targets, offenders and guardians; certainly, the notion of a target needs further exploration in terms of cybercrime. In general, the target in RAT is in essence an opportunity to commit a crime, which also often includes the notion of a victim. For cybercrimes, the opportunity presents itself to a potential offender, but as we have already noted, the harm caused by the offender's actions is very unlikely to take place within the offender's vicinity, and the offender does not have to be in any contact with the victim or the victim's physical possessions – a cybercrime may be effectively extended through time and space. This however is of no consequence to the applicability of RAT if the notion of a target is narrowed to that of an opportunity and excludes any notion of a victim within the vicinity of the offender. For a potential cyber-offender, the RAT target of a crime presents simply as an opportunity to commit a crime.

Adapted and 're-tooled' versions of RAT have been used with some success to analyse online phenomena such as 'cyber-stalking' and online fraud. For example, Reyns et al. (2011) applied 'cyberlifestyle-routine activities theory' and found that the risk of cyber-stalking victimisation (amongst a sample of around a thousand college students) was positively associated with online proximity to motivated offenders and online target attractiveness, and negatively associated with online guardianship. They concluded that RAT could be successfully adapted to cyberspace to explain online forms of victimisation (ibid., p. 1164). Pratt et al. (2010) applied a 'generalised' and 'digitalised' version of RAT ('Routine Online Theory') to internet fraud (using a sample of 900 plus adults from Florida) and concluded by noting that their findings supported the routine activity perspective (ibid., p. 268). Kigerl (2012) attempted to apply RAT at the level of 'high cyber-crime countries' rather than individual offender behaviour but his conclusions were more concerned with the effects of unemployment on cybercrime activity (ibid., pp. 483–4).

Psychological Perspectives

Whereas the criminological theory discussed above is normally concerned with crime as a phenomenon, psychological perspectives are often based on the behaviour and motivation of the individual. Put simplistically, psychology is rooted more in 'criminals' than in 'crimes'.

General psychological perspectives on the policing of digital crime usually arise from four main traditions: Psychodynamic Theories, Behaviourist Theories, Cognitive Theories and Personality Theories. Most of these traditions arose in the early to mid-twentieth century. Psychodynamic theories are often associated with their founder, Sigmund Freud (1859–1939). Freud himself had little to say about crime but one of his followers, John Bowlby (1907–1990), developed an influential 'maternal deprivation' thesis which was firmly rooted in the psychodynamic tradition. Behaviourist theories originated with the well-known classical conditioning experiments of Ivan Pavlov (1848–1939) and were then extensively developed by John Watson (1878–1958) and B.F. Skinner (1904–1990). Cognitive social psychology theories are usually associated with Ulric Neisser (1928–2012) – particularly in the US, and Lawrence Kohlberg's (1927–1987) notion of 'moral reasoning' has been particularly influential psychology of crime, as has the extensive contribution of Albert Bandura (1929–). Personality theories are normally associated with the work of Hans Eysenck (1916–1990). We provide an overview of the four main traditions in Table 2.2, which also includes some possible examples as illustrations.

Table 2.2   Psychological Traditions and Digital Crime

	Key features	Example of a possible application to digital crime
Psychodynamic	The subconscious; the id, ego and superego. Criminal behaviour is a consequence of disruption of the psyche due to inadequate development of the superego.	Understanding of motivation of 'ego' cyber-criminals, for example hacking as electronic vandalism
Behaviourist	The concepts of stimulus and response, reinforcement (negative and positive) and punishment. Classical conditioning and operant conditioning.	The reinforcement of a cyber-stalker's behaviour by the observable fear of a victim via a SNS

	Key features	Example of a possible application to digital crime
Cognitive Social	Humans are sentient beings with perception, memory and reasoning.	Online child abuse groomers may repeat a consistent 'cognitive script' to themselves, to rationalise and direct their behaviour
Personality	Individuals differ in terms of personality. For example Eysenk found differences in extraversion, neuroticism and psychoticism. High extraversion (a need for external stimulation) associated with some forms of criminality.	The desire of some individuals to promote their criminal activity via social networks.

There is a wide range of crimes that fall under the heading of 'digital crime' and often many disparate sub-groups within the groups of people who engage in virtual forms of criminality. Therefore psychological theory needs to be applied in specific ways to specific contexts if it is to provide meaningful insights.

A long-standing question in criminal psychology is whether those who commit crime are in some way 'different' to those who do not; for example, are there significant personality differences between the two groups? Obviously there can never be an ambiguous 'yes' or 'no' answer to such a question. For example, there is often no clear binary distinction per se between those that do, and those that do not commit crime, given that crime itself is a social construct. Even if there were to be a clear distinction it would be impossible to separate cause and effect. A corollary to this, and perhaps an even more challenging question, is whether the personality traits of those who undertake specifically digital crime differ from both the law abiding population as a whole, and/or from those who undertake more traditional forms of crime (see Chapter 1). A potentially important question is how the behaviour and motivation of cyber-criminals (or even cyber-terrorists) might parallel or differ from that of 'conventional' criminals. This is a subject of significant research at the time of writing. Indeed, in 2012 the UK government offered research funding to investigate these kinds of questions (EPSRC, 2012). There has also been significant investment in the US.

Theories from each of the psychological traditions continue to exert influence, to a greater or less extent, on the policing of digital crime. The psychodynamic perspective is currently perhaps the least applied in practice, apart from its use in studying online child abuse. Personality theories, and in particular trait theory, is the subject of a lively research agenda within digital criminology. This is partly because as Hollin notes, there is 'empirical evidence in favour of Eysenck's theory' (Hollin, in Maguire et al., 2002, p. 155) but also perhaps because these theories lend themselves more readily to understanding online behaviours.

Applying Criminology and Psychology to Digital Crime

In this section we briefly examine two applications of criminology and psychology to digital crime; neutralisation and de-individuation (or 'de-individualisation'). This is not to suggest that these two theories are in some way more important than others; we have chosen them to illustrate the way that theories can be applied in practice.

The theory of neutralisation was developed by Graham Sykes and David Matza in the 1950s as part of their work into Sutherland's differential association (see above). It is worth noting that much of their interest was in 'juvenile delinquency' in the US. They began with the observation that most people are aware of 'right' and 'wrong' and generally respect law-abiding individuals, but that some people will 'drift away' from law-abiding activities towards illegal alternatives, adopting 'neutralisation' techniques to justify and legitimise their illegal actions. Sykes and Matza identified five techniques of neutralisation as shown in Table 2.3.

Table 2.3   Techniques of Neutralisation

Technique of neutralisation	Description
Denial of responsibility	It was not the offender's fault and ultimately the blame lies elsewhere
Denial of injury	Assertion that nobody was really harmed or hurt by the act
Denial of victim	Argument that the victim deserved what happened
Condemnation of the condemners	Sees those that condemn the act as 'just as bad' in their own ways
Appeal to greater good*	Illegal acts are needed to achieve the greater good

(Adapted from Sykes and Matza, 1957 but the author's interpretation and description. * In the original Sykes and Matza, 'Appeal to higher loyalties'.)

As Yar (2005a, p. 392) notes, the 1980s hackers' own accounts of their activities clearly employ a number of the techniques of neutralisation described by Sykes and Matza. Certainly, the current well-known 'Anonymous' group of hackers (a loosely coordinated online community that began in the 1980s and is notorious for launching coordinated DDoS attacks) would appear to employ a number of such techniques. For example, in 2012 the FBI closed down the Megaupload website that had been facilitating illegal file-sharing. The Anonymous group retaliated by launching major DDoS attacks against the FBI, the US Department of Justice and a number of recording industry companies and associations, resulting in some websites becoming inaccessible for several days. Anonymous has also claimed responsibility for earlier attacks against PayPal, MasterCard and Visa, carried out after these companies froze the accounts belonging to Julian Assange's WikiLeaks. In response to comments made by an FBI Director about the dangers of the internet becoming the 'Wild West', Anonymous issued a statement in 2011 which included clear elements of a 'denial of responsibility' and 'appeal to greater good', for example (cited by Epstein 2011):

'You see, most people do not behave like bandits if they have no reason to. We become bandits on the Internet because you have forced our hand.'

'These governments and corporations are our enemy. And we will continue to fight them, with all methods we have at our disposal, and that certainly includes breaking into their websites and exposing their lies.'

However, this form of justification by hackers is not universal. For example, the notorious hacker group LulzSec (loosely associated with Anonymous) rarely employed any techniques of neutralisation:

For the past 50 days we've been disrupting and exposing corporations, governments, often the general population itself, and quite possibly everything in between, just because we could. All to selflessly entertain others - vanity, fame, recognition, all of these things are shadowed by our desire for that which we all love. The raw, uninterrupted, chaotic thrill of entertainment and anarchy. (Statement from Lulzsec cited by Business Insider, 2011).

Interesting, Zamoon and Curley (2008) also identified a number of Sykes and Matza's techniques of neutralisation in the attitudes adopted by the popular press towards software piracy (both 'for' and 'against').

When individuals inhabit the internet they often become part of an online 'crowd', albeit a crowd that they rarely, if ever, interact with face-to-face. A number of psychological theories have been formulated which attempt to conceptualise how the behaviour of individuals might change when joining a crowd. An early, but still very influential approach to 'crowd psychology' was adopted by Gustave Le Bon in the late nineteenth century in his book 'The Crowd: A Study of the Popular Mind'. Le Bon argued that people could be 'submerged' within the identity of the crowd through a process of contagion, and then lose their sense of individual identity and adopt irrational and violent behaviour. Although Le Bon's ideas in their original formulation have not withstood academic scrutiny, the concept of a loss or loosening of a sense of individual identity formed the basis of the later theory of deindividuation, developed in the 1950s by Festinger and others (notably Zimbardo) in which an individual feels less like an individual and more disinhibited. Deindividuation normally requires (but is not an inevitable consequence of) three factors: anonymity of the individual, sharing of responsibility with others, and being part of a group (the larger the group the more the effect). In certain situations the process of deindividuation can lead to increased likelihood of anti-social behaviour, aggression and violence. A classic example of deindividuation from psychological research is the 1970s 'Halloween' experiment (Beaman et al., 1979) in which a bowl of sweets (candy) would be offered to child 'trick-or-treaters'. The person answering (under the direction of the experimenters) would tell the children to take just one sweet but would then place the sweet on a nearby shelf and leave the hallway. The experimenter found that the children who were part of a group and who believed themselves to be 'anonymous' (e.g. wearing a mask) were more likely to take more than one sweet when compared with a single child or children who had reason to believe they could be identified. Another possible and more recent example of deindividuation could be the riots that spread through England in the summer of 2011(but this is certainly debatable).

There are many examples of apparent diminution of the sense of personal responsibility and a change in the usual norms of behaviour of individuals inhabiting online environments. This is perhaps due to not being able to easily see the implications and consequences of our actions, and a tendency towards 'impulsivity' – see Chapter 1. Online examples of the effect of deindividuation include software piracy and aspects of cyber-bullying (although not all online examples necessarily conform to the 'classic' conditions required for deindividuation, such as anonymity). More recently the 'social identity model of deindividuation effects' (the 'SIDE' model) has been developed (by Spears and Lee, 1994 and others in later years), partly as a result of the lack of empirical research backing the classic model of deindividuation but also to take account the phenomenon of online environments. Underlying the SIDE model is the paradigm that an individual's sense of identity resides, at any one time, on a continuum, with personal identity at one extreme and social identity at the other. When anonymity is more salient within an online environment this tends to encourage behaviour on an individual level; when social identity is more salient then group identity tends to dominate.

When examining theories of deindividuation it is important to see online environments within the wider context of the personal and social environments we inhabit. Take for example the phenomenon of 'sick' jokes or 'off colour' humour; humour that flows from an unfortunate or even tragic event that might be the subject of much media and public interest, even if only for a short period of time, or humour that is based for example on a well-known person's physical or mental disability. An example of a tragic newsworthy event would be the death of a member of the Royal Family in the UK, such as Princess Diana or Queen Elizabeth the Queen Mother. In the past these jokes would circulate widely by word of mouth, and be shared amongst small groups of people or on a one-to-one basis, normally through personal social contacts of friendship, family or kinship. On those occasions when these sick jokes 'strayed' from private to public (as was the case for the late US comic Richard Pryor or the current-day UK comedian Frankie Boyle) it often caused controversy but rarely resulted in any form of legal process involving prosecution. There were perhaps two recognisable, parallel but distinct spheres of discourse: the private (which embraced trusted, intimate and private interactions involving direct personal contact) and the public (larger groups of unfamiliar people, organisational communication, and traditional forms of media such as newspapers or television). The divisions between the private and public were reasonably clear, and in the main people had a reasonable understanding of the implications of their actions. Put more prosaically, most people understood that the same off-colour joke told between intimates over a drink at the local bar would be unacceptable if told as part of an address to a school assembly. However, the social rules and distinctions that underpinned the telling of 'sick' jokes in the past have not transferred comfortably to new online social networks. In 2012 a teenager in the UK received a 12-week jail sentence for making jokes on Facebook about a missing abducted child (BBC, 2012a). The teenager pleaded guilty to the charge of 'sending by means of a public electronic communications network a message or other matter that is grossly offensive' (under s 127 of the UK's 2003 Communication Act). Before sentencing by the Magistrate, the teenager's legal representative explained that his client "[...] did seem genuinely remorseful and regretful for what he had done. At the time he posted these comments not once did he think he would find himself where he is today."

An Extended Example – Online Child Sexual Abuse Imagery

There is a long history of the manufacture, distribution and use of child sexual abuse imagery (CSAI, or 'child pornography' as it sometimes known, although this phrase is not favoured by professionals in the field – see for example, Taylor and Quayle, 2003), most of which predates the internet. Examples included line drawings of children in eroticised poses and narratives involving children as sexual objects, some of which were shared by like-minded individuals. In the twentieth Century photographic CSAI began to appear. However, until relatively recently photography involved developing prints from negatives and was largely undertaken by high street commercial providers, or by post. This posed obvious dangers for those intent on making and sharing imagery of child sexual abuse. The advent of instant contact printing (such as the 'Polaroid' camera) and then the revolution in digital photography removed these particular inhibitory factors. Indeed, there is a long history of the 'early adoption' of new technologies by those who produce, distribute, consume and share CSAI. For example, by the year 2000 there were already a number 'alt.binary' usenet groups where CSAI was being posted and downloaded (Goode, 2011, p. 26).

The advent of the internet and widespread broadband 'dramatically changed the underground world of child pornography' (Siegfried et al., 2008, p. 286). CSAI became more accessible, more voluminous and variegated, and for the offender the apparent anonymity of the internet seemed to reduce the likelihood of being detected; in essence the internet is now 'a vital part of the child pornographer's criminal tradecraft' (ibid., p. 287).

In any discussion concerning online CSAI there is likely to be discussion of the precise meanings of 'child' and 'sexual'. There are obvious difficulties inherent with the definitions of these terms, and not just in terms of the law. In the case of sex-offending, a relatively common approach (when seeking to understand the psychological motives and actions of an offender) is to consider that a 'child' is a person before, or at, the stage of pubescence. This does not convert easily into chronological age, and most countries prefer to use the certainty of specifying an age in years in their laws and conventions. For example, the U.S. Federal Code (as amended by the Child Pornography Prevention Act 1996 and the Protection Act 2003) makes unlawful the production, receipt, distribution, possession, transportation, mailing and advertising of any 'visual depiction' involving the use of a minor, and a minor is in turn described as somebody under the age of 18. Similarly, the term 'sexual' is open to a wide range of interpretation. In the UK the CPS and others refer more usually to 'indecent' imagery.

The very existence of online CSAI understandably produces strong media, political and public response and concern. However, it is important to note that not all users of online CSAI are active 'contact' paedophiles; nor do all paedophiles use such imagery for stimulus or grooming purposes. More fundamentally, not all people who commit sexual offences against children are paedophiles, according to most scientific and technical definitions of the term. (The definitions are often based on the persistent sexual preference for prepubescent or pubescent children. There are some pathological offenders who will sexually abuse people, including children, but their offences against children arise because of the vulnerability of the victim rather than the age of the victim). Nor, for a number of reasons, will removing all CSAI from the internet (even if this were possible) necessarily lead to a decrease in the incidence of contact offending against children. Firstly, the links between consumption of CSAI and the acting out of fantasy in terms of actual (physical) contact sexual abuse of children is tenuous. Almost all research conducted, and regardless of the country concerned, has shown that only a small minority of known users of online CSAI have been convicted of contact child sexual abuse offences (Lee et al., 2012, pp. 2–3; Endrass et al., 2009). Reconviction rates for UK-based convicted CSAI offenders are also lower than those for contact child sex offenders (Osborn et al., 2010).Of course, it might be that detected CSAI offenders are not representative of the group as a whole (that is, all CSAI users), but this seems unlikely. The existence of CSAI may have little impact of a predisposition to contact offend against children; as Carter et al. noted in 1987 'if an individual is prone to act on his fantasies, it is likely that he will do so irrespective of the availability of or exposure to pornography' (Carter et al., 1987, p. 207). The UK's Child Exploitation and Online Protection Centre (CEOP) however, in a review of the academic literature, concluded that 'there is a clear correlation between [indecent images of children] offending and contact sexual offending against children' (CEOP, 2012b, p. 6), although they do also note that 'causation cannot be established' (ibid.). Secondly, even if there is a link between the use of offensive imagery and physical action, legitimate forms of imagery involving children (such as advertising imagery involving children in their underwear, or Disney films involving children) will still be widely available. Indeed, research cited by Niveau (2010, p. 570) claims that contact paedophiles actually prefer 'soft-core' images easily accessible from television advertisements and similar sources, rather than explicit 'hard-core' child abuse imagery.

Whatever the degree of correlation between use of CSAI and contact sexual offences, the policing and investigation of online child abuse imagery is important in its own right. This is because it will presumably reduce the likelihood of further harm to the child victims, and punish those engaged (motivated often for economic reasons) in the production and distribution of such images.

It is difficult to assess the extent of the problem in terms of the volume of imagery and the numbers of people accessing CSAI, partly due to the inherently rapidly changing nature of online environments and the readiness of some users to adopt and adapt to new forms of online communication. An additional problem is that some producers and sharers use technological means to deliberately conceal the existence of online child abuse imagery (see 'steganography' in Chapter 1). In 2011 the Internet Watch Foundation (IWF, 2012) took action against almost 13,000 publically available internet sites which contained child sexual abuse imagery (IWF, 2012). However, there are likely to be significantly more images available in the so-called 'dark web' (see Chapter 10), the parts of the internet which are not publicly accessible (special software is required to access it) and password-protected sites. CEOP claims that there are millions of indecent images of children in circulation on the internet, with 'police forces reporting seizures of up to 2.5 million images in single collections alone' (CEOP, 2012b, p. 4).

In terms of a theoretical understanding, Elliott and Beech (2009, p. 181), in a review of sexual offence theory and internet offenders, outline four groups of typologies of individuals accessing online CSAI:

- the 'periodically prurient' (sporadic offenders acting out of a sense of curiosity, perhaps within the context of broader interest in extreme pornography);
- 'fantasy only' offenders (those who access and/sometimes trade imagery for fantasy sexual reasons but do not commit contact sexual offences against children);
- 'direct victimisation' offenders (where child pornography use is part of a wider pattern of grooming and contact offences against children); and
- 'commercial exploitation' offenders (those motivated by the criminal intent of making money by producing and collecting imagery to trade).

Differentiating between these groups is important in terms of both the policing and investigation of online CSAI crime.

Little is known with any degree of certainty concerning the demography of online CSAI offenders. However, apart from gender (offenders are usually male) those that are convicted of downloading online CSAI are more likely to be employed and more highly educated than those that commit contact sexual offences against children (Burke et al., 2001). A popular claim, particularly in the US, is that the offence of downloading CSAI is a 'white collar' (as distinct from a 'blue collar') crime, but this is almost certainly an over-simplification. However, Witt (2010, p. 4) observed that 'studies have found that child pornography offenders are generally more educated, more intelligent, and have more stable work and relationship histories than contact sex offenders'. There is some evidence that online CSAI offenders are 'socially anxious and emotionally lonely' and also exhibit features of 'compulsion and obsession' (Marshall et al., 2012, p. 41). Compared to other offenders (not only sex offenders), online CSAI offenders were younger than average, normally single, and lived alone (Reijnen et al. 2009, although the sample size for this particular study was small). The limited evidence available that attempts to differentiate between contact and non-contact offenders within the population of users of CSAI suggests that the former are more likely to show anti-social behaviour and have more problems with substance abuse (McCarthy, 2010).

The demography of the victims of online CSAI is somewhat more confidently assessed, at least in the UK. In 2011, Quayle and Jones analysed CEOP's database of CSAI (over 240,000 images gathered from police seizures in the UK). Most of the child victims were female and white, although there were significant differences in the proportion of males to females according to age of victim (Quayle and Jones, 2011).

There have been numerous attempts to conceptualise the process leading to (and, to a lesser extent, the reasons for) child sexual abuse. Influential models include Finklelhor's (1984) stepwise model in which four preconditions are required for a person to carry out child sexual abuse. The perpetrator must:

- experience a strong motivation to commit the acts (a strong desire, fantasising);
- overcome his internal inhibitions to realising the motivation (making excuses);
- overcome external inhibitors (gaining access to children); and
- overcome the child's resistance (grooming).

Online child sexual abuse imagery may feature at a number of stages described within the preconditions model, for example it can be shown to the child as part of the grooming process in an attempt to present the abuse as a 'normal' activity.

Ward and Hudson (1998, 2000) and Ward et al. (2004) developed the Self-Regulation Model (SRM) in relation to sexual offending in general. It is a 'metatheoretical' framework which aims to integrate the various theory-building approaches. Previous models had incorrectly assumed that 'one size fits all', and also for example, that sex-offenders have deficient coping strategies which predispose them to commit offences. However, Ward and Hudson found that the latter to be incorrect as many offenders actively seek to offend, and develop sophisticated strategies to do so. Ward and Hudson went on to suggest that offenders adopt one of two attitudes; either an 'approach-goal' where they want to commit the offences, or an 'avoidance-goal' where they see their offending in a negative light and would prefer not to commit the offences. This categorisation is important for investigating, managing and preventing offending behaviour, and is explained in more detail below.

The SRM posits nine phases involved in sexual offending as shown in Table 2.4.

Table 2.4   The Nine Phases in the Self-regulation Model

Phase	Description	Explanation
1	Triggering life event	The offender experiences a significant life event, the appraisal of which 'triggers' phase 2.
2	Desire for offending sexual activity, arising by direct or indirect 'motives'	Direct – explicitly linked with sexual fantasy and impulses. Indirect – related to other emotions such as anger.
3	The offender's attitude ('goal') is either approach or avoidance	Approach-goal; committing the abuse is seen as desirable and achievable, more likely to be from phase 2 direct route. Avoidance-goal; committing the abuse is seen as bad and to be avoided, more likely to be from phase 2 indirect route.
4	Selection of planning strategy	Approach-goal strategies plan how to commit offences. Avoidance-goal strategies plan to prevent offending.
5	High risk situations encountered	Opportunities to commit offences, for example situations where potential victims might be encountered.
6	Lapse	Intention to offend, 'avoidance' offenders claim a 'lapse' in self-control and switch to using 'approach' pathways.
7	Committing an offence(s)	When committing an offence an offender may have: • a self-focus (own needs dominate); • a victim-focus ('care' for the victim); or • a mutual-focus (a 'relationship' with the victim).
8	Evaluation of offending act(s)	Approach offenders might blame the victim. Avoidance offenders feel guilt, shame and cognitive dissonance.
9	Intentions with future offending	Approach offenders are buoyed by their 'success' and might even refine their offending strategies. Avoidance offenders may either determine not to offend again, or accept inevitability and adopt an approach goal.

Table based on Ward and Hudson (1998, 2000) and Ward et al. (2004) but author's own description and explanation.

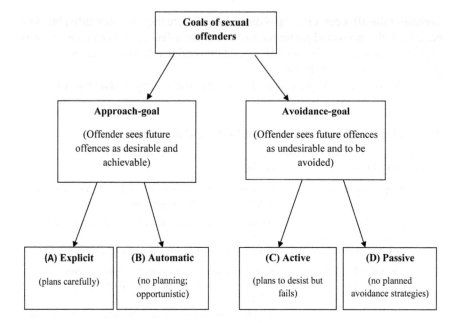

Figure 2.1   The Self-regulation Model Pathways to Offending

The SRM proposes the existence of four distinct offending pathways from Phase 3 onwards. The pathway taken will depend on offender's attitude or goal (approach or avoidance, see Phase 3 above), and also his planning and self-regulation skills. The resulting four offence pathways are shown in Figure 2.1 (authors' interpretation), and explained in more detail below.

The four 'pathways to offending' are thus:

(A) The approach-explicit offender who actively wishes to undertake offending behaviour and will plan his offending, seeking out victims, undertaking grooming and taking steps to avoid detection. These offenders tend to view their offending activities in a positive light and may even 'learn' from their offending, and devise yet more effective strategies.

(B) The approach-automatic offender who has a number of similarities with the approach-explicit offender in that he consciously desires to undertake offending sexual behaviour, but they differ in their lack of planning and preparation. This type of offender will likely offend if the opportunity presents itself, given that they also lack self-regulation and have poor coping skills.

(C) The avoidant-active offender who will often take steps to try to avoid offending. However, these avoidance strategies (such as using online non-obscene child imagery, such as children in underwear) are often counter-productive in that they tend to reinforce offending behaviour rather than eliminate it ('mis-regulation').

(D) The avoidant-passive offender who also wishes to stop offending but lacks the effective skills to do so, (through a lack of confidence or because of their impulsive personality). They do not even attempt to put in place strategies to avoid offending. Although they feel negatively about their offending in general terms, the psychological rewards of the offence are positive and strong ('under-regulation').

The SRM has received support from a number of empirical studies (for example, Bickley and Beech, 2002), and although the SRM was formulated originally for 'conventional' sex offending such as contact child molestation, Elliott and Beech note the 'benefits of applying the S-R model [SRM] to internet sexual offending' (2009, p. 188). These benefits, they suggest, particularly reside in the distinction the SRM provides between offenders showing passive under-regulation and those showing active mis-regulation of behaviour. The former would be characteristic of avoidant-passive internet sex offenders (for example, demonstrating impulsive access of online CSAI, blaming the 'internet' for their behaviour), while the latter could be offenders using online CSAI to address current personal problems such as boredom or depression (ibid., pp. 188–9). More generally, the SRM may be of potential value to law enforcement agencies in a number of ways. For example, if it is indeed a valid and workable model then it would suggest that approach offenders (rather than avoidant offenders) pose the greater investigative challenges to law enforcement and are possibly more likely to be involved in very serious crime. We could put this more crudely: the avoidance fish is an easier catch, but the approach fish would be a more valuable catch.

There are however limitations in the application of the SRM to the phenomenon of online CSAI. Elliott and Beech observe that the SRM (as outlined by Ward and Hudson) seems to suggest that an offender's use of CSAI for fantasy and masturbation is essentially maladaptive, because such strategies may make an offender more, rather than less likely to relapse. However, the statistical evidence contradicts this as it seems to suggest that most offenders successfully restrict themselves to the use of CSAI, and do not in fact go on to commit contact offences against children (ibid., p. 189).

Chapter 3

Preventing Digital Crime

David Bennett with Paul Stephens

Introduction

It is perhaps now a cliché to say that 'prevention is better than cure', but if this observation retains any merit it must surely do so when applied to digital crime. For example if a person uses the same insecure password for many different purposes (for accessing a home PC and carrying out online transactions) and the password is stolen, putting right the resulting financial and security injury can present a considerable challenge. It is relatively straightforward to implement simple security measures, and these can be effective in preventing such crimes. However, the struggle continues between law-abiding individuals and organisations working to prevent digital crime (such as the digital security industry), and the criminals who are trying to perpetrate such crimes. In 2013 yet more reports of organised cyber-espionage began to emerge, further adding to the existing litany of cyber-security breaches.

'Digital crime prevention' per se is not always seen as an integral component of 'policing digital crime'. However, in more general and theoretical terms, 'crime prevention' is an intrinsic part of the pluralistic model of modern policing now adopted by many countries, for example it was a component of 'third party' policing in 1990s Australia (Buerger and Mazerolle, 1998). Although the emphasis within the media is often on the 'crime fighting' aspects of policing, the reality is that crime prevention has always been a long-standing function of most police organisations. For example, police forces offer advice to local organisations and people on general crime prevention (protecting their property, safety online), but also in relation to specific threats (for example the presence of 'distraction' burglars in an area). In the UK CEOP runs the 'ThinkUKnow' campaign to increase young people's understanding of online safety (CEOP, 2013), which is in fact one of the most commonly used and disseminated e-education packages (Barnard-Wills, 2012, p. 239).

The emphasis within this chapter is the prevention of digital crimes related to gaining unlawful access to systems and networks through circumventing control mechanisms. This is not to suggest that preventing other crimes and behaviour (disseminating online child sexual abuse imagery, cyber-bullying, online fraud) is not important. However, preventing crimes of illegal access is a relatively well-researched area, and one that is also common to many other digital policing contexts. It also provides a good basis for discussing some of the wider issues involved.

Crime Prevention Theory and Digital Crime

At the outset it is important to acknowledge that there has been comparatively little development of specific digital crime prevention theory, and the number of applications of existing crime prevention theory to digital crime is also relatively small. As Lewis and Lewis (2011, p. 757) note: '[t]hough technology has changed the information and communication practices of society [...] crime prevention theories have not evolved to account for how technology use affects criminal behavior or victimization'. Where theory does it exist it tends to flow from two main presumptions of traditional crime prevention theory (see also Chapter 2 on routine activities theory), that crime is prevented by:

- decreasing the vulnerability of the potential victim or system ('defending the target'); and/or
- reducing the attractiveness of the criminal act to an offender ('dissuading the attacker').

Hence we hear regular calls to 'harden' information system targets from possible attack by would-be hackers, and governments are urged to increase the penalties for online intellectual property crimes to dissuade potential offenders.

General deterrence theory would include the idea of 'dissuading the attacker'. The theory arose from the observations of Beccaria and Bentham in the eighteenth century and is based on the premise that offenders are 'rational actors' who make decisions based upon the benefits and costs to them, and that they are deterred where the likely response to an illegal act ('retaliation') outweighs the benefits. Within this paradigm, decisive factors for the offender are:

- the likely benefit to the offender;
- the offender's perception of the likelihood of detection ('certainty');
- how quickly any punishment would follow an offence ('celerity'); and
- the degree of punishment meted out ('severity').

General deterrence theory usually holds that certainty and celerity are more important than severity in a person's decision-making: that is the degree of certainty of being caught and being quickly penalised in some way (for example, being restrained) is more important than the longer term severity of any punishment on conviction. It would then follow that crime is more likely to be prevented when the actual immediate costs are particularly high (and potentially outweigh any benefits that would accrue), and the would-be offender perceives that a swift retaliation would follow detection.

Modern general deterrence theory is located within behavioural psychology, but there are also links with game theory (particularly in terms of 'cyber-deterrence', for example Libicki, 2009). General deterrence theory also derives from rational choice theory in criminology (see Chapter 2) and would appear to be a promising basis for preventing at least some forms of digital crime. For example, most online fraudsters are intent upon 'monetising' their phishing attacks against individuals. By making this more difficult (for instance by cutting off payment sources), the cost-benefit balance for the offender is shifted. One of the UK 'Cyber Crime Strategy' objectives (see below) is for the Home Office to work with other agencies to ensure that 'criminals are deterred from exploiting the online environment'(Cabinet Office, 2011, p. 18). The use of deterrence as a tactic for prevention is seen most clearly however in discussions surrounding so-called 'cyber-espionage' (such as the alleged China-based hacking incidents in 2013) and even 'cyber-warfare'. As Holt and Kilger (2012, p. 799) observe 'Policy makers have increasingly focused on deterring cyber-attacks performed by state-sponsored actors'.

Situational crime prevention theory provides an alternative approach to crime prevention, but compared with general deterrence theory it places more emphasis on defending the target than deterring the attacker. The concepts underpinning situational crime prevention are based on environmental criminology and routine activities theory (see Chapter 2). As one of the main architects of situational crime prevention theory, Ronald V Clarke explained, it is 'focused on the settings for crime, rather than upon those committing criminal acts' (Clarke, 1997, p. 2). Situational crime prevention places particular emphasis on:

- increasing the effort needed to commit the crime;
- increasing the risks of being caught;
- reducing the rewards available through the crime; and
- reducing the number of 'excuses' open to those who might wish to justify their crime.

For example, the use of secure passwords (see below) usually increases the amount of effort required for an offender to gain unauthorised access to information. The use of cameras to monitor ATMs for the possibility of the installation of illegal 'Lebanese loop' devices is a clear example of increasing the risk. The theory has been applied in practice for cybercrime, for example Newman and Clarke (2003) have applied it comprehensively for crime prevention in e-commerce.

Organisational and Individual Responsibility for Preventing Cybercrime

As Garland (1996) and others since have argued, in the economically developed parts of the world we have witnessed a shift in the discourse about where the responsibility for countering crime might reside. From being the exclusive remit of governments and official law enforcement agencies there is now more emphasis on the sharing of responsibility, including at the level of communities, organisations and the individual. Crime is becoming 'normalised', and this amounts in effect to a realisation that the future emphasis will be on preventing as much crime as is possible (and mitigating its effects if it does occur), rather than on 'winning the war on crime'. Hence communities and individuals are expected to assume more of the responsibility for reducing crime, and it is seen as a reasonable expectation that citizens should protect their own property by installing forms of security, locking doors and windows and so on. The argument runs that a similar level of responsibility should also be expected of our online 'netizens', for example in terms of using virus checkers and being aware of online fraud (Krohn et al., 2009, p. 580). Many internet-based organisations and companies also point towards the need for individuals to assume greater responsibility. PayPal for example, complain that:

> [m]any Internet users are simply not aware that their actions, or lack thereof, have an impact on others and the Internet itself. This lack of awareness can be traced to a lack of education [...]. Computer (Internet) security simply has not been part of our curriculum. (Barrett et al., 2012, p. 6)

Brenner and Clarke go yet further, and even suggest there should be a system of 'distributed' security 'that uses criminal sanctions that require (i) computer users [...] to employ reasonable security measures to prevent the commission of cybercrimes' (Brenner and Clarke, 2006, p. 659).

A number of organisations have met accredited standards such as ISO27001 for Information Security Management Systems (ISO, 2005). However, as O'Connor (2009) notes, this alone is insufficient because a security management standard is not the same as a security standard. The former is about managing risk, and ensuring that risks that are identified are controlled, and that the controls remain effective over time. It does not set a 'gold standard' for the security itself. However, the dynamic approach (reacting to risks as their importance increases) appears to work well for organisations with ISO27001 certification, and that have set the risk factors appropriately. Official security standards do exist per se, but these generally apply for specific components of the overall security infrastructure. For example, the FIPS 140 Standards developed in the US relate to the requirements for implementing cryptographic algorithms in software and hardware that might fit into larger systems (NIST, 1994). However, adherence to this clearly does not necessarily mean that the whole system is secure.

Finally, we have the issue of organisations such as Dropbox being able to access data that users have stored with them. Dropbox have a policy of securing data with a cryptosystem, but some of their employees are able to access the information stored in users' accounts. This would usually be within the context of a specific criminal allegation about the owner of the account, and Dropbox have policies to protect users' data (Dropbox, 2012). But the significant point here is that the data is encrypted at the server end, and not at the client end: users send and receive files in plain text, albeit over a secure channel, but the encryption occurs on the Dropbox systems. And furthermore, Dropbox uses Amazon servers to store the data, which increases its potential vulnerability to unauthorised access: an attack on Amazon's storage facilities could also capture information from Dropbox users. The initial assumption is that the data is secure, and while this is largely true, as to how secure it remains is beyond a user's control.

Other problems may arise with staff suitability, for example security may be threatened if a company employs a system administrator with criminal intent. Appropriate policies are needed to try to prevent such a situation arising, for example by checking references thoroughly before engaging employees. Further protection can be provided through security audits performed by independent persons who will check that appropriate systems have been put in place.

In some organisations (but by no means all) the work practices of those staff members who have access to information is a matter of policy and regulation. For example allowing staff to take data away from a site on USB pen drives can create vulnerabilities for an organisation and leave them open to criminal exploitation. There are numerous stories in the press of devices containing insecure data being left in taxis, on trains, or lost in the post (BBC News, 2009, BBC News, 2010), or even being stolen along with the relevant security keys for accessing the data (BBC News, 2009). This is likely to be a significant problem, with estimates for example of more than 60,000 items being left in London Taxis within a six month period in 2008. Many of the items were mobile phones, but with such devices being able to store increasingly large amounts of data this is not without consequence (BBC News, 2008a). It has been estimated that over the past three years there have been over a thousand incidents in London hospitals where patient data has been lost or stolen, generally due to a misplaced laptop or USB pen drive (Goodchild, 2011). In a recent case a USB pen drive containing unprotected sensitive data about serious crime and witnesses was stolen from a police detective's home (BBC News, 2012f) and Greater Manchester Police were fined £120,000 by the Information Commissioner's Office for a failure to protect personal data. The level of fine was in part was influenced, it is reported, by the force's failure to 'sufficiently re-train staff'; the policy of not removing insecure data from police premises was in place, but it was not adhered to. This is not uncommon. In many cases organisations are found to have policies in place to prohibit such activities, but the requirements are simply not followed.

National Cyber-crime Strategies

Many governments have developed cyber-security strategies in response to the perceived risks presented by digital crime, particularly cybercrime. Both the UK and US governments have developed such strategies but with significantly different foci, emphases and priorities.

The UK government's 'Cyber Crime Strategy' is wide-ranging and promotes the government's 'vision for the UK' for the year 2015 (Cabinet Office, 2011). It has four main objectives:

- to tackle cybercrime and for the UK to be one of the most secure places in the world to do business in cyberspace;
- to be more resilient to cyber-attacks and better able to protect UK interests in cyberspace;
- to have helped shape an open, stable and vibrant cyberspace which the UK public can use safely, and which supports open societies; and
- to have the cross-cutting knowledge, skills and capabilities the UK needs to underpin its cyber-security objectives.

The last of these objectives is very broad and is essentially a pre-requisite for the preceding three. The overall strategy is apparently founded on a risk-reduction approach, with working partnerships between government and private and public sector organisations as well as international partnership between governments. The strategy claims to balance security with freedom and privacy. Fifty-seven actions have been specified to support implementation of the strategy, with different government departments (including the Home Office, MoD and Department for Culture Media and Sport) being responsible for different actions. It is likely therefore have a wide influence. However, the required actions show considerable variation in content and specificity. Some of the more specific actions (for example Objective 3, Action 11) are aimed at directly improving the security of individual users, by, inter alia, requiring internet service providers to help customers to identify, address and protect against malicious activity. But less specifically, Objective 1 Action 6 is concerned with the promotion of greater levels of international co-operation on cybercrime, but there is no suggestion of how this might even be approached, putting aside how it will be achieved in practice.

The UK's proposed strategy has been broadly welcomed, if only because it is seen to take the threat posed by cybercrime as serious, and it is also an ambitious attempt at an integrated response. However, there are some criticisms of the lack of detail in some areas (Ashford, 2011), and there are already questions over possible 'slippage' in meeting the objectives, for example in relation to Action 4.3 on improving educational involvement in relation to cyber-security, for which the work was to be completed by March 2012. A follow-up report (UK Cyber Security Strategy: 3 December 2012 – one year on) is unclear on whether this objective was in fact achieved, or how it has been deployed (Cabinet Office, 2012). The report highlights 10 areas where progress has been made, but regrettably these are not linked back to the original actions. It can be seen that a number of the actions relate to education, but while these operate at 'all levels' as specified by the original document, it is unclear what research underpins these actions. The report contains outcomes that relate to world class research, PhD studentships, and work at GCSE (secondary school) level with the 'Behind the screens initiative', alongside apprenticeships for school age and undergraduate students. The issue is not so much with the actions, nor the original intent, but the lack of traceability from the plan to the actions and outcomes. Sommer (2012) has noted that out of a total of £650 million for the whole project the 'getsafeonline' programme has received just under £400,000, and that it is 'disappointing that the National Cyber Security Programme placed so little emphasis on helping individuals and businesses help themselves' (ibid., p. 99).

The US has a parallel framework and associated legislation, the 'Comprehensive National Cybersecurity Initiative'. This is structured as 12 overlapping and mutually reinforcing initiatives (National Security Council, n.d.) and aims to defend against current threats, predict and protect against future threats, and also increase the robustness of the cyber-security environment. Table 3.1 shows the 12 initiatives, with our commentary in italics.

Table 3.1   The US Comprehensive National Cybersecurity Initiative

Initiative	Commentary
Manage the Federal Enterprise Network as a single network enterprise with Trusted Internet Connections.	*This would involve standardising the mechanisms used by government agencies to connect and work with the internet, and should allow for common security solutions which would make them more robust.*
Deploy an intrusion detection system of sensors across the Federal enterprise.	*If implemented, this should help prevent security breaches by identifying unauthorised-access incidents. This should be done in real time so that investigators can try to capture sufficient information to prevent the attack or to capture the criminals.*
Pursue deployment of intrusion prevention systems across the Federal enterprise.	*This initiative includes detecting intrusions and protecting the systems in use.*
Coordinate and redirect research and development (R&D) efforts.	*This initiative is concerned with how R&D money is spent, to ensure that outcomes are effective against known and expected future threats.*
Connect current cyber ops centers to enhance situational awareness.	*Put simply, enhancing communications between organisations should improve resilience by communicating about threats and perceived future threats as well as defence mechanisms.*
Develop and implement a government-wide cyber counterintelligence (CI) plan.	*This area looks at the defence of the US government and private sector organisations against attacks mounted by foreign governments and foreign government-backed individuals.*
Increase the security of classified networks.	*This aims to improve the security of networks used for military, diplomatic and law enforcement purposes.*
Expand cyber education.	*Put simply, it is recognised that there are insufficient numbers of cyber-security experts and more will be required to protect the national interest, not only for government purposes but also for companies and individuals at different levels. Further, there is a need to educate decision makers about the risks and needs to improve cyber-security*

continued ...

Initiative	Commentary
Define and develop enduring "leap-ahead" technology, strategies, and programs.	*This will consider R&D that produces new and alternative solutions to replace current approaches to particular problems, or where there are no solutions at present, to try to improve the security of cyberspace. Some commentators have observed that this might include development and deployment of mechanisms such as Stuxnet, a ' worm' which appears to have been designed to interfere with Iran's nuclear programme.*
Define and develop enduring deterrence strategies and programs.	*This complements other initiatives listed here by producing the technology and developing the strategies that will protect against cyberattack. As such attacks can be perpetrated at very low cost compared to other types of war, it can be carried out by very small groups; the deterrent effect of Mutually Assured Destruction of the nuclear age no longer applies.*
Develop multi-pronged approaches to supply chain risk management.	*This area looks at helping to protect the ICT infrastructure from damage and appropriation of information by means of installed equipment. Equipment made and brought in from overseas could be modified by agents introducing mechanisms for interruption of damage of communications or data. Many commentators refer to the predominance of China (and countries strongly influenced by China) as being the big risk here, but there are others.*
Define the Federal role for extending cyber-security into critical infrastructure domains.	*This area will consider the extent to which the government can work with and potentially interfere with private and other public sector organisations to ensure security of cyber infrastructure. One example given is that Google Mail is being used by the US Department of the Interior* (Gewirtz, 2012). *There would be an interest in how secure Google has made its system, and Google might be pressurised to adhere to particular government requirements.*

There are marked similarities between the US and UK strategies, for example UK Objective 2 (to be more resilient to cyber-attack) can be seen to encompass many of the US initiatives (1, 2, 3, 6, 7 and 10). The UK Strategy makes many more direct references to users at all levels (private individuals through to private businesses and government), and the US strategy is more focussed on federal infrastructure, but nonetheless the underlying objectives are similar. Both, for example, see important roles for education, training and research.

Security through Controlling Access

An information system consists of hardware, software, data and networking, and the security of such a system is only as good as its weakest point. Information systems inevitably contain vulnerabilities which are subject to threats, some of which will be human mediated and known as attacks. Hardware is vulnerable to logical attacks, for example the firmware of a device can be altered, and software is also vulnerable; it can be stopped, deleted, altered or 'enhanced' with the addition of malicious code (Pfleeger and Pfleeger, 2007, pp. 15–16). Data is also vulnerable; its security may be breached, for example when unauthorised users gain access to it; its integrity may be compromised when it is altered without authorisation; or its availability may be blocked, as in a distributed denial of service (DDoS) attack.

'Controls' are preventative measures that are implemented in order to protect a system by blocking the exploitation of vulnerabilities. The effectiveness of a particular control depends on awareness of the problem, the likelihood of the control system being used, whether overlapping controls are employed, and periodic review (ibid., pp. 24–9). Usability is a key factor for any control measure as people are unlikely to use a control that is difficult to implement (Pedersen, 2010). We consider here some of the technological means by which criminal activities can be prevented. There is however an ever continuing cycle of advances in defences, subsequent attacks and then circumvention of the new defences, amounting in effect to a digital 'arms-race'. For example, in the 1990s it was argued that cryptography might provide a relatively permanent solution to the security-crime nexus, with Schneier (1996) for instance observing in the preface of his book, *Applied Cryptography* that 'It is insufficient to protect ourselves with laws; we need to protect ourselves with mathematics'. But just four years on Schneier felt that cryptography-based solutions alone were no longer sufficient for protecting users against criminal attack (Schneier, 2000). The main reason for his change of view is that security has many interlinked components in practice, and all the components of the chain need to be equally strong; just one weak link will allow a criminal to act. Simple reliance on the law or purely technical solutions ignores the fact that the human element can make a significant contribution to security.

One major area to consider is the motivation of people and organisations to use the technologies and applications that are already available. For example, one of the most commonly used communication methods on computers is email, and it is generally perceived as insecure. There were an estimated 3.1 billion email accounts in 2011, and this figure is likely to rise to 4.1 billion in 2015 (Radicati Group, 2011). Other estimates suggest that in 2013, approximately 500 billion messages will sent each day (Pierce, 2011). The proportion of these which might be considered as 'secure' is almost impossible to determine from publically available resources, but it is likely to be very small. There are a variety of reasons for email being routinely insecure, for example the contents are usually in plaintext and encryption is not routinely employed. There is therefore no message integrity (the contents may be changed without notice by anyone who can access the email), nor is there any reliable author authentication (anyone can fake an email to look as though it has been sent by another person). Technological solutions for making email secure have been available for some time, and could be used on almost all computing devices, from smartphones to even low powered desktop computers. They include for example, implementations of the S/MIME (Internet Engineering Task Force (IETF), n.d.) or PGP mail protocols (Zimmerman, 1995), and the cost of using such solutions is remarkably low; free versions of PGP have been available for use by individuals (and at low cost to businesses) ever since its initial development in 1991. All companies of a reasonable size could incorporate secure email into their IT systems, but almost none have done so. As Ou (2005) noted more than 12 years ago, 'While both S/MIME and PGP are certified by the NIST, neither solution has any penetration in the mass computing market'. There is little evidence that the situation is any different today. Such security features could also be included in almost all the current cloud-based web services, albeit with the possible disadvantage that the hosting organisations could in principle read sent and received emails. In fact, it is likely that some kind of security is added to cloud-based email transmission by using the STARTTLS command (see FastMail, 2012) rather than PGP or S/MIME, but this is does not amount to 'end-to-end' security. (See Chapter 1 on the 'Market for Lemons' for discussion on the possible reasons for non-adoption).

Many digital crimes are committed through vulnerabilities resulting from human fallibility, and only some of these 'people problems' can be addressed by technological solutions. Education and training on identifying and countering criminal methods could play a key part in the defence, together with the development of best practice and appropriate organisational policies. As noted earlier, advice for individuals is available online from sources such as getsafeonline.org (backed by government departments), major computer security companies, banks, and law enforcement agencies. As for all crime prevention, the necessary technical mechanisms, the policies and the best practices will inevitably change over time. Inevitably, we consider here the current approaches to the prevention of digital crime, rather than speculation concerning the future.

User Authentication

Authentication is the process by which an information system allows or denies a user access, and normally depends on the inputs entered by, or read from, a user (Smith, 2002). Note, however, that authentication is not the same as identification; a system cannot identify an individual unless the inputs or readings from a person are unique, but it can authenticate a person by matching his or her data against stored values (Pfleeger and Pfleeger, 2007, pp. 234–5). An information system can authenticate a user by testing what they know (for example a password or PIN number), by what they possess (for example a hardware dongle required to run specialised software) or by their physical human characteristics, such as fingerprints (Ciampa, forthcoming 2014). Secondary authentication involves the use of two systems in parallel where both have to be satisfied to grant access. So for example an authentication method could involve mobile phone keystroke analysis (Clarke and Furnell, 2007) in conjunction with a password. Authentication usually works positively; the system will allow authentication requests that require an affirmative response, for example 'does the password entered match the stored password?' It should be noted however, that negative filtering may also be useful (rejecting authentication requests that require a negative response, for example 'does this log-on request come from a blacklisted host?'), but its implementation is in its infancy (Dasgupta and Saha, 2010).

There have been security lapses with respect to authentication, for example a bug in a Dropbox update allowed unauthenticated users to access the contents of other users' accounts (Agarwal, 2012). The problem was quickly fixed, but unsurprisingly the incident still caused considerable concern at the time. The details of individual authentication methods are provided below.

Passwords

Passwords are commonly used in conjunction with a user-ID to control access to computer systems. Note however, that a password-protected system is not inherently secure, for example the WEP protocol for wifi uses passwords, but the system is flawed and a password can be ascertained relatively easily, usually within a minute of the first attempt. Further, with increasing hyper-connectivity, most users now regularly employ a large number of user-ID/password pairs which can be difficult to remember, so many people use the same passwords across a number of websites. This can seriously compromise cyber-security: the overall level of security will be reduced to the lowest level of all the sites accessed (Bonneau and Preibusch, 2010), because the shared password could be cracked on a low security site and then used to access the other sites.

While it seems unlikely that a reputable e-business would be interested in using a legitimately stored password to attempt to access another site, it is not beyond the scope of criminal activity to try to obtain passwords for this purpose. Passwords could be obtained by criminals using phishing attacks or even through a website which has been set up for other activity that required registration, such as a forum. Once obtained, a criminal may then attempt to use a password on other sites the compromised user is judged likely to access. For example, on obtaining a password for an Amazon account a cyber-criminal could employ an automated process for trying the password on other sites such as eBay, PayPal, Facebook, Gmail, and Yahoo. Problems are confounded once an attacker gains access to one system, because his or her first action will often be to change the password to prevent the original owner or law enforcement officials from accessing the account. The use of a shared password between systems could easily result in the hapless user losing control of many accounts within a short period of time. Although passwords are vitally important for many systems, the option of using additional means for authentication is becoming more and more common.

The popular and technical literature often includes discussion about the necessity to choose and use a 'good' password. However a good password in terms of security is one that contains apparently random features, while a key feature of a good password from a user's perspective is one that is easy to remember. These two requirements are often inherently contradictory because a random sequence of letters, digits and symbols can be difficult to remember. In addition, the use of the term 'password' has not promoted security (see Natarajan, 2011 for a discussion), because it inadvertently encourages people to conceptualise a 'password' as consisting of a single pronounceable word, and this is not good practice because such choices are susceptible to dictionary attacks. Secure systems guard against these vulnerabilities by requiring users to enter characters other than letters and by disallowing groups of characters that may identify the user in certain ways. However, simple substitutions of certain letters for numbers (such as the digit '3' for the letter 'E') and simple pre-fixes or suffixes of one or two digits do not help to strengthen passwords as much as is typically believed.

Research has found that many users will choose the same password as others, for example in 2012 SplashData claimed that the top ten passwords were (in order of frequency of use): password, 123456, 12345678, abc123, qwerty, monkey, letmein, dragon, 111111 and baseball (compiled from files containing millions of stolen passwords, posted online by hackers (SplashData, 2012)). Information concerning popular choices of passwords is of interest not only to criminals wishing to compromise the security of a system, but also to a law enforcement-mediated recovery of encrypted information that may have been used for criminal purposes.

To form a strong password there are two main approaches; the XKCD approach developed by Randall Munroe, and the 'Schneier approach'. The XKCD method suggests it is generally best to use a 'passphrase' (xkcd, n.d.) because the combination of two or more memorable but unrelated words of reasonable length provides more security. The XKCD website includes the example 'correct horse battery staple' (XKCD, 2013), which for most people will be easier to remember than multiple substitutions of alternative symbols within a single word. However, care is needed because certain phrases such as, 'iloveyou' and 'letmein' (see above) are commonly used, and would weaken any multi-word password. The alternative approach (from, Schneier, (2008)), suggests using the first letter, or pair of letters from each word of a phrase. A simple root phrase, such as, 'A safe Computer is a secure Computer' can be turned into a passphrase such as 'AsCisasecureC'. This is a strong password: thirteen characters have been used and it is unlikely to be included as a possibility in any dictionary-based attack.

Many users partially reuse passwords, and add prefixes or suffixes that relate to the particular function. For example the 'strong' thirteen character password described above could be used as a stem for two further passwords such as 'AsCisasecureCeBay' and 'AsCisasecureCFacebook'. But predictability is the enemy of randomness: if one password is revealed, the others are now reasonably easy to guess. (See Kirchoff's Principle, which states that the security of cryptography is a function more of key management and less of the inherent secrecy of the system employed). It would of course be more secure to use a random word associated with each site for the respective passwords, for example the appended word for eBay could be 'Apple', and for Facebook 'Crate'. However, this would be still vulnerable as an attacker would only need to look for the use of an appended dictionary word. We cover password cracking in Chapter 6.

Security consultant Bruce Schneier recommends that users write down their passwords (Schneier, 2005). This initially seems counter-intuitive and is indeed something that is often said to represent poor security practice, but the idea is not without merit, because long and complex passwords which are not easily memorable could be used. Writing down a password and then leaving it available for anyone to read would obviously be foolish, but if the note is stored securely then it may be a reasonable solution, and it would be even better to note just a hint to aid its recall. However writing down a password in any form creates a risk of devastating loss if an unscrupulous person obtains the written record and realises its value. From a law enforcement perspective, as with password cracking, a suspect's written records of passwords would obviously of great potential use in cases that might involve encrypted files with incriminating evidence.

Passwords can also of course be stored electronically, but they are obviously vulnerable if 'hidden' within a simple text file and the device on which they are stored is hacked or stolen. To counter this eventuality, computer programs known as 'password wallets' or 'password managers' are available (Fisher, n.d.). These allow a user to store a number of passwords and the names of their associated systems securely in one place, protected by just one password to access them all. A freely available open source project to this end is PasswordSafe (Password Safe, n.d.), but other systems exist on a variety of platforms including smartphones, tablets and desktop operating systems.

Some systems require the user to change their password at regular intervals supposedly making them harder to crack as the window of exposure to work on a particular password is smaller. However, regular password changes can also lead to poorer password choices as users find them difficult to remember (Schneier, 2010).

The system an organisation uses for storing passwords may reduce security, for example, if they are stored in plaintext anyone gaining access to the website's system area can potentially read any user's password. Thirty-two million passwords stored in plaintext were released by a social media application RockYou (Leyden, 2010). They were revealed to hackers of the site by an SQL injection attack, a security loophole in the site's code. For the hackers, the analysis of the passwords no doubt provided a large amount of very useful statistical information. However, in this case the issue was not so much that millions of passwords were released but rather that they should never have been stored in plain text.

Most sites at least encrypt passwords but there is always the possibility that two users share the same password, and if one of the users views the password file they are able to deduce that users employing the same encryption method will have a matching password. This can be avoided by using a *salt*, which is a random number often based on the system time, that is added to the password before it is encrypted (Stallings, 2010). However, such encryption methods can also be a point of weakness, for example old implementations of the Unix function *crypt* truncate passwords to eight characters (Bonneau, 2011). Modern systems use more sophisticated processes for storage of passwords, which are resistant against dictionary and brute force attacks (see below), for all but the simplest of passwords. An example of this would be the bcrypt function, which uses a salted digest, but also has a 'work function' which regulates how hard it is to turn a password into its securely stored form.

Single-use passwords can be generated by cryptographic systems, and these improve security as they are only used once, as secondary authentication. They are transmitted to the user via a secure sending protocol. Online banking security (see below) frequently involves the use of single-use passwords as do public access computer facilities such as those used with two stage authentication by Google, where a text message may be sent to a user's phone. They have however been shown to be vulnerable to attack (Molloy and Li, 2011).

Security for Banking Transactions

Chip and PIN credit and debit cards are frequently used for retail transactions and withdrawing cash from ATMs. The Personal Identification Number (PIN) entered by the user is normally limited to a small number of digits, typically four, and is in effect an impoverished form of password with limited size and range of available characters. The standard security considerations apply; 1111 or 1234 are easily guessable as a PIN. There are 10,000 possible different four digit PINs, but it is claimed that just 20 account for 27% of all the PINs in circulation (DataGenetics, 2012). A PIN can be memorised from the shape or pattern of the digits, or the digits can be associated with letters from a secretly selected word. All written records of a PIN should use some form of code as protection.

The online verification of a credit or debit card can involve the use of a password, as well as the standard procedure involving the primary account number (the PAN) and the expiry date (on the front of the card) together with the customer verification security code (the CVC, normally three digits) from the card's signature strip (on the reverse). However, since the introduction of chip and PIN for in-person card transactions, the use of 'card not present' (CNP) fraud has increased and now accounts for more than half of all card fraud in the UK (FFA, 2012). The main response from industry has been to introduce new systems that use a password, such as 3-D Secure ('Verified by Visa' and 'MasterCard Secure Code'). When performing online card transactions an additional password entry form must be completed, but this approach has been criticised as being vulnerable to attack due to, amongst other things, its inconsistent authentication methods (Murdoch and Anderson, 2010).

Online-banking systems often employ single-use passwords that need to be entered into a dedicated device supplied by the bank. There are a variety of such systems and devices, for example the RSA SecurID (EMC, 2012) and the CAP/ DPA chip and PIN card devices (EMC Corporation, 2012), (Visa, 2006). The RSA SecurID system device displays a different number on its LCD display each minute, and has an inbuilt battery which is intended to last indefinitely. The device is also designed to be tamper-proof. The authentication process involves the user entering the displayed number and a password into the relevant system. The system is able to predict the number the device will display at a given time, and if this matches the number entered by the user, then it is assumed that the device must be physically present with the user. This system does not of course protect against so-called 'man-in-the-middle' attacks, where a rogue intermediary requests information of the genuine user, which is then used to access the customer's account. The two other main security systems are CAP and DPA, respectively the Chip Authentication Program (Mastercard) and the Dynamic Passcode Authentication system (VISA). For these, the device provided by the bank has a slot for receiving a chip and PIN card, a small display, and a numeric keypad with a few additional symbols. To carry out a transaction the customer must insert their card into the device and enter a valid PIN. Once a function is requested by the banking system, the customer selects this manually on the device. The device then often requests further information, the precise nature of which is determined by the system, based on the function chosen at the time. The device will then calculate a number using the card details and transaction details, and return this transformation result to the customer for entry. This is the authenticator. If the wrong card or details are used, the authentication code will be incorrect and the transaction will not proceed. The user is requested to enter different information on different occasions and this creates varying authenticating responses on each occasion. However, research by Drimer, et al. (2009) has identified vulnerabilities with the system, and these may lead to abuse by criminals. A further online banking security system involves the installation of additional software on a user's computer, for example 'Trusteer Rapport' (Trusteer, 2012). This has a number of security functions including ensuring that bank login details are only entered on the genuine bank website.

Biometric Authentication

Biometric authentication systems record the biometric details of authorised users and store the records in a database. When a user is to be authenticated the system will scan his or her biometric details and try to find a match with previously recorded data. Fingerprint recognition along with other biometric authentication methods relies on the assumption of uniqueness, i.e. that no two fingerprints are ever the same. The supposed uniqueness of fingerprints is a largely a product of inductive reasoning. However even if every fingerprint is in fact unique, it does not mean that every representation of a fingerprint stored in a biometric recognition system is unique since such representations are always abstract finite representations of the actual anatomical fingerprint (Vacca, 2009). Every such system will inevitably have two associated error rates: the false-accept rate (this is how often the system authenticates someone when it should not), and the false-reject rate (how often the system does not authenticate someone when it should) (Smith, 2007).

The more popular and implemented technologies for biometric authentication use fingerprints but other features can be used such as hand geometry, iris recognition and facial recognition (Smith, 2007). Finger vein analysis systems are already available for example for bank ATMs in other countries (Kleinman, 2013). Gait analysis is being developed for forensic purposes, but could also potentially be developed for use in biometric authentication.

Biometric authentication systems are vulnerable to attacks in a number of ways. An attacker may alter his or her features that are used for biometric authentication, either physically or by accessing and changing the stored digital record of a personal feature. Attackers may also attempt to hack into the controlling system and change it so it permits access. There are possible security issues with finger print systems as it is relatively easy to produce fake prints. Traces of latent fingerprints are often obtainable from surfaces that users have touched with their fingers, and spoofing attempts include making gelatine or graphite copies of real fingerprints (Brooks, 2010). If an attacker manages to circumvent a fingerprint recognition system the compromised user will no longer be able to use their fingerprints on that system (Vacca, 2009), and this can present problems which do not apply for non-biometric authentication systems.

CAPTCHA System Authentication

CAPTCHA is an acronym for 'Completely Automated Public Turing Test to Tell Computers and Humans Apart', and such systems have been developed to help prevent automated use of facilities. (The reference to 'Turing Test' is to a well-known test developed by the mathematician Alan Turing in the 1950s which tested the ability of a machine to 'fool' a human that actual human communication was being used). The CAPTCHA tests are deliberately designed to be easy for humans to solve but difficult for a machine or computer to answer, such as recognising characters that are distorted and irregularly positioned. Unfortunately, it has been shown that the CAPTCHA systems of major websites can be deceived (Yan and El Ahmad, 2008).

Authentication using Patterns and Images

The Android operating system for smartphones uses an alternative authentication mechanism which requires the user to enter a correctly swiped gesture on a 3x3 grid (Angulo and Wästlund, 2011). The main advantages of this are the speed of entry (the finger does not need to be lifted between points) and the fact that it is easy to remember (the user can choose a gesture shape that is attractive and memorable). However, there are disadvantages – primarily that the user's fingers leave a visible grease trail mark on the phone, and as the entry gesture is entered frequently its trail is often the most pronounced on the screen. Thus, unless the screen is cleaned carefully after each unlock activity, then the actual security provided is quite low. German researchers have also claimed that freezing an Android phone can bypass the encryption system employed, provided the freezing is undertaken within a certain period of time (BBC, 2013).

Encryption

Data can be encrypted for secure storage on digital devices, and a user will need to use an authentication process to access it. Encryption protects data by converting 'cleartext' (or 'plaintext') into 'ciphertext', which is unreadable without a 'key'. An algorithm and one or more keys (passwords) are used to encode the original message into an unreadable form via a series of steps which are very difficult to reverse by trial and error. The process of decryption is performed by the intended recipient using a corresponding algorithm and key(s), and a number of different encryption algorithms are available. The level of security each provides depends on the length of the key and the details of cryptographic system. The type of encryption most currently used today is so strong that a user who is later unable to complete the authentication process may permanently lose access to the data. However, the use of such systems is often seriously considered and often used by both individuals and organisations, for large volumes of data stored on computer systems, and for transporting data for example on laptops or USB pen drives.

One commonly used system is 'public key cryptography'. Each user in a communication group must have two mathematically related keys: a public key and a private key. A public key is not kept secret, and will be available to all users within a communication group, but a private key is known to just one person. Any message encrypted by the public key can only be decrypted by the corresponding private key, and any message encrypted by the private key can be decrypted by the corresponding public key. Imagine that Alice wishes to send an encrypted message to Bob; she would use Bob's public key (available to anybody) to encrypt the message, but only he can decode it as he would need to use his private key (available only to him). A worked example illustrating the mathematics of this encryption process is given in Chapter 10.

Such a system also allows for digital signatures, the electronic signing of digital messages by users. Alice could include a digital signature with the message to Bob by producing a digest of the message using a hash function then encrypting this using her own private key. When Bob receives this digital signature he can decrypt it using Alice's public key (Solomon and Chapple, 2005). Public key cryptography can also be used to create digital watermarks. These are created by trusted third parties ('certification authorities') using public keys and digital signatures. The watermarks identify the copyright owner of the digital content (Das, 2009).

BitLocker is an encryption product installed on recent and more expensive versions of the Microsoft operating system. It allows a user to encrypt a drive of information to prevent its unauthorised reading, and is highly secure but not infallible (Broersma, 2009). It is not available on the operating system in general home use. There are many alternatives to this type of built-in system, including a number of open source systems, for example the TrueCrypt tool released in 2004 (TrueCrypt, 2012). Either a whole drive or a segment of a drive in a fixed size file can be encrypted, and the secure area is used for storing all important information, and copies of files in the insecure area are also made. (The drive segment option is sometimes employed if the use of a whole drive for higher security information is inconvenient or not required.) A software program must be run to subsequently access the data, and this inevitably requires extra time and effort. It is relatively easy for a user (including those intent on hiding incriminating material) to forget to do this, for example, when automatically running software such as the Microsoft Office packages if the option to make automatic backups of data to a location outside of the encrypted area has been chosen.

For transporting stored data, USB devices with automatic built-in encryption mechanisms can be used. Products such as Inmation IronKey USB pen drives (Imation, n.d.) provide automatic password protection for stored files, and other security features such as a secure browser. However, the initial purchase cost of these security-enhanced devices is significantly higher than for a non-secured device. Of course Truecrypt can be used on a USB pen drive, but this is not a common practice.

Data Security for Discarded, Stolen and In-transit Digital Devices

Digital devices are often discarded by their users and owners with much data still present and accessible on the device. Research in 2009 found that 54 per cent of second hand USB devices contained forensically recoverable data (Jones, et al., 2009), although this figure now appears to be falling (Szewczyk and Sansurooah, 2011). Computers may also contain sensitive stored information such as financial transaction records and automatically stored passwords for websites. It is possible to securely remove data so that it is completely erased, and cannot be recovered with computer forensic tools. For traditional hard drives data removal can be performed either physically or with software. Breaking up a hard drive, or other storage device with implements such as a hammer and chisel will generally prevent any meaningful data from being removed, but also prevents re-use of the storage medium. Software such as BCwipe (Jetico Inc. Oy., 2012) will remove data stored in currently unallocated areas of drives, and can also securely delete data related to website password storage, web caches and similar. Some devices, such as mobile phones with the Android operating system, even have such a mode built in, so that users do not have to seek out third party systems in order to carry out a major data removal operation. For modern solid-state drives using Windows 7 there is a very low chance of recovering data once it has been deleted (King and Vidas, 2011), and this has serious implications for digital forensics, as explained in Chapter 10.

With the advent of truly mobile computing, the number of devices in transit has increased significantly and this provides new opportunities for crime. In some cases the technology itself can aid its discovery and appropriation. An example of this is the use of Bluetooth on some computers, where they would 'wake' from standby on receiving a Bluetooth wake-up signal. Criminals were using cheap Bluetooth signal strength detectors to wake the devices and then hone in on expensive laptops left in parked cars (New South Wales Government, n.d.).

This technique has generally been well publicised to business computer users, and many organisations now have policies that try to prevent its execution. Even if a device is stolen, many smartphones have tracking apps installed (for example, 'Where's My Droid?' Alienman Tech, 2012) which allow remote data deletion to help prevent identity theft and other crimes. For some devices, the owner of a stolen phone can even remotely install an app on the device after the theft, in order to aid its recovery.

Malware

Malware is any piece of software which has been designed with a malicious intent, for example spyware, viruses, worms and Trojans. These pieces of code can allow an attacker to gain some level of control over a user's personal information and system. If malicious software or an attacker infiltrates a system then there is significant potential for data loss. Advice is often that back-up copies should be made on a separate device, for example on removable media. Most modern operating systems include a way of easily backing up and restoring data, and backups can also be made to cloud storage on the internet.

One way in which malware is spread is through users downloading and running software. Until relatively recently a popular protocol for downloading from the internet was File Transfer Protocol (FTP). This had to be deliberately invoked so it was difficult for the user to be unaware that downloading was in process. Nowadays users will more usually download simply by clicking on a hypertext link, although many operating systems will warn the user of the dangers. Peer-to-peer (P2P) networks and supporting software are also often used for downloading: users make files on their computers available to other users for download (and this often includes illegal copies of intellectual property). However some downloaded files may be malicious in intent, and the provenance of some may be difficult to determine, because even if the immediate source of a file is a well-meaning individual, they might still have been the victim of a cyber-attack. Anti-virus software can be used (see below) to scan downloaded data to help ensure it is not malicious, but it cannot identify malicious software with complete certainty. With respect to software checks for tablet computer and smartphone apps, different approaches are taken by different manufacturers. Apple is quite stringent and performs some security validation on apps before they are made available to users through their AppStore. Google (the Android operating system) is more relaxed and it is widely assumed that they do not perform the same level of checks on software (Mitchell, 2010). Indeed on Android based phones it is quite possible to upload software from outside the 'official' application marketplace by un-ticking a box in the options; no checks on the software will necessarily have been made by the manufacturer.

Spyware protection, anti-virus software and a firewall all reduce the risk from malware. A firewall helps to make a system less 'visible' on the internet, for example by ensuring that the programs running are not 'advertised' to potential attackers, and by preventing some malicious types of network traffic. Some criminals will try to circumnavigate security software by persuading a user to install other software without the user knowing it will disable or remove the security software. The approach may be made through emails, messages on social media sites or even phone calls. In a typical phone scam the caller will claim to be from Microsoft and to be responding to an automatic message about a problem with the user's computer. The caller will try to persuade the user to install some software from the internet to resolve the problem; indeed a user may even be charged for this service. However, the new software is malicious, and could even allow the criminal to remotely control the computer without the user's knowledge.

Optional User-implemented Controls

Ease-of-use and protection from security threats are two important issues for prospective purchasers of digital technology. Often however, there is a tension between these two factors as the added security procedures tend to complicate the user's experience of digital devices. In the past much commercially available technology tended to favour ease-of-use over security. Indeed, early versions of the Windows operating system were notoriously insecure, leading computer security expert, Gene Spafford, to claim that 'Securing an environment of Windows platforms from abuse – external or internal – is akin to trying to install sprinklers in a fireworks factory where smoking on the job is permitted' (Spafford, no date).

Internet service providers (ISPs) will often supply internet connection equipment to home users with minimal security features enabled, and provide little in the way of documentation on how to activate such features. This could be justified as pragmatic because the reduced security results in an easier set-up procedure. But at the same time software and hardware manufacturers often make a marketing virtue of the security of their systems, and this encourages users to believe that connecting a computer system to the internet is just like plugging in any other kind of electrical appliance. However, users will need to sacrifice some of their system's ease-of-use if they wish to remain secure, because deliberate attackers and malicious software continually scan the internet, searching for vulnerable systems. An attacker may intend fraudulent use of a user's details, or to use a hacked computer for storing illicit files on the hard disk or for mounting attacks on other computer systems.

When software vulnerabilities are discovered the company that makes the software will usually release a 'patch', another piece of code to resolve or fix the problem. This is known as an automatic update. Most operating systems and modern applications have a way to enable automatic updating so that any patches released are then automatically installed.

Chapter 4

Law and Digital Crime

Ed Day with Robin Bryant

Introduction

Between 2006 and 2010 there were only 90 convictions in the UK under the Computer Misuse Act 1990 (total derived from data given in Hansard, 2012). Further, the number of convictions per year actually fell between 2006 and 2010 (from 25 to 10, ibid.). Yet it seems inconceivable that this small absolute number and relative decline is the result of fewer 'computer crimes' being committed. Part of the explanation for this apparent paradox is that many of the crimes within the UK that occur online, or with other digital characteristics, are prosecuted under alternative legislation such as the Fraud Act 2006. For example, hacking is covered explicitly by the Computer Misuse Act 1990 (CMA), and although it might be involved in enacting extortion (for example), it is the extortion that is likely to be prosecuted as this will carry the heavier penalty on conviction.

Deciding how to make best use of the inevitably limited resources for tackling digital crime is a key aspect of a pertinent debate. It is estimated that the amount spent on defending against cybercrime (for example the cost of anti-virus software) is far higher than the amount spent on policing cybercrime (the actual apprehension and prosecution of offenders). However, research suggests that a small number of criminal networks are responsible for a large number of cybercrime incidents, so the money might be better spent on targeting these groups rather than trying to defend against the incidents in the first instance. If this is the case then legislation will have key role to play in the efficient policing of digital crime, and it is vital that the legislation be appropriate, reasonable and logically targeted.

Many difficulties arise when using legislation for targeting crimes committed in rapidly changing technical contexts, not least of which is that it is difficult for the details of new legislation to keep pace with technological change. In addition the multi-jurisdictional nature of much digital crime presents additional challenges, as does the fact that legislation has to exist within complex political systems, for example the UK must follow European Union directives when creating legislation to combat much cybercrime. There are also debates on the necessary extent and the nature of such regulation. Many argue that there is too much legislation (Wilson, 2010) but others insist that more laws are required to protect individuals, e-commerce and society. Regulation of course may have unintended effects, for example on privacy (Busch, 2012), and this further colours the debate on how far cyberspace should be regulated.

The question of who will carry out the regulation also needs to be addressed. It is rare for a country to operate an extreme stance on regulation, so 'no regulation' or 'full state regulation' is the exception. Co-regulation of cyberspace is far more common, and this combining legislation with delegated self-regulation. Examples of self-regulation include industry codes of practice, and organisations such as the Internet Watch Foundation (Marsden, 2011).

There is also dispute about how much *new* legislation is really needed. This is partly because of uncertainty over the extent to which the advent of the internet has given rise to new forms of criminality (see Chapter 1). But is it true that most digital crime is just 'real world crime' in a different guise; 'old wine in new bottles'? (Grabosky, 2001). Consider for example the 2004 case in which Armin Meiwes killed and ate Bernd Jürgen Brandes with his consent (Jewkes, 2007, p. 1). Meiwes had advertised for a victim in online groups such as Cannibal Café (Franky, 2002) and of course murder is a very ancient crime, but would Meiwes have been able to find a compliant victim before the advent of the internet? And more pertinently, can the existing legislation and other forms of regulation adequately address the mediating effects the internet has provided for many forms of human behaviour?

It has been argued that legislation changes at a much slower pace than technology. The history of publications relating to computer and cybercrimes dates back at least to the early 1970s, and there are other accounts of such crimes dating back to the 1950s (van Tassel, 1970). The legislative output in the period since has of course varied, and has had to play 'catch-up' due to the evolution of such crimes over the decades, especially with respect to the huge impact made by the internet. As hacking evolved from an 'innocent' pastime to an economically motivated criminal activity, the need for legislation and the regulation of cyberspace and computing was seen by many as vital (Walden, 2007, pp. 25–6). During the 1980s an increase in hacking and virus writing was seen, and the legislation in the UK was not suited to addressing the emerging threat (Fafinski, 2009, p. 21).

The Regulation of Cyberspace

How cyberspace is governed and regulated, or indeed whether it could or should be controlled at all, is a complex topic covering multiple areas: technical standards, censorship, and net neutrality. It also involves many stakeholders and actors: nation states, public and private organisations, and movements such as the hacktivist group 'Anonymous'.

Indeed some argue that the rise of the internet has weakened the traditional power of the nation-state by changing the scale and scope of communication, and has led to the rise of new transnational organisations of a distributed nature. Examples of this shift in governance are the 'Internet Engineering Task Force' the (IETF) which standardises the internet's protocols via memos known as 'Request for Comments' (RFCs), and the 'Internet Corporation for Assigned Names and Numbers' (ICANN), created in 1998 to administer IP addresses and the DNS system (Mueller, 2010). Further, the transnationality, intangibility and the fast rate of change of internet communication combine to make the formulation, enactment and implementation of digital crime legislation inherently problematic, even at the level of the nation state (van Dijk, 2012).

Control of the Internet

The history of the development of the internet provides useful insights into its changing nature and the many different interests which complicate its regulation. The internet began as the ARPANET in 1969 when four universities in the US (UCLA, University of California Santa Barbara, Stanford Research Institute (SRI) and the University of Utah) became nodes in the world's first packet switching network. (Packet switching allows for communications to be split into chunks and for each chunk to be routed via a number of network paths, as opposed to the alternative of circuit switching which requires a dedicated circuit). The ARPANET was initially under the control of the US Defense Department's Advanced Research Projects Agency (DARPA), but in 1975 control was transferred to the US Defense Communications Agency (DCA, Hafner and Lyon, 1996). The differences between the underlying networks required the development of a standard communications protocol. In 1983 the ARPANET began using the 'Internet Protocol' and the 'Domain Name System' was created. The DCA then separated off part of the network into a military-only MILNET, leaving the remainder still as ARPANET. In 1986 the National Science Foundation (NSF) created the NSFNET, a research and academic network that used TCP/IP. The Foundation took over the role of 'internet backbone' from the ARPANET, which ceased to exist in 1990. NSFNET itself was subsequently replaced by commercial internet providers' networks, before closing in 1995. During the late 1980s and early 1990s, connections to European and Asian TCP/IP networks converted the internet to a worldwide rather than a 'US-centric' network, and in 1990 Tim Berners-Lee and Robert Cailliau proposed the World Wide Web (Gromov, 2002).

The world-wide nature of the internet leads, perhaps inevitably, to the very principle of control of the internet being contested. Indeed some argue there is a veritable 'cold war' being fought over internet governance. For example, Kleinwächter (2013) argues that there are two opposing conglomerates in this 'war': China, Russia, Iran, Pakistan, Saudi Arabia, the United Arab Emirates, Sudan together with some other Arab, African and Central Asian countries 'against' the US and its Western allies (presumably including the UK). The first group prioritise state control over their citizen's use of the internet using legislation and other means, to defend their national sovereignty. Untrammelled, uncensored and ubiquitous use of the internet is not seen as a 'human right'. The polar opposite of this is the 'US model' where there is cooperation between government and others towards an open approach to securing the internet. Between these two poles are countries such as India, Brazil, South Africa, Egypt, Kenya, Ghana and others that are anti-censorship but disagree with the US government's role in ICANN and the domination of the internet economy by US corporations (Kleinwächter, 2013).

Although characterising the differences over governance of the internet as a 'cold war' is probably veering towards caricature, there are nonetheless clear and real examples of tensions, with some countries such as Russia and China making controversial proposals to increase their control over the internet. But they withdrew the proposals, following protests from others at WCIT 2012 (the International Telecommunication Union's World Conference in 2012, convened to update the International Telecommunication Regulations, a binding global treaty dating from 1988).

There is also a debate about whether so-called 'net neutrality' (the idea that all data should be treated equally whatever its source, destination and purpose), should be protected through legislation. Currently in some countries ISPs may 'throttle' data at the request of government or other interested parties for reasons such as copyright infringement or censorship.

Criminal Law and Criminal Justice Systems

There are many differences between the criminal justice systems in countries across the world: there may be a panel of judges rather than a jury, and the accused may be questioned by an investigating judge and not by a prosecuting counsel. All these differences can be a significant complicating factor in cross-border criminal investigations. The form of justice used in England and Wales is often referred to as 'adversarial' (and in the US an 'adversary' system is also applied for most criminal cases). Some European countries (for example France and the Netherlands) use the 'inquisitorial' system instead. Other differences include that in some European countries, and elsewhere in the world, guilt is presumed and innocence has to be proven, whereas in the UK, there is a presumption of innocence and the onus is on the prosecution to prove guilt.

In the main the criminal law of England and Wales adopts the principle of *'actus non facit reus, nisi sit mens rea'* which we can translate as 'an act does not make a person criminally liable unless it is accompanied by a guilty mindset'. There are therefore usually two elements of criminal liability: *actus reus* and *mens rea*. (Note however that there are exceptions to this requirement).

In the UK, and many other countries, there are several different forms of law: common law, statute law, case law, Acts of Parliament, Statutory Instruments, and by-laws. In terms of digital crime, statute law is probably of the greatest relevance (a well-known example of a statute law being the Computer Misuse Act 1990). Statute law is written law, and is the foundation of the current legal system in England and Wales. It is derived from Acts of Parliament and can be accessed electronically via the online UK Statute Law Database.

Case law helps establish the precise meaning of legislation through a 'doctrine of precedent' which sets out how that piece of legislation should be used by a court of law when applying it to similar circumstances. Although the specific circumstances of the case might change, the court should use the same reasoning

Table 4.1 *Actus Reus* and *Mens Rea*

	Overview	Explanation	Examples
Actus Reus	The action that the defendant carried out, proved beyond reasonable doubt	• acted criminally in some way • omitted to do an act which brought about a criminal outcome • caused a state of affairs to happen • failed to do an act which was required, and as such brought about a criminal outcome	Sending by means of a public electronic communications network a message or other matter that is grossly offensive or of an indent, obscene or menacing character (Communications Act 2003, s 127)

Mens Rea	An intention to commit the crime	Different terms are used in a number of offences to indicate intent:
		  • 'dishonestly'
		  • 'wilfully'
		  • 'recklessly'
		  • 'with intent'
			The offence of unauthorised access to a computer (an offence under s 1 of the CMA) requires proof of two mens rea elements:
			(1) Knowledge that the intended access was unauthorised; and
			(2) An intention to obtain information about a program or data held by a computer

(or *ratio decidendi*) that was used by previous courts to reach a decision. An example of case law from the UK concerned an individual, Alban Fellows who was storing and accessing child sexual abuse imagery on his employer's computer. Fellows made the imagery available via the internet but access was controlled by a password he provided to other people (including one Steven Arnold). Fellows was convicted on four counts of possessing indecent photographs of children (counter to the UK's Children's Act 1978) but appealed. In the subsequent appeal (*Fellows and Arnold* [1997] 1 Cr App R 244) it was held that providing another person with the password to access pornographic data stored on a computer amounted to 'showing' the data to the other person and hence the appeal was dismissed.

However, in many legal systems a simple one-to-one correspondence between a specific criminal act and a single offence under the law does not often exist. For example, when considering the crime of the dissemination of malware via a peer-to-peer network the UK police and CPS might consider the CMA sections concerning the modification of computer materials, or unauthorised access with the intent to commit or facilitate the commission of further criminal offences such as theft or fraud), but they might also consider the Police and Justice Act 2006 (PJA) which deals with the making, supplying or obtaining articles for use in computer misuse offences (Taylor et al. 2011).

Classification of UK Offences and the Courts

Criminal offences in the UK are classified as either summary, indictable or either-way, according to their seriousness and at which court they can be tried. Either way offences can be tried either summarily or on indictment, depending on the circumstances, as follows:

- Summary-only offences can only be tried in a magistrates' court. An example would be the persistent use of a communications network for the purpose of causing annoyance, inconvenience or needless anxiety (s 127(1) of the Communications Act 2003).
- Indictment-only offences can only be dealt with in a Crown Court and are the most serious cases. An example would be an individual prosecuted for inciting others to commit serious offences (believing that one or more offences would be committed) under s 46 of the Serious Crime Act 2007 (see the cases of Blackshaw and Sutcliffe, sentenced in 2011 to four years in prison for using Facebook to incite 'rioting' in Cheshire. They created an event on Facebook called 'SMASH DWN IN NORTHWICH TOWN' with an invitation to join the 'MOB HILL MASSIVE NORTHWICH LOOTIN' with the first comment from Blackshaw being 'WE'LL NEED TO GET ON THIS KICKIN OFF ALL OVER' (CPS, 2012)).
- Either-way offences may be tried in a magistrates' court or a Crown Court; the magistrate decides. An example of an either-way offence in England and Wales would be unblocking a stolen mobile phone (by changing the IMEI number) that had been 'switched off' by a provider. The offence would have been committed under s 1(1) of the Mobile Telephones (Re-Programming) Act 2002 for which the sentence on summary conviction is a fine or a maximum of six months imprisonment, but the maximum sentence on indictment is a fine or a maximum of five years imprisonment.

In the UK a magistrates' court conducts summary trials and deals with less serious criminal cases. The Crown Court hears more serious criminal cases including indictable offences such as murder, rape and manslaughter. It also tries appeals from magistrates' courts, and 'either-way' cases referred by magistrates' courts. The trial in a Crown Court takes place before a judge and a jury, and members of the public may have to attend as witnesses. There are about 90 Crown Courts across the UK. On matters of fact and law, it is possible to appeal from the Crown Court to the Criminal Division of the Court of Appeal.

The Court of Appeal considers appeals from the Crown Court (criminal cases) and the High Court (civil cases) but it also takes a few appeals from magistrates' and youth courts. The Supreme Court is the final instance of appeal on points of law on important legal disputes for criminal and civil cases in England and Wales. A youth court is normally used for defendants aged between 10 and 17 years.

Digital Crime Legislation in the UK

A wide range of digitally-related activities are regarded as either criminal in themselves or as contributing to a criminal act. However, precisely which law and legislation is applicable to particular criminal behaviours is a complex issue. Even the *actus reus* (see above) presents problems in suspected digital offences since there may be no physical act per se in an automated process. The *mens rea* is also problematic, for example with respect to causation (did the act cause the crime, and/or was it intended?). There are further questions, for example does the specific legislation require intention (such as for murder) or is negligence sufficient, or alternatively, (as for strict liability offences) is no intention required at all? Does specific codified legislation (e.g. Acts of Parliament) and case law apply, and are there any possible conflicts between these different sources of law and their interpretation?

As well as the innate complexity of legislation in a common law system such as that of the UK, there are also varying levels of political complexity. The UK comprises England and Wales, Scotland and Northern Ireland and there are often differences between the jurisdictions. As well as being made of up four states the UK is also bound by EU law. UK law is challengeable if it is deemed to conflict with EU law.

Digital crime is not constrained by physical or legal boundaries and often involves technology situated in many countries. There are therefore important issues concerning both *material jurisdiction* (under which jurisdiction was the offence committed?) and *procedural jurisdiction* (the procedural rules of which jurisdiction govern the investigation and evidence?) (Walden, 2007, pp. 298 and 310). In order to avoid (or minimise) the potential complexities and conflicts that are likely to arise when prosecuting or investigating digital crimes that span national borders, a number of harmonisation initiatives have been attempted. The Council of Europe, G8, the United Nations, the Commonwealth and the European Union have all created initiatives that seek to harmonise digital crime legislation and provide for mutual legal assistance (Walden, 2007, p. 328).

The rules regarding cooperation between the UK and EU states differ from those governing cooperation between the UK and non-EU states. One of the aims of the Council of Europe is the harmonisation of legislation within its 47 European member countries, and it creates conventions and international treaties with this aim (Council of Europe, 2012). However such treaties are not legally binding (Walden, 2007, pp. 329–30) because the Council of Europe is a separate organisation from the EU. A memorandum of understanding promotes close cooperation between the EU and the Council of Europe (European Union, 2008).

For cooperation between the UK and the EU, the key piece of legislation is the Crime (International Co-operation) Act 2003. This implements the European Convention on Mutual Assistance in Criminal Matters (1959) and its subsequent amendments. It does not, however, specify any criminal law; it only addresses how states should cooperate in the process of applying law. The main EU agreement which sets out the EU's stance on criminal computer law (both substantively and procedurally) is the Council of Europe's Convention on Cybercrime (Convention on Cybercrime ETS No: 185). The Convention on Cybercrime was initially open for signatures in 2001, and came into force in 2004 (Walden, 2007, p. 330). The slow pace of ratification of the treaty has been criticised as potentially providing 'safe havens' for criminals (Carstensen, 2011). The UK finally ratified the convention in 2011, ten years after signing it (Council of Europe Treaty Office, 2012).

The globalisation of digital crime necessitates cooperation between legal systems, for example suspects may need to be extradited between nations. Treaties such as the Convention on Cybercrime and the Extradition Act (2003) allow for extradition to (but not from) the US, but these treaties are sometimes criticised for being heavy-handed and infringing on an individual's rights. Two cases of UK hackers awaiting extradition to the United States have highlighted concerns over the use of such legislation. For example Gary McKinnon was arrested in 2005 for hacking into US military computers and it was argued that as a sufferer of Asperger's syndrome, extradition would increase his suicide risk (Travis, 2012). The extradition has since been blocked by the Home Secretary Teresa May (BBC, 2012c). The Sheffield Hallam University student, Richard O'Dwyer, fought extradition to the US where he faced charges of copyright infringement in relation to his website 'tvshack.net', which provided links to copyrighted materials. His case was controversial since, amongst other things, any alleged infringement was not deemed sufficient for any UK prosecution (Ball and Travis, 2012). His case was settled when he agreed to a 'deferred prosecution' and to pay £20,000 in compensation.

Criminal Law and Internet-related Crime

As we noted in Chapter 1, Wall (2001) argued that the internet has impacted on crime in four broad areas of criminality:

- Cyber-trespass (this includes hacking, which can range from ethical hacking to information warfare, and would also include unauthorised access and modification of computer systems)
- Cyber-thefts (fraud, appropriation of intellectual property etc.)
- Cyber-obscenities (which includes pornography, sex-trade)
- Cyber-violence (which includes stalking, hate-speech etc.)

Wall's categories were specifically aimed at delineating the types of crimes and deviant behaviours mediated by the use of the internet (hence 'cyber'). These divisions also apply equally well for many 'digital behaviours' (as opposed to strictly internet based ones). For example the creation of child sex abuse images using a smartphone would obviously reside in the obscenity category. It should be noted that not every crime will fit neatly into just one category, and indeed there may be some debate concerning the categorisation of particular activities, but trespass, theft, obscenity and violence are useful categories for summarising UK criminal law.

Cyber-trespass

Prior to the introduction of the CMA 1990, other legislation was sometimes be used to prosecute certain forms of digital crime. For example the Criminal Damage Act 1971 (CDA) was used in the case of *Cox v. Riley* (1986) 83 Cr App R 54 (DC) (Fafinski, 2009, pp. 21–8). The defendant had allegedly erased the computer programmes on a plastic circuit card required for the operation of a computer-controlled saw. The initial judgment concluded that the plastic card was tangible and therefore counted as 'property' under the CDA. Riley appealed, arguing that the programmes were not tangible, but the appeal was dismissed when the Divisional Court agreed that the card as tangible property (Fafinski, 2009, pp. 22–3). The difficulty was resolved by the introduction of the CMA 1990, and its section 3 offence of '[u]nauthorised acts with intent to impair, or with recklessness as to impairing, operation of computer, etc.' (Bainbridge, 2008).

The appropriateness of the CDA was also challenged in the case of *R v. Whiteley* (1991) 93 Cr App R 381. Whiteley had hacked into and altered information on the JANET academic network. In the appeal *R v. Whiteley* (1991) 93 Cr. App. R. 25 (CA) the defence argued that there should be a distinction drawn between the physical disks themselves and any information stored on them, but the Court of Appeal rejected this argument noting that disks and their magnetic particles are both parts of the same entity. It was argued that, despite the fact that the particles were invisible, the damage had indeed occurred to tangible property (the requirement under the CDA, rather than the damage itself being tangible) (Bainbridge, 2008, p. 455).

'Tangibility' was also an issue in the case of *R v Gold & Schifreen* (1988) 1 AC 1063. The defendants were accuse of gaining unauthorised access to BT's Prestel network, and subsequently altering data in, amongst other places, the private mailbox of Prince Philip, the Duke of Edinburgh (Fafinski, 2009, pp. 26–7). The defendants were convicted under section 1(1) of the Forgery and Counterfeiting Act 1981, which requires the making of a 'false instrument.' On appeal both the Court of Appeal and House of Lords found for the defendants, in essence the argument being that a false instrument needed to be stored for some time, and the entry of a user-ID and password were fleeting in nature (since both were immediately deleted after validation) so did not meet this requirement (Bainbridge, 2008).

Another piece of legislation that could be used for the prosecution of early occurrences of digital crime was the Theft Act 1968, which contains the offence of the abstraction of electricity (Bainbridge, 1989). But it has been argued since that this was (and is) a 'clumsy' form of prosecution because the amount of electricity 'stolen' is very likely to be insignificant compared with to the damage done to a computer system, and also the theft of the electricity would occur whether the hackers motives were malign or not (Fafinski, 2009).

By the late 1980s many considered the existing legislation to be insufficient to cope with computer crime. Following a Law Commission of England and Wales report in 1989, the CMA (Computer Misuse Act 1990) was introduced as a private member's bill by the late Michael Colvin MP, and it became legislation on 29 June 1990. It also applies to both Scotland and Northern Ireland. Interestingly, it makes no attempt to define the term 'computer' due to the complexity of such a definition (Law Commission, 1989) and this provides a certain amount of flexibility when applying the legislation to cases involving devices such as modern smartphones. These would have not have been considered by the Act when it was drafted, but most certainly are targets of unauthorised access and modification today.

The Act created three new offences:

- Section 1: 'Unauthorised access to computer material'.
- Section 2: 'Unauthorised access with intent to commit or facilitate commission of further offences'.
- Section 3: 'Unauthorised modification of computer material' (as originally enacted)

The question of authorisation, what is and is not authorised behaviour is a complex issue. For example the case of Lennon (*Lennon* [2005] ECLR 5(5), 3 and *DPP v. Lennon* [2006] All ER (D) 147 (May)) discussed authorisation in relation to a DoS attack. Lennon performed a DoS attack against Domestic and General Group ('D & G'), bombarding the company's mail server with approximately 5 million emails. The original judgement found for Lennon, the judge arguing that D & G's mail server authorised each individual email sent, but the Director of Public Prosecutions was successful on appeal when the Divisional Court found that there are limits to implied consent and that the owners of the mail server's company would not have consented to transmitting emails intended to disrupt its own service (Walden, 2007, p. 161, p. 180). For an in-depth discussion of authorisation in relation to computer law in general, see Walden (2007, pp. 160–67) or Kerr (2003).

Section 1 offences were originally summary-only offences and the penalties were limited to a maximum 6 months' imprisonment or a £5000 fine. Section 35 of the Police and Justice Act 2006 (PJA) amended the CMA to increase the penalty to 12 months, and also made the section 1 offence an either-way offence, the indictable tariff being two years' imprisonment. The new indictable nature of the offence brought the CMA into compliance with the EU Framework Decision 2005/222/JHA, which requires penalties of between two and five years if the offence is committed as part of a criminal organisation (Walden, 2007, p. 170).

To meet the requirements of a section 1 offence the perpetrator must have *intended* to access the unauthorised system, as well as have *known* that such access is unauthorised (Walden, 2007). If these aspects of the *mens rea* had not been included with respect to unauthorised access then a person who had accidentally accessed a system without proper authorisation could be convicted of a criminal offence. However the current requirement for intention might allow defences which claim ignorance, although warnings on login screens make it difficult to argue that someone who accesses such a system did not have both knowledge and intent of wrong-doing. A successful defence against a section 1 offence was a claimed 'addiction to hacking' when Paul Bedworth and two other defendants were charged with amending a database owned by the Financial Times and affecting work of the European Organisation for the Research and Treatment of Cancer (Southwark Crown Court, 17 March 1993; Fafinski, 2008). Addiction is not an allowable defence under English law, yet a jury found Bedworth not guilty of section 1 and 3 offences due to his proclaimed addiction to hacking. This seems to be merely an 'erroneous verdict' on the part of the jury rather than a signal that intention should be removed as a requirement from the CMA. If intent was removed it might make the merely clumsy criminally liable when they mistakenly or unknowingly access systems without authorisation (Bainbridge, 2008). The CMA was amended by the PJA (s 35) to make it an offence 'to enable any such access to be secured,' which it has been argued might criminalise the use of so-called 'hacking tools' even though they have legitimate uses (Walden, 2007, p. 168). This is discussed further below.

A recent example of a successful prosecution under section 1 was the case of Glenn Mangham, who admitted hacking into Facebook servers and downloading source code between April and May 2011 (BBC, 2012e). Mangham has since been released (after his sentence was reduced on appeal), and he disputes that his actions were malicious and is also sceptical of the claim that Facebook incurred costs of $200,000 investigating his actions (Mangham, 2012).

In the US the situation is a little different to the UK's section 1 unauthorised access offence. At the federal level a threshold of a $5,000 loss in one year must be met for an access offence to occur (Walden, 2007, p. 171, Computer Fraud and Abuse Act, 18 U.S.C. § 1030). However as well as the Federal statutes there are also varying state laws, for example Leon Walker was charged with hacking into his wife's Gmail account under Michigan state law (Brasier, 2011), although the hacking charges were eventually dropped (Brasier, 2012).

Jurisdiction was an issue for a section 1 CMA 1990 offence in the case of *R v Tomsett* [1985] Crim LR 369. Tomsett was a telex operator working in London who sent a telex to attempt to move money from a New York bank account to another account under his control in Geneva. The Court of Appeal ruled that if Tomsett had succeeded the crime would have taken place in New York, and under English common law the UK courts would have had no jurisdiction. To counter this problem the CMA addresses jurisdiction, so that a section 1 or 3 offence applies if the computer which was the target of the prohibited behaviour was situated in the UK, or if the perpetrator was in the UK when committing the prohibited behaviour. For a suspected section 2 offence, if the act that is considered as the further offence takes place outside the UK, it must be an offence in both the UK and the country in which it occurs, an example of the legal principle known as dual criminality (Bainbridge, 2008), discussed further in Chapter 6.

For a section 2 offence ('unauthorised access with intent to commit or facilitate commission of further offences') the perpetrator must have *intended* to access the unauthorised system, as well as have *known* that such access is unauthorised, but also there must be intention to commit a further offence; one which has a sentence fixed by law, or one for which the maximum sentence is five or more years' imprisonment (Walden, 2007, p. 171). An example of a successful section 2 prosecution occurred in *R v. Delamare* [2003] EWCA Crim 424 when Delamare, an employee of Barclays Bank at Poole in the UK, was asked by an acquaintance to provide the details of two customers from the bank's computer. These details were later used by Delamare's acquaintance to attempt fraud by impersonating one of the customers and attempting to withdraw £10,000 from the bank (Fafinski, 2008). The further offence does not have to be possible (Walden, 2007) since s 2 (4) of the CMA 1990 states that '[a] person may be guilty of an offence under this section even though the facts are such that the commission of the further offence is impossible' (CMA, s 2 (4)). This means that a hacker who gains unauthorised access to an organisation's database with the intention of stealing intellectual property who then finds nothing of value is still liable.

The case of *Cox v. Riley* highlighted the ambiguity of the CDA with respect to computer data and tangible property. To clarify the situation in the UK, section 3 of the CMA specifically mentions modification of the 'contents of any computer', thus making the offence applicable for any electronic data held on a computer (Bainbridge, 2008). Indeed the CMA 1990 specifically mentions the disjuncture with the CDA when it states '[f]or the purposes of the [1971 c. 48.] Criminal Damage Act 1971 a modification of the contents of a computer shall not be regarded as damaging any computer or computer storage medium unless its effect on that computer or computer storage medium impairs its physical condition' (CMA, s 3 (6)).

For an offence to have occurred under section 3 of the CMA, in its original form (before the PJA modifications) again both intention and knowledge of an act 'which causes an unauthorised modification of the contents of any computer' (CMA, s 3 (2)) are required, and specifically intent:

> ... to cause a modification of the contents of any computer and by so doing—
> (a) to impair the operation of any computer;
> (b) to prevent or hinder access to any program or data held in any computer; or
> (c) to impair the operation of any such program or the reliability of any such data. (CMA 1990, s 3 (2))

The intent does not need to be towards any specific computer, data or program nor does any specific type of modification need to be intended (CMA, s 3 (3)), nor does it have to be a permanent modification (CMA, s 3 (5)). Section 3 offences are either-way offences originally punishable by a maximum six months' imprisonment and/or a fine for a summary offence, and by a maximum 12 months' imprisonment and/or a fine for an indictable offence. The PJA (s 36) doubled each of the terms of imprisonment, except for summary conviction in Scotland which remained at six months.

Goulden (1992, unreported Southwark Crown Court) was an early case of a successful prosecution under section 3 of the CMA. Goulden claimed that a company for whom he had installed software owed him money, and to force the company to pay him he had added a requirement for a password to access the company's machine on which he had installed software. Since the company were unable to access this machine they claimed they had lost £36,000 of business, and indeed went into liquidation (Akdeniz, 1996). Another example of a section 3 prosecution was the case of *R v Pile* (Plymouth Crown Court 15/11/1995). The defendant (also known as the 'Black Baron') had written two computer viruses known as Pathogen and Queeg. Pile was charged under sections 1 and 3 of the CMA, and was also charged with the common law offence of incitement since he encouraged others to pass on the viruses. He pleaded guilty and was sentenced to 18 months imprisonment; the first person to be jailed under the CMA 1990 in relation to writing a virus (Fafinski, 2008, p. 59).

The changes to the CMA introduced by the PJA were drafted largely in response to the perceived inability of the CMA to deal with denial of service (DoS) attacks (Fafinski, 2008). The CMA's section 3 offence '[u]nauthorised modification of computer material' requiring 'unauthorised modification of the contents of any computer' (CMA, s 3 (1)) was replaced by the a new section 3 offence: '[u] nauthorised acts with intent to impair, or with recklessness as to impairing, operation of computer, etc.' which broadened the scope for 'any unauthorised act in relation to a computer' (PJA, s 36). It was argued that DoS attacks would be easier to prosecute because formerly it might be argued that sending of emails was not '[u]nauthorised modification of computer material' (such as was ultimately unsuccessfully argued in Lennon's defence). Instead, the sending of emails could be classed as '[u]nauthorised acts with intent to impair' (Walden, 2007, pp. 180–81) and could therefore be prosecuted under the revised CMA.

The making, supplying or obtaining of articles for use in cyber-trespass is also covered by the CMA. Section 36 of the PJA amended section 3 of the CMA to include enablement, (as for the CMA section 1 offence modified by s 35 of the PJA, see above). The PJA (s 37) also created a new section 3A which addresses '[m]aking, supplying or obtaining articles for use in offence under section 1 or 3'. The prohibited behaviours in this new section are:

(1) A person is guilty of an offence if he makes, adapts, supplies or offers to supply any article intending it to be used to commit, or to assist in the commission of, an offence under section 1 or 3.

(2) A person is guilty of an offence if he supplies or offers to supply any article believing that it is likely to be used to commit, or to assist in the commission of, an offence under section 1 or 3.

(3) A person is guilty of an offence if he obtains any article with a view to its being supplied for use to commit, or to assist in the commission of, an offence under section 1 or 3.

(4) In this section 'article' includes any program or data held in electronic form.

The section 3A offences carry the same penalties as the equivalent section 3 offences.

As previously noted, there is some debate about the PJA's role in the possible criminalisation of the use of so-called 'hacking tools' (Walden, 2007). Many such tools can have both legitimate and malign uses, for example automated penetration testing tools (PTT) in essence probe computer systems looking for weaknesses, and have an existing list of known weaknesses and the software patches designed to fix them. If a system has not applied a particular patch then the PTT notes the weakness. A hacker would use the same tool, but is more likely to exploit the weakness to gain unauthorised access (Sommer, 2006). It has been argued (Sommer, 2006) that some tools such as virus creation kits do not have this dual-use function, but likewise it could also be argued that even these could be used legitimately, in order to understand and counter threats. Whether such fears are justified or not, the UK's Crown Prosecution Service (CPS) asks prosecutors to be mindful of potential legitimate uses for such software: '[p]rosecutors should be aware that there is a legitimate industry concerned with the security of computer systems that generates 'articles' (this includes any program or data held in electronic form) to test and/or audit hardware and software. Some articles will therefore have a dual use and prosecutors need to ascertain that the suspect has a criminal intent' (CPS, 2011).

The new section 3A arose due to the UK's attempt to comply with the EU's 2001 Convention on Cybercrime which requires signatories (Convention on Cybercrime, Art. 6) to criminalise (via new or existing domestic legislation):

> ... a. the production, sale, procurement for use, import, distribution or otherwise making available of:
>
> > i. a device, including a computer program, designed or adapted primarily for the purpose of committing any of the offences established in accordance with Articles 2 through 5;
> >
> > ii. a computer password, access code, or similar data by which the whole or any part of a computer system is capable of being accessed, with intent that it be used for the purpose of committing any of the offences established in Articles 2 through 5; and...

This criminalises, inter alia, the passing on of knowledge about vulnerabilities that could be used to access, or in other ways exploit, computer systems, and it seems that section 3A of the CMA provides this legislation in UK law (Walden, 2007, pp. 193–5).

As noted earlier there have been comparatively few cases brought to successful prosecution under CMA. Although only 214 cases were brought using the CMA in England and Wales in the 16-year period from 1990 to 2006 (All Party Parliamentary Internet Group, 2004), there were however 161 convictions from these 214 cases, so although the CMA was used infrequently, when it was used it was used successfully (MacEwan, 2008).

Further changes to the CMA may be required in the near future since in 2010 the European Commission released the 'Proposal for a Directive on attacks against information systems, repealing Framework Decision 2005/222/JHA' (Cash, 2011). This new proposal is designed to repeal the existing 2005 EU Council Framework Decision on attacks against information systems (2005/222/JHA) which addressed 'Illegal access to information systems,' 'Illegal system interference,' and 'Illegal data interference' and to harmonise EU law across member states with regard to this problem (Directive, E.U.C. 2005). The European Commission felt a new directive was necessary for two main reasons, the first of which was the rapid changes in technology since 2005; new threats have since emerged, in particular the use of botnets in large-scale attacks was not foreseen when the original legislation was drafted. The second reason for the new directive is related to the implementation of such directives, since not all EU states follow the 2005 directive. In addition the Commission has new powers to ensure member states follow EU rules, and can refer them to the European Court of Justice if they do not (EU Commission, 2010). As well as increasing penalties for offences listed under the 2005 directive, the 2010 legislation: 'penalises the production, sale, procurement for use, import, distribution or otherwise making available of devices/tools used for committing the offences' (European Commission, 2010). This presents similar issues to the effective ban on hacking tools under the revised CMA (see above): might the legitimate use of devices or tools for attacks on information systems become criminalised? After all botnets can have benign uses, such as when non-criminal tasks require large amounts of computing power. For example SETILive, a project administered by the Search for Extraterrestrial Intelligence organisation, harnesses large numbers of PCs connected as a botnet to detect signals potentially sent by alien civilisations (SETI, 2012). Might SETI's work be criminalised under the EU 2010 directive?

The UK's Terrorism Act 2000 also provides legislation similar to the CMA but in relation to terrorist acts. Section 1 (2) (e) of the Terrorism Act 2000 requires that an act 'is designed seriously to interfere with or seriously to disrupt an electronic system' so no great harm need be caused for an offence to be committed under this legislation (Hardy, 2011). Section 57 also states 'A person commits an offence if he possesses an article in circumstances which give rise to a reasonable suspicion that his possession is for a purpose connected with the commission, preparation or instigation of an act of terrorism' (s 57 (1)) and section 58 makes it an offence to collect or possess information 'likely to be useful to a person committing or preparing an act of terrorism' (s 58 (1) (a)) thus potentially criminalising ownership of software or access codes (Walden, 2007, p. 183). Other than the fact that such actions or possession apply to terrorist acts, these offences are similar to those under the CMA, but they carry far higher penalties (Walden, 2007, p. 183).

Cyber-theft and associated activities

There is wide-spread and on-going debate regarding regulation and control of digital technology in relation to the infringement of intellectual property rights

(IPR). Intellectual Properties (IP) are products formed from creative endeavour, innovation and other original intellectual work, and would include a recording of a song, a film, or a new design of jeans. IPR are those legal rights that are intended to protect the originators (for example individuals or companies) that have created the IP. The term 'Piracy' is often used to denote copyright infringement, hence 'cyber-piracy' referring to activities that contravene copyright laws via the internet, such as downloading copyrighted music without permission from the rights' holder. The term 'counterfeiting' is commonly used for trade mark infringement such as selling fake branded goods on eBay (Cornish et al., 2010).

IPR comprises an array of legal devices, which may be categorised into:

- Patents: a new invention that usually has to be 'industrially applicable', for example a 'Dyson' vacuum cleaner.
- Trade marking: a sign that distinguishes a company, for example the 'McDonalds' logo.
- Designs: the 'overall visual appearance' of a product, for example a type of 'Nike' trainer. The design may include 'lines, contours, colours, shape, texture, materials and the ornamentation of the product.'
- Copyright: economic rights over material such as music, for example. a particular song may be copyrighted, so if you buy a CD you own the CD but not its musical content (Wall and Yar, 2009), and
- Other forms of IPR: for example, plant breeders' rights.

IP crime often transgresses the law surrounding more than one of these categories as in the case of counterfeit goods. There are both civil and criminal legislative remedies to IPR infringement, but criminal sanctions only apply in the UK for copyright and trademarks, and not for patent or design rights (Cornish et al., 2010). IPR covers intangible intellectual endeavour as opposed to tangible; that is, 'real' property and attributes. In the digital realm IPR applies to intangible products too. This new 'digital property' is easily disseminated via global networks due to the ability to perfectly reproduce the data and the low cost of the necessary copying equipment (see Chapter 1). This has the concomitant effect of making it easy to circumvent traditional controls, and thus making digital property extremely easy to 'steal' (Wall and Yar, 2009).

The US was far ahead of the UK in terms of digital IPR legislation. In the first case that addressed mass copying in the US in 1984 – the so-called Betamax decision – copying technologies were deemed to be not necessarily illegal if they have legitimate uses (*Sony Corp. of Am. v. Universal City Studios, Inc.* 464 U.S. 417, 442 (1984)). (A similar provision, that of 'fair dealing', exists in UK law under the Copyright, Designs and Patents Act 1988). The Betamax decision was held to apply until Peer-to-Peer (P2P) file-sharing became widespread and changed the IPR infringement landscape.

P2P file-sharing via the internet has been greatly facilitated by the reduction in file sizes afforded by compression technologies such as MP3 for audio and

MPEG-4 for video. The smaller file sizes along with increased bandwidth and the growth in file-sharing software based on P2P protocols has seen an exponential rise in the amount of material shared both legally and illegally via the internet. Before the advent of P2P, 'old' computer paradigms for large-scale applications consisted of mainframe and/or client server systems. For such systems much of the processing was performed by a large centralised resource, and accessed by terminal or client machines. P2P computing is a different architecture model in that each computer in a P2P network is a peer of any other and the processing load is shared by 'equal' (although some may be more equal than others!) machines. The chief piece of US legislation for countering illegal file-sharing is the Digital Millennium Copyright Act (17 U.S.C. § 512 (1998); DMCA) which has a 'safe harbor' provision, section 512, which protects sites such as Youtube from copyright infringement activity of their users.

In 1999, Napster became the first P2P file-sharing network. It had a central server which contained indexes of song files, but much of the work was undertaken by peer nodes on an equal basis. The Napster server informed the nodes which pieces of files could be found on which peer machines, and the nodes then transferred file pieces from one to another. In the case of *A&M Records v. Napster Inc.* (239 F.3d 1004, 1025 (9th Cir. 2001)) it was ruled that Napster failed to police infringements, a requirement under the 'safe harbor' provision of the DMCA. In 2000 the file-sharing network Grokster began using FastTrack software which decentralised searches. In the 2005 case of *MGM Studios Inc. v. Grokster, Ltd* (545 U.S. 913, 928 (2005)) Grokster were found to have *induced* copyright infringements (Corsaro, 2012).

Since these cases BitTorrent (BT) has become the most prevalent P2P protocol. Some sites are BT trackers which only store metadata, not copyrighted material, so some would argue that these sites are therefore legal. However legal pressure (usually backed by trade associations, especially the Motion Picture Association of America (MPAA) and Recording Industry Association of America (RIAA)) has led to the closure of many such BT tracker sites.

In the UK the key legislation in terms of copyright is the:

- Copyright, Designs and Patents Act 1988 (CDPA), later amended by the Copyright and Trade Marks (Offences and Enforcement) Act 2002 which provided for increased penalties.
- Copyright and Related Rights Regulations 2003 (CRRR) the aim of which was to make minor changes to UK copyright legislation in order to implement the European Union Copyright Directive.

Unauthorised file-sharing and the use of unauthorised decoders (for example for obtaining Sky TV for free) are illegal under both the CDPA and the CRRR.

Probably the most well-known case of a BT tracker site is Pirate Bay, based in Sweden. In April 2009 a Swedish court found the four men behind the Pirate Bay website guilty of breaking copyright law. They were sentenced to jail terms and received a $4.5m (£3m) fine. On appeal the jail terms were reduced but the fine increased (Cheng, 2010). The UK High Court has since ordered ISPs to block Pirate Bay under the CDPA (*Dramatico Entertainment Ltd & Ors v British Sky Broadcasting Ltd & Ors* [2012] EWHC 1152 (Ch)) although there are criticisms of the effectiveness of such blocks as it seems that the number of Pirate Bay users has increased since the High Court injunction and there are a number of proxy sites allowing indirect but technically straightforward access to Pirate Bay. The claim that blocking such sites leads to increased legitimate music sales is highly contested (Kaye, 2012; Yar, 2006). In part to deflect legal attacks the Pirate Bay defaulted to using magnet links (instead of torrent files), enabling users to find out about files from other peers rather than via a torrent file hosted on a Pirate Bay server (Halliday, 2012). A magnet link does not point to any location but instead contains the hash value of the file to be downloaded. Its main 'advantage' in terms of avoiding legal attacks is that it is simply a link, and so unlike a torrent file does not have to be stored on a torrent tracker site.

The afore-mentioned cases involve *secondary* liability, but the primary liability for copyright infringement lies with the users. In the US the RIAA/MPAA have targeted colleges and students, and the British Phonographic Industry (BPI, the British music industry's trade association) have targeted UK users. In 2006 in the first court case of its kind in UK, two men were ordered by high court to pay the BPI fines for downloading (BBC, 2006), and in 2010 a woman in the US was ordered to pay $2m (since reduced to $54,000) for sharing 24 songs over the internet (BBC, 2010).

Much of the current legislation takes a graduated response or 'three strikes and you're out' approach to persistent downloading. For example in France the government agency that polices online IP infringement (HADOPI) has passed a so-called 'HADOPI law' which includes a 'three strikes' provision that ultimately requires an ISP to remove a persistent offender's internet access (Constitutional Council, 2009). Amusingly, the agency created to enforce the HADOPI law launched with a logo created in a font that was owned by France Telecom, thus infringing their copyright (Daily Telegraph, 2010). In the UK, the Digital Economy Act 2010, creates a similar 'three strikes' provision. There has been much criticism of this legislation and OfCom (the regulator for the UK communication industries) has yet to provide the details on how it will be policed (Moody, 2012). The various legislative attempts are all aimed at online file-sharing yet there is some evidence that in fact 'offline' file-sharing might be a more significant economic threat to the creative industries than online file-sharing, (BOP Consulting, 2010).

There is also much criticism of, and opposition to, IPR related legislation on a wider scale. For example the Anti-Counterfeiting Trade Agreement (ACTA) was recently rejected by the EU, after it earlier rejected any compulsory 'three strikes' provisions (Barron, 2011). And in the US the Stop Online Piracy Act (SOPA) and the Protect IP Act (Preventing Real Online Threats to Economic Creativity and Theft of Intellectual Property Act) (PIPA) were also defeated (Rushe, 2012).

In relation to other forms of cyber-theft, the UK's Fraud Act 2006 became law on 15 Jan 2007 and this legislation is more effective for addressing computer crime than the Theft Acts of 1968 and 1978. For example under the new legislation the act of phishing is clearly a criminal offence (Bainbridge, 2008, p. 424). At its inception the Fraud Act 2006 was expected to lead to the repeal of the common law offence of conspiracy to defraud (Bainbridge, 2008, p. 432), yet it is still being used.

Section 126 of the Communications Act 2003 legislates against 'Dishonestly obtaining electronic communication services' (although it does not cover TV conditional access service theft; this is covered under the CDPA (Communications Act 2003, s 125 (1) & (2))). Section 126 of the Communications Act 2003 has been used to successfully prosecute the behaviour known as 'war driving' which is searching for an unsecured wifi access (not necessarily while driving a vehicle!) and then using the wifi without authorisation. Gregory Straszkiewicz was accused of 'piggybacking' the wifi of an Ealing household (Wakefield, 2005). Despite his conviction, prosecutions under this Act are not clear-cut as there is an issue over whether there really was any intent to avoid a charge, when there is in fact no charge in place for accessing a home network (Mac Síthigh, 2009).

A mobile phone is uniquely identified by its International Mobile Equipment Identity (IMEI) number and network service providers can use this to blacklist stolen phones. A stolen phone with a blocked IMEI will not work on a network, so criminals will often seek to change the IMEI so the phone can be used again (Willassen, 2003). Specific legislation under the Mobile Telephones (Re-programming) Act 2002 (MTRA) makes it an offence:

- to alter an IMEI (s 1);
- to own equipment for re-programming a phone (s 2 (1));
- to supply such equipment (s 2(2)); or
- to offer to supply such equipment (s 2 (3)).

Other countries have varying legislation regarding this issue; for example there is no such legislation in the US; IMEI alteration is legal in the US (Fitchard, 2012).

Cyber-obscenity

What is classified as 'obscene' material is to some extent subjective. Most would argue that paedophilia is obscene, yet even here there are some grey areas. For example the police use a modified version of the Combating Paedophile Information Networks in Europe (COPINE) scale which grades paedophilic images as to their severity (Quayle, 2012). How should a potentially innocuous image (for example, a child in underwear taken from a clothing catalogue, which would be at the low level of the COPINE scale) be treated when found in possession of a suspect? Also, at what age is a person still a 'child'? Is it a child's legal age or their apparent age, and if it is the legal age, should this be the age of consent? This also causes jurisdictional issues since, for example, the age of consent in Spain is 13 (unless 'deceit' is used in gaining consent).

Whatever the definition, the main legislation in the UK regarding obscenity pre-dating the internet is the Obscene Publications Acts (OPA) of 1959 and 1964, which make the distribution of obscene articles illegal. Obscene articles are those that would 'deprave and corrupt' (OPA 1964, s 1(1)), and the Acts provide powers to search for and seize such articles (OPA 1964, s 3). These Acts were amended by the Criminal Justice and Public Order Act 1994 (CJPOA) to include computer disks as 'articles' and electronic transmission as 'distribution' (Edwards et al., 2010).

The OPA 1959 provides a 'Defence of Public Good' (OPA 1959, s 4) which considers work of artistic merit as potentially protected. No such protection is afforded by section 1 of the Protection of Children Act 1978 (PCA) which prohibits taking, permitting to be taken, distributing, showing, advertising or possessing for distribution indecent photographs or pseudo-photographs of a child originally under the age of 16 (s 2). This was amended by the Sexual Offences Act 2003 (SOA) which increased the age of a child to those under 18 but provided defences for those in possession of images of 16 or 17 year olds if they were married or in a partnership with the child (s 45 (4)), or if an indecent image or pseudo-image of a child under 18 was required for law enforcement purposes (s 46).

The CJPOA (s 84) expanded the remit of the legislation by amending the PCA to cover pseudo- photographs: that is 'an image, whether made by computer-graphics or otherwise howsoever, which appears to be a photograph.' As well as the ban on pseudo-photographs, legislation in the Coroners and Justice Act 2009 (sections 62 to 68) prohibits indecent drawings or computer-generated images of children.

Prior to the Criminal Justice Act 1988 (CJA) possession of was not an offence but section 160 of the CJA changed this by creating 'an offence for a person to have any indecent photograph of a child (meaning in this section a person under the age of 16) in his possession.' (s 160 (1) as enacted). This was later amended to a person under 18 by the SOA, with a marriage/partnership defence (similar to the changes in the PCA 1978).

The Communications Act 2003 also provides legislation that is relevant to countering obscenity through digital means. Section 127 of the Communications Act 2003 prohibits the sending of indecent messages through 'a public electronic communications network' (s 127 (1) (a)).

Issues of intent with respect to images were considered in *Atkins & Goodland v Director of Public Prosecutions* [2000] 2 All ER 425. In this case Atkins had indecent images of children stored in a computer cache. At issue was whether such images could be regarded as 'possessed' under the CJA. The Queen's Bench Divisional Court found on appeal that intent was necessary for possession i.e. he would need to have been aware of the images. He denied this and his appeal was successful (Walden, 2007 p. 143).

Whether deleted photos are possessed was discussed in *R v Ross, Warwick & Porter* [2006] EWCA Crim 560, [2006] 1 WLR 2633, where Porter was found to have thumbnails of indecent images of children on his computer, even after deleting the files and emptying his recycle bin (see Chapter 8). It was judged that unless the defendant had specialist software (which he did not), he would not be able to access the images and so he did not 'possess' them (Walden, 2007, pp. 143–4).

'Grooming', another internet-mediated child abuse behaviour, has been explicitly targeted by legislation, specifically s 15 SOA which criminalises the meeting of a child following sexual grooming and 'is intended to cover situations where an adult (A) establishes contact with a child through, for example, meetings, telephone conversations or communications on the Internet, and gains the child's trust and confidence so that he can arrange to meet the child for the purpose of committing a 'relevant offence' against the child.' (Explanatory Notes to the SOA 2003). There has been some criticism of this legislation as it potentially criminalises behaviour even if no actual sexual abuse occurs (Edwards et al., 2010, p. 420).

As well as paedophilia and grooming, extreme pornography has been targeted by legislation. Section 63 of the Criminal Justice and Immigration Act 2008 made the possession of an 'extreme pornographic image' an offence (s 63 (1)). As is common with such legislation the definition of images that would constitute an offence is open to some interpretation. They must be 'grossly offensive, disgusting or otherwise of an obscene character' (s 63 (6) (b)), and they must portray 'in an explicit and realistic way' (s 63 (7)) one of:

(a) an act which threatens a person's life;
(b) an act which results, or is likely to result, in serious injury to a person's anus, breasts or genitals;
(c) an act which involves sexual interference with a human corpse; or
(d) a person performing an act of intercourse or oral sex with an animal (whether dead or alive) and a reasonable person looking at the image would think that any such person or animal was real.

The imprecise and subjective notion of what is extreme is an obvious weakness to this act, for example Simon Walsh was found not guilty of possessing extreme images under the act in August 2012. He possessed images showing 'urethral sounding', where the urethra at the tip of the penis is stretched, and 'anal fisting' where a person inserts his/her arm into the anus of another person. He was acquitted by a jury after his defence argued these images were not depicting serious injury (Davies, 2012).

New digital social media are of particular concern in terms of privacy in sexual offence cases. For example in a recent case the Sheffield United footballer Ched Evans was found guilty of rape, and people tweeted the name of the victim on the social network Twitter. They were charged under Sexual Offences (Amendment) Act 1992 which protects the privacy of rape victims, and also charged with 'malicious communication' (Dowell, 2012; see also the violence section below).

Cyber-violence

Three forms of criminal behaviour will be discussed in this section: hate-speech, malicious communications and terrorism. There may of course be some overlap between these, for example an SMS text message referring to a person by a racial epithet might be regarded as either hate speech or malicious communications, or as both.

The regulation of 'hate speech' – the victimisation of marginalised groups by written or oral means – is a relatively recent phenomenon and there are some differences in how it is treated in different jurisdictions. For example, the definition of who can be a victim of a hate crime is not consistent within the EU: in the UK anyone can be a victim of hate crime, whereas in Sweden a member of a majority community cannot be the victim of a hate crime if attacked by a minority member (Garland and Chakraborti, 2012). There is also a problem with whether hate is actually needed as part of the *mens rea* for a hate crime. The Convention on Cybercrime attempts to address racism mediated by the internet, and has references to 'hate' in Articles 2, 5 and 6, but this is a strong requirement that is not generally seen in most hate crimes (Garland and Chakraborti, 2012).

In the UK, section 21 of the Public Order Act 1986 (POA) makes it an offence for a person to distribute, show or play, visual or audio recordings that are 'threatening, abusive or insulting' and by which:

(a)   he intends thereby to stir up racial hatred, or
(b)   having regard to all the circumstances racial hatred is likely to be stirred up thereby, (s 21 (1))

There have been suggestions that the word 'insulting' should be removed since it may lead to curtailment of free speech (Strickland, 2012). Free speech issues in the United States however are very different; the First Amendment to the US constitution protects free speech, and this includes hate speech. This difference with regard to free speech was at issue in the case of *R v Sheppard and Whittle* [2010] EWCA Crim 65 in which the defendants were successfully prosecuted under POA for publishing holocaust denying material on a website. Whilst in England, Sheppard had uploaded the material in to a server based in California. The original judge ruled the English courts had jurisdiction as most of the acts related to the publishing of the material (including its creation, editing and uploading) had occurred in England. The Court of Appeal agreed with this ruling and upheld the defendants' convictions (Gillespie, 2010).

The Racial and Religious Hatred Act 2006 (RRHA) amended the POA and extended the protections already provided for racial groups to religious groups (in England and Wales only). Prior to its enactment RRHA appeared to deny the right to criticise religion; but s 29J was added to provide 'protection of freedom of expression', allowing for inter alia criticism and insults directed at belief systems (Barendt, 2011). The Crime and Disorder Act 1998 created a number of racially aggravated criminal offences including harassment and threatening behaviour. It was later amended by the Anti-terrorism Crime and Security Act 2001, which included similar offences pertaining to religious groups (CPS, n.d.).

Malicious communications is addressed by specific legislation, whether or not it contains hate speech. There is however frequently some overlap between hate speech and malicious communications. Section 1 of the Malicious Communications Act 1988 (MCA) made it an offence to send 'letters etc. with intent to cause distress or anxiety' (s 1). The MCA was later amended by the Criminal Justice and Police Act 2001 to clearly identify 'electronic communication' as one of the forms of prohibited behaviour. There is no requirement under the Act for the intended (or any) recipient to receive the message. The Communications Act 2003 (s 127 (2)) contains similar provisions although is more aimed at prohibiting the use of a public network than protecting an individual (Walden, 2007, p. 151). Paul Chambers recently succeeded in a High Court Appeal against his prosecution under section 127(1) of the Communications Act 2003. In 2010 he had tweeted: 'Crap! Robin Hood airport is closed. You've got a week and a bit to get your shit together otherwise I'm blowing the airport sky high!!' which was originally ruled to be menacing (Bowcott, 2012). The Protection From Harassment Act 1997 provides protection similar to the MCA but for a series (two or more) of malicious communications, and it also contains provision for the issuing of restraining orders (s 2).

The definition of terrorism and identifying terrorist organisations are contentious issues (Blackburn, 2011). Under UK law, digital acts related to threats or acts of terrorism are covered by the Terrorism Act 2000 which defines terrorism as including an action which 'is designed seriously to interfere with or seriously to disrupt an electronic system' (s 1 (2) (e)). It is also an offence to belong or profess to belong to a proscribed organisation (s 11), and s 12 prohibits various forms of supporting proscribed organisations such as arranging a meeting. As discussed earlier, s 57 of the Act prohibits possession of articles which are intended for use in terrorist acts and s 58 makes the collecting or recording of information used for terrorist purposes an offence. Five Muslim men Irfan Raja, Awaab Iqbal, Aitzaz Zafar, Usman Malik and Akbar Butt were found guilty of offences under ss 57 and 58 for downloading and sharing extremist videos and literature in support of proscribed groups. The Court of Appeal quashed their sentences stating that there was no evidence that possession of the articles was related to planning terrorist acts and the CPS was criticised for using the law as a 'blunt instrument' (BBC, 2008b).

Cyber-warfare occurs where government sponsored hackers are employed in an attempt to interfere with another country's digital infrastructure. Governments may seek to protect their technological resources from such attacks from other governments and from terrorist organisations, such as Al Qaeda. In the wake of an alleged attack by Russian agencies on the Estonian state (Traynor, 2007), NATO created the Cooperative Cyber Defence Centre of Excellence in Tallinn, Estonia (NATO, 2011 and see Chapter 5) in order to '... enhance the capability, cooperation and information sharing among NATO, NATO nations and partners in cyber-defence by virtue of education, research and development, lessons learned and consultation' (op. cit). The ubiquitous globalisation of activities and communication afforded by the internet was addressed by the Criminal Justice (Terrorism and Conspiracy) Act 1998. This added a s 1A to the Criminal Law Act 1977, creating the offence of 'Conspiracy to commit offences outside the United Kingdom'.

Legislation and Investigation

Depending on the nature of an investigation, evidence can be obtained coercively (such as by searching a premises), or covertly (such as interception of data packets). Often both these techniques will be used (Walden, 2007, p. 203). The obtaining of digital evidence generally follows a pattern: first it is obtained by covert surveillance of a suspect, then from a Communications Service Provider (CSP), and finally using search and seizure powers (Walden, 2007, p. 204). In the 2012 UK the ACPO rules for electronic evidence recovery (ACPO, 2012) help provide guidelines to collecting data that will be more likely to withstand scrutiny in court. A number of other jurisdictions in the world have similar sets of guidelines (as discussed in a number of chapters).

In the UK, Part 2 of the Regulation of Investigatory Powers Act 2000 (RIPA) is the main piece of legislation governing surveillance by *public* bodies. It applies to: '(a) directed surveillance, (b) intrusive surveillance; and (c) the conduct and use of covert human intelligence sources' (s 26 (1)).

Directed surveillance must not be intrusive, it must be for a specific investigation, it must be likely to provide 'private information about a person', and it must not be a reaction to spontaneous events (RIPA s 26 (10); Walden, 2007, pp. 216–17). Authorisation is required from a police officer of rank Superintendent or higher, or from other similar officers in the military and prison service. The surveillance can last for up to three months (Harfield and Harfield, 2012).

Intrusive surveillance differs from directed surveillance in that it occurs in a private residence or vehicle and uses a surveillance device. An obvious example in digital investigation would be the installation of a key-logger on a suspect's PC. Potential infringements of the surveillance target's rights can become somewhat complex, and authorisations may be required under provisions of the Police Act 1997 and/or the Intelligence Services Act 1994.

The use of covert human intelligence sources (a 'CHIS') also requires authorisation under RIPA, along with designation of the source's handler and tasks they are authorised to carry out. The Serious Organised Crime and Police Act 2005 allows for the possibility of immunity from prosecution of a source. There is further discussion of the use of covert techniques in Chapter 6.

Interception of Communications Legislation

In the UK, Part I, Chapter I of RIPA governs the interception of the *contents* of private communications. The interception is illegal unless at least one of the following four conditions is met (Edwards et al, 2010):

  i.   Both sender and recipient have given permission;
  ii. The CSP needs to intercept in order to provide the service;
  iii. The CSP needs to intercept to meet legal requirements;
  iv. The Secretary of State deems an interception necessary for 'RIPA purposes'.

The purposes referred to in (iv) above are listed in RIPA section 5 (3) as:

(a)   in the interests of national security;

(b)   for the purpose of preventing or detecting serious crime;

(c)   for the purpose of safeguarding the economic well-being of the UK; or

(d)   for the purpose, in circumstances appearing to the Secretary of State to be equivalent to those in which he would issue a warrant by virtue of paragraph (b), of giving effect to the provisions of any international mutual assistance agreement.

However, a number of commentators have criticised the list of purposes as being too broad and lacking the oversight of the judiciary (Edwards et al, 2010).

Whether both sender and recipient had given permission for the contents of their private web browsing to be intercepted was at issue in 2009 when BT Group plc trialled software made by a company called Phorm. The software analysed the browsing habits of BT's ISP customers in order to send them targeted advertising. RIPA refers to 'implied consent' and it was argued that this analysis of customers' browsing habits was therefore legal. The EU sued the UK claiming RIPA did not follow the directive on privacy and electronic communications 2002/58/EC which requires 'free and informed consent'. As a result RIPA has since been amended to comply with 2002/58/EC (Baker, 2012).

Communications data is also regulated by RIPA. This regulation concerns the communication itself (for example when it took place) rather than its content. For telephone calls this would include the caller's telephone number and the number of the receiving telephone. Part I, Chapter II of RIPA details how communications data can be acquired, by whom, and for what purposes. Law enforcement organisations for example may ask a CSP to divulge communications data for crime prevention purposes. Communications data is also covered by the Data Retention (EC Directive) Regulations 2009 (DRECDR) for fixed and mobile telephony, VoIP and email. This is UK legislation that implements the EU Data Retention Directive 2006/24/EC. It requires a CSP, when notified by the Secretary of State, to retain communication information for 12 months (Walker, 2009) and this is likely to be implemented under the Communications Capabilities Development Programme (Mitchell, 2012).

Search and Seizure Procedures Legislation

The main piece of legislation which governs investigative procedure is the Police and Criminal Evidence Act 1984 (PACE). This controls inter alia powers to search persons after arrest (s 18); powers of seizure, including hard copy print outs of information stored on computers (s 19); the extension of powers of seizure to computerised information (s 20) and searches of premises in which a person has been arrested (s 32). Sections 50 and 51 of the Criminal Justice and Police Act 2001 provide powers of 'searching and sifting', so can be used to seize a hard drive for later searching for files that may be of interest. Procedures at digital crime scenes are described in detail in Chapter 7.

Expert Evidence

In court there are often matters beyond the expertise of the prosecution, defence, judge and jury. Such situations often occur in regard to digital evidence, and both the prosecution and defence may call on the services of 'expert witnesses'. Experts cannot provide evidence for matters that the judge and jury could decide without assistance: 'the purpose of expert evidence is to provide the Court with information which is outside the experience and knowledge of a judge and jury' (*R v Turner* [1975] 1 QB 834). In the UK witnesses are generally barred from providing opinion testimony and can only give evidence that helps decide facts. Expert witnesses are an exception to this rule (Dwyer, 2003) and the seminal case allowing for expert opinion is *Folkes v Chadd* (1782) 3 Doug KB 157, wherein experts gave conflicting scientific testimony on the silting up of Wells harbour (Golan 2004). Inevitably this leads to the problem of determining who can be regarded as an 'expert' and in which instances an expert is needed. In the UK both of these issues are currently decided by the judge.

Very often expert evidence is based on scientific methods, yet this is not always the case even in the field of digital analysis. An expert giving evidence on hacker subcultures for instance might provide ethnographic accounts of hacker behaviour, which although unscientific might provide valuable insights that are relevant to the case. Nevertheless much forensic testimony is based on one or more scientific methods or principles. While the nature of what makes something scientific is contested (Nola and Sankey, 2000), normally, scientific methods must at least be both reliable and valid. A method is reliable if it produces the same results for different trials with the same input, and valid if the method does what it purports to do. No scientific method is perfectly valid or reliable, but for it to be generally accepted within a scientific community, it must be highly reliable and have a high degree of validity. These requirements are difficult to translate to legislation.

The case of *Frye v United States* 293 F 1013 (DC Cir 1923) in the US led to the 'general acceptance' test: expert evidence is admissible if it is generally acceptable by the scientific community. In this case, the reliability and validity of a 'systolic blood pressure deception test' was used, which purports to indicate whether a person is lying by measuring their systolic blood pressure. It was decided that such a test was not generally accepted by the wider scientific community.

The general acceptance test was largely superseded in 1993 by *Daubert v. Merrell Dow Pharmaceuticals, Inc.* 509 U.S. 579, 1993). At their original trial the plaintiffs were not allowed to present expert evidence (alleging a link between the drug Benedictin and birth defects) because of the Frye general acceptance test. This ruling was reversed on appeal and four factors were introduced:

1. whether the theory or technique has been/can be tested;

2. whether the theory or technique has been subject to peer review;
3. whether the theory or technique has known or potential error rates; and
4. whether the theory or technique is accepted within the relevant scientific community. (Cheng and Yoon, 2005)

Thus the judge became the 'gatekeeper' with respect to scientific testimony (and in *Kumho Tire Co v Carmichael* 526 U.S. 137 (1999) Daubert was extended to cover 'non-scientific expert testimony). In the US the Daubert standard is used at the federal level, while at the state level some states use Daubert, some Frye, some neither (Keierleber and Bohan, 2005).

In the UK the situation is somewhat different. In 2011 the Law commission produced a report 'Expert Evidence in Criminal Proceedings in England and Wales' (Law Com No 325) which examined the existing UK law regarding experts (Wilson, 2012). They noted problems with Daubert since ' it provides the trial judge with a wide discretion in the determination of evidentiary reliability and that appeals in relation to the application of this test are judged against a very narrow 'abuse of discretion' standard of review' (Law Com 325; 5.91). Rather than moving to the Daubert tests, the report recommended that the current common law test of 'sufficiently reliable' opinion evidence being admissible should be retained. The report then takes 50 pages to illustrate three factors that determine 'sufficient reliability'. These are in summary (Law Com 325; 3 6 (2)):

(a) the evidence is predicated on sound principles, techniques and assumptions;
(b) those principles, techniques and assumptions have been properly applied to the facts of the case; and
(c) the evidence is supported by [that is, logically in keeping with] those principles, techniques and assumptions as applied to the facts of the case.

There is further discussion concerning expert evidence in Chapter 10.

Legal Tactics for Reducing Digital Crime

Finally, in a book entitled 'Policing Digital Crime' we should not neglect the use of legal tactics to help reduce the prevalence of digital crime. When the Bredolan botnet was closed down by the Dutch National Crime Squad's High Tech Crime Team, a report by Fortinet suggested that global spam levels dropped by 26 per cent within a week (Info Security, 2010). It is reported that the botnet was used predominantly to send out spam emails advertising fraudulent pharmaceutical products.

Another legal tactic is the use of 'cease and desist' letters. It is reported that many individuals have received a cease and desist letter, but clear statistics are hard to come by. Such letters can be used to try to prevent illegal file-sharing of copyright materials, typically popular music and films. Information is gathered by an individual's ISP and a letter is sent in suspicious cases (in the US, typically from the FBI). Individuals may also be taken to court, and in the first legal case to proceed and stand before a jury several major record labels were awarded damages. The level awarded has varied over time, but has ranged from $54,000 to almost $2million, depending on appeals and counter appeals (United States Court of Appeals, 2012). The date of the first prosecution of an individual for this offence was 2006 and the last appeal judgement was filed in 2012, with the defendant also banned by court order from 'making recording available for distribution to the public through online media distribution systems' (op. cit). Cease and desist letters are also sent to deter sellers of counterfeit goods on auction sites, such as eBay. The intention is that by effective imposition of penalties for illegal activity will deter others, as well as the prosecuted parties from future illegal acts.

One area where the legal process has been used to extensive effect is in relation to combating the distribution of indecent images of children. A successful prosecution generally attracts a custodial sentence. The sentencing manual presented by the Crown Prosecution Service of the UK for this crime (Crown Prosecution Service, 2012) provides for sentences from four weeks to nine years depending on the severity of the crime and any aggravating and mitigating factors. In addition, offenders may also receive as part of their sentence an order banning them from unsupervised use of the internet. Again the intention would be to prevent future criminal acts by the offender and also to act as a deterrent to others. Further, those convicted of this crime will find it difficult to work in certain careers owing to their inclusion on a Sex Offenders Register.

Other criminal prosecutions have occurred in the fields of fraud, for example a large eBay auction fraud scheme with a total value of over $700,000 has been prosecuted in the US (United States Department of Justice, n.d.).

Chapter 5
Policing Digital Crime: the International and Organisational Context

Robin Bryant with Paul Stephens

Introduction

In this chapter we examine international cooperation in relation to the policing of digital crime, together with how different nations each organise their formal response to cybercrime and other digital crimes. In terms of the latter the emphasis is on European and UK organisational responses, but reference is also made to other jurisdictions.

International Cooperation

Two often encountered clichés in policing are that 'digital crime knows no international boundaries' and 'cybercrime respects no borders'. These reflect a long-held truism that major digital crime investigation and some less serious investigations will often involve an international dimension (Grabosky and Smith, 2001). For example, in 2006 a UK Internet Service Provider (ISP) contacted the Computer Crime Unit at the Metropolitan Police Service (the MPS, London's police force) to report suspicions that 'botnets' had taken control of approximately 19,000 of their customers' PCs (Metropolitan Police Authority, 2009). Although the compromised server controlling the PCs was located in Acton in London, the Canadian offender quickly switched control to a server in Germany, then Korea and finally to the US (ibid.). The investigation involved the MPS Computer Crime Unit together with German, Norwegian, Australian, Korean, US, Brazilian and Canadian Police agencies. As Clough (2012, p. 4) notes: 'No matter how effective a country's local laws, the global nature of cybercrime means that international cooperation is inevitable. This may be in order to secure evidence of offending, or to secure the offenders themselves'. Clough continues by citing a recent example, where law enforcement agencies across a total of 13 countries uncovered an online network of suspected child sex offenders (using the forum 'boylover.net') with an estimated 70,000 members worldwide.

During the attempted seizure of a suspect's PC and its data a suspect might voluntarily reveal using online data storage through a cloud service. In such circumstances the investigator will need to fully research the cloud provider to establish the company's identity and its geographical location (for example, although the suspect's PC might be located in the UK, much of the data might be processed by data centres in multiple locations abroad). An application for this data might be required at a later stage, and there could well be issues concerning data protection. The implications of cloud computing for digital forensic investigation are discussed further in Chapter 10.

Macro, Meso and Micro Levels of Cooperation

In general terms, international cooperation between law enforcement agencies engaged in countering or investigating digital crime can occur at one of three levels: macro, meso or micro (terms adopted and adapted from Benyon et al., 1993, pp. 12–13). At the macro level, cooperation is typically between governments and international organisations, including through the agencies of Europol and Interpol (see below). For example, Interpol maintains a National Central Reference Points (NCRPs) network of cybercrime investigators to 'facilitate operational contact among member countries as quickly as possible' (Interpol, 2013). At the meso level, the cooperation is likely to be between police forces or law enforcement agencies located in different nation states, for example between the PcEU in the UK and the FBI in the US. At the micro level the cooperation will often be informal and take the form of contact between individual investigators.

A notable example of macro-level cooperation is the 2001 Council of Europe Cybercrime Convention (otherwise known as the 'Budapest Convention on Cybercrime' or the 'Treaty of Budapest') and often referred to in other chapters of this book. The Convention intends to, inter alia 'help establish a fast and effective regime of international cooperation' (Convention on Cybercrime CETS No: 185, Council of Europe, 2001). To date (August 2013), 40 countries had ratified the convention and nine remained as signatories, the latter group including Turkey; new countries are frequently added to the list. In June 2013 'Guidance Notes' to the Convention were issued by the Council of Europe on malware, botnets, DDoS attacks, identity theft, DDoS and critical information and infrastructure attacks. It should be noted however that in some parts of the world the Convention is considered as too specific to Western Europe to be suitable as a model for general adoption.

In 2010 the 'Digital Agenda for Europe' (May 2010) established the European Cybercrime Platform, the 'ECCP' comprising the Internet Crime Reporting System (ICROS), the Internet Financial Crime Database (AWF) and a repository of best practice (IFOREX). Also in 2010 there was a new EU Directive on attacks against information systems which intended to improve European police cooperation by strengthening the existing structure of 24/7 contact points, and also included the obligation to respond to urgent requests within eight hours. In 2012 the new European Cybercrime Centre (with an operational capability) was established by Europol in Den Haag (see below).

There are also a number of formal multilateral conventions which provide a basis for international cooperation in an investigation; these include (but are not limited to) the1959 European Convention on Mutual Assistance in Criminal Matters, and the supplement to the 1959 convention, namely the Convention on Mutual Assistance in Criminal Matters between Member States of the European Union of May 29, 2000. In addition there are bilateral agreements in place between many countries and these include the 1994 Treaty between the UK and the US for Mutual Legal Assistance in Criminal Matters. As noted in Chapter 4, some states base their approach to mutual legal assistance on the principle of the need to demonstrate 'dual criminality' between the countries involved – that is, the alleged acts should be offences in both countries. In terms of crimes such as online child sexual abuse imagery this is almost always the case but for other crimes, such as online 'hate' crimes, the dual criminality criteria will not normally be met.

Cooperation at the meso level often occurs between police forces in different countries, if only on an ad hoc basis to meet a specific operational need. Europol, for example, is able to organise 'Joint Investigation Teams' (JITs) consisting of police staff from European countries for the investigation of cross-border crime, although it has to be said that in practice these do not frequently appear to be instigated. There are also other examples of formalised meso level cooperation: the UK's Serious and Organised Crime Agency (SOCA, many functions of which will soon be subsumed within a new National Crime Agency) has a number of Cyber (or Cybercrime) Liaison Officers in overseas locations, including the US (for example, based in the Greater Pittsburgh Area).

One practical problem encountered by police investigators at the meso level is knowing who, or what organisation to contact in another country to take forward a digital crime investigation that has an international dimension. Part of the difficulty is a lack of standardisation in the name of the unit with the responsibility for policing and investigating digital crime within another country. They may be known variously as 'Digital Crime Units', 'High Tech Crime Units' or be part of a more general criminal investigation unit, as is the case, for example, in Albania (Directorate against Financial Crime under the Department against Organised and Serious Crime, General Directorate of State Police).

At the micro level cooperation will often be of an informal nature, and occur through the usual means of direct contact, face-to-face, by phone or by email. This cooperation is often facilitated through links between individuals that have already been established through previous cooperation on criminal cases or by joint attendance at multinational training events (see below). Investigators in the UK however are also mindful of the rules of legal disclosure, as even such informal communication is likely to fall within the requirements of CPIA.

However, none of this means that international cooperation will necessarily be forthcoming when needed or requested. There are a plethora of reasons why problems might be encountered in practice, and these range from the legal (for example, in some countries the possession of child abuse imagery does not constitute an offence) and political, to the cultural, and might also include simple inadequacy. China for example, claims that it requested cooperation from the FBI concerning 'fake banking sites and child sexual abuse imagery websites' but received no support from the US (Jian, 2010). Not all the Interpol NCRPs (see above) offered 24 hour support in the past (González, 2007) and it is unclear whether the position has changed since. There is also the inherent problem of widely differing practices in digital forensic investigation in different national states; even within Europe practice will differ. For example, in Romania, in order for an electronic search of a computer to be conducted both the owner and witnesses have to be present; whereas in some other countries this form of searching would normally not be permitted and certainly not encouraged (see Chapter 7). Cultural norms vary between nations and this can also affect law enforcement agencies as well as the more general 'conflict between the moral, political or constitutional differences among nations' (Marion, 2010, p. 699, citing Shapiro, 1999 and Swire, 2005). In summary, although we might wish the micro, meso and macro levels to complement each other, in practice this is rarely the case.

International Cooperation Between Law Enforcement Agencies

As Brenner (2010, p. 174) notes, there are currently no international law enforcement agencies (LEAs) tasked with carrying out cybercrime investigation, nor does there appear to be an appetite amongst nation states to create one. However, many national agencies responsible for policing digital crime will also collaborate with other LEAs at an international level. In terms of influence and reach, two of the most important channels of cooperation are Interpol and Europol. Interpol has 190 member countries worldwide. Its proclaimed mission is to prevent and fight against crime by encouraging international cooperation between law enforcement agencies through offering technical and operational support (Interpol, 2012). Their Financial and High Tech Crime Sub-Directorate has a responsibility for coordinating responses to digital crime, including financial crime, high tech crime, counterfeit credit cards and currency and IPR crime. Interpol is currently involved in establishing a Digital Crime Centre in Singapore, scheduled to open in May 2014.

Europol is the European law enforcement agency, and is responsible for assisting member states of the European Union with countering serious international organised crime and terrorism (Europol, 2012a). Until recently Europol had a dedicated High Tech Crime Centre which dealt with digital crime but it has now been subsumed with a new European-wide centre (see below).

In addition to Europol and Interpol there are a number of other agencies that enhance cooperation across international borders including:

- the United Nations Office on Drugs and Crime (UNODC), which offers technical assistance to member states to counter cybercrime, together with 'capacity building' (under UN Resolution 20/7) and, in cooperation with the Korean Institute of Criminology, has established a 'Virtual Forum against Cybercrime';

- the Organization for Security and Co-operation in Europe (OSCE) organises a number of law enforcement cybercrime investigation courses in Europe (for example, in Serbia);
- Eurojust, the European Union's Judicial Cooperation Unit is made up of seconded national prosecutors, magistrates and police officers from EU member states and its remit includes assisting the member states to deal with cybercrime;
- the Commonwealth Cybercrime Initiative (CGI), made up of 54 Commonwealth countries (19 from Africa; eight from Asia; three from the Americas; ten from the Caribbean; three from Europe and 11 from the South Pacific). It aims to assist developing Commonwealth countries 'to build their institutional, human and technical capacities with respect to [...] investigation and law enforcement with the aim of, making their jurisdictions more secure by denying safe havens to cyber criminals [...]' (CGI, 2011).
- the G8 24/7 High Tech crime network has points of contact in approximately 50 countries that offer urgent assistance with investigations involving electronic evidence;
- the Organisation of American States (the OAS, which includes the US, Canada and 32 other states such as Argentina, Brazil, Colombia, Chile and Venezuela) has assisted in the creation of 14 cybercrime investigation units;
- the Russian Federation has a Department 'K' (effectively the Ministry of Interior's cybercrime unit) that links together 87 cybercrime units in the Federation with the IT sector, Interpol and G8 24/7 (see above);
- other multi- and bilateral- organisations such as the 2012 agreement between Russia and Austria, the Shanghai Cooperation Organisation (Russia, China, Kazakhstan), and the Collective Security Treaty Organisation (Russia, Belarus, Armenia, Kazakhstan. Kyrgyzstan, Tajikistan and Uzbekistan) have committed to cooperation in combating cybercrime, and in some cases carry out join operations and investigations.

The FBI has a number of 'embedded' full-time agents in digital crime units around the world, in countries such as Estonia, the Netherlands, Romania, Ukraine and Columbia (Snow, 2011). The 'Cooperative Cyber Defence Centre of Excellence' (the CCDCOE) is based in Tallinn, the capital of Estonia and has support from Estonia, Latvia, Lithuania, Germany, Hungary, Italy, Poland, Slovakia, Spain, the Netherlands and the US (with Turkey also intending to join) (NATO, 2011). In 2012 France joined the CCDCOE and the UK signalled its intention to do so in January 2013. The CCDCOE has a self-declared remit to 'enhance the capability, cooperation and information sharing [...] among NATO nations [...] by virtue of education, research and development' (CCDCOE, 2013). It is funded by the sponsoring nations (ibid.) and presents itself as largely an organisation with an interest in conducting research (NATO, 2013) and joint 'cyber defence exercises' and delivering conferences and training courses (rather than as an organisation with an operational and incident capability; Lorents, 2011). The CCDCOE appears to be taking an increasing interest in 'cyber-warfare' which is perhaps not unexpected given the allegations of state-supported cyber-attacks made in 2012 and 2013.

In early 2013 the new European Cybercrime Centre (EC³) based within Europol's headquarters in Den Haag (The Hague) opened with the intention of becoming 'the focal point in the EU's fight against cybercrime' (Europol, 2013). It is expected to be fully functional by 2015 but already appears well-equipped, with specialist facilities such as a 'Faraday room' to enable digital devices to be forensically examined without the risk of being affected by outside electronic interference. The emphasis of the new Centre appears to be very much on detection, investigation and supporting member states in prosecuting cybercrime; a 'guiding principle' will be an emphasis 'less in anticipation of computer crime (on anti-virus, firewalls etc) [and] an awful lot more on catching and punishing the perpetrators' (Europol, 2012b, p. 8). A particular target for the new Centre will be online organised crime (especially when these groups target e-banking and other forms of financial activity), online child sexual exploitation, and attempts to adversely affect the critical information systems of the EU (European Commission, 2013). Operational support for member nations (in terms of digital forensic analysis and coordinating criminal investigations) appears to be a key priority although the centre has also been given a remit for strategic trend analysis (emerging cybercrime threats), 'data fusion' (which includes collecting and analysing intelligence on cybercrime) and finally, the analysis of training needs and the delivery of training. The Centre is staffed by a combination of seconded cybercrime investigators from EU member countries and staff directly under the employ of Europol, about 40 in all in 2013, with plans to increase this in the future. However, the EU is expecting to make further budget cuts and as one of the Commissioners for Home Affairs noted at the launch of the Centre, 'The EU agencies are in general expected to cut staff, not to get more people' (Malmström, cited by Brewster, 2013).

Private Sector and Voluntary Organisations at the International Level

There are also a number of other organisations involved specifically involved in the general 'policing' of the internet but which are not LEAs. The Internet Corporation for Assigned Names and Numbers (ICANN) controls the Domain Name System (DNS): the system (often compared to use of a 'phone book') for associating the recognisable names we see on the internet into IP addresses (for example, the Google website, http://www.google.com has a number IP addresses including 173.194.46.16). The abuse of the DNS occurs in a number of types of digital crime, including online fraud. As Easton (2012, p. 273) notes, ICANN's role is also crucial in maintaining the stability and interoperability of the internet. In 2011 ICANN established formal links with Interpol.

The Virtual Global Taskforce (VGT) has nine full members: the Australian Federal Police, the UK's CEOP, Europol, Interpol, the Italian Postal and

Communication Police Service, the National Child Exploitation Coordination Centre (within the Royal Canadian Mounted Police), the New Zealand Police, the Ministry of Interior for the United Arab Emirates and the US Immigration and Customs Enforcement (VGT, 2013). The VGT currently has nine private sector partners including PayPal and Research in Motion (RIM, the developer of Blackberry).

One of the express aims of the UK's Internet Watch Foundation (IWF) is to tackle the distribution of child sexual abuse images via the internet. The IWF has in excess of 60 financially contributing members including Google, a number of ISPs (e.g. Virgin Media, AOL), Facebook, the BBC and Cisco (IWF, 2013a), and the IWF has links with CEOP, the MPS, local police forces and a 'service-level' agreement with the Association of Chief Police Officers (ACPO). The IWF are part funded by the EU through the EU Safer Internet Programme (IWF, 2013b). The IWF provides a clear example of a government/private enterprise partnership model which is relatively common approach in attempting to counter digital crime in many countries. Undoubtedly the IWF undertakes an important task in terms of protecting the public and supporting law enforcement. However, Laidlaw (2012, p. 312) argues that although the IWF carries out work of critical importance 'if unchecked its operations can have a significant impact on the right to freedom of expression'.

There is also a large private enterprise sector that promotes products that are aimed at protecting against internet-based digital crimes. This would include software that protects against viruses, botnets and rootkits; firewall software that prevents unauthorised access; and penetration testing services that aim to check security of networks and websites (Yar, 2010). Some of the major software corporations and vendors such as Microsoft also play a wider role in supporting the policing of digital crime. For example, the Microsoft Digital Crimes Unit (the DCU) focuses on two main areas: malicious software crimes and child exploitation crimes (Microsoft, 2013a). The DCU also shares with LEAs (free of charge) its 'Computer Online Forensic Evidence Extractor' (COFEE) software for first responders at digital crime scenes (see Chapter 7). In March 2013 Microsoft announced that it would be combining the DCU with its 'Internet piracy unit' to form a new Microsoft 'Cybercrime Center' (Microsoft, 2013b). In effect this combines Microsoft's community support activity with the protection of its own IPR, and it remains to be seen whether this will result in a change of emphasis.

The Organisation of Digital Crime Units

There is significant variation within Europe in terms of the organisation, structure and even function of digital crime units. Although there has been some coalescing around the concept of the 'cybercrime unit' in recent years, 'high tech crime units' and 'computer forensic units' amongst a myriad of other terms are still frequently encountered. Albania has its 'Sector against Cybercrime' (within the Directorate against Financial Crime) under the Department against Organised and Serious Crime, General Directorate of State Police (Council of Europe, 2011, p. 9), and in Romania a growth in online card fraud gave rise in the first instance to new legislation, and then to the creation of a specialist cybercrime police unit in 2003. These specialist units typically have a work load which is a combination of 'pure' cybercrime investigation and the provision of support for a more traditional criminal investigation which feature digital intelligence and evidence, however, not all European digital crime investigation units have a digital forensics capability. The European Network and Information Security Agency (ENISA) also provides aid to European member states in addressing information security issues (ENISA, 2011).

In terms of the training of digital forensic investigators in Europe, inevitably this varies from country to country, often reflecting local circumstances and need. However, there have been a number of attempts to harmonise training (and associated professional accreditation) across the European Union, most notably under the aegis of Cepol (the European Police College) and Europol. European-wide training programmes have been funded by the European Commission and others. For example, the ISEC 2008 (and subsequent ISEC funding rounds) cybercrime project 'Developing and disseminating an accredited international training programme for the future' involved Europol, Interpol, the UNODC, the national Irish police service, *An Garda Siochana*, the UK's National Policing Improvement Agency, and the *Landesamt für Ausbildung, Fortbildung und Personalangelegenheiten der Polizei NRW* from Germany (Bryant et al., 2012). The project aimed to harmonise cybercrime investigation international training through the production and dissemination of academically accredited digital forensics training courses. Ten courses were developed by the Agis projects: Introductory IT Forensics and Network Investigations; Applied NTFS Forensics; Intermediate Internet Investigations; Intermediate Network Investigations; Linux as an Investigative Tool; Mobile Phone Forensics; Forensic Scripting Using Bash; Live Data Forensics; Wireless LANs and VoIP; and Malware Analysis and Investigations. Microsoft has subsequently funded upgrades of seven of these courses. Responsibility for the courses now resides with the European Cybercrime Education and Training Group (ECTEG) hosted by Europol.

In the UK the work of a digital crime investigator at a local level is normally situated within a 'High Tech Crime Unit', a 'Computer Crime Unit', 'Digital Forensics Unit' (for example, Kent Police) or even within an 'Economic Crime Unit'. These units have often evolved from earlier force 'Fraud Squads', and tend to be relatively small in terms of the number of staff and allocation of resources. With UK county police forces such as Essex Police and Kent Police each unit has between approximately 10 and 20 members of staff, typically a mix of managers, digital forensic analysts and forensic 'imagers', with most staff being police staff rather than police officers; indeed, the proportion of non-police officer staff appears to be steadily increasing. Most of the workload for these units arises from criminal investigations being conducted by the local police force where an investigator has encountered a digital device (for example, a PC, mobile phone or CCTV camera).

Some sub-contraction of the workload to non-police private contractors occurs on a 'needs as' basis, but practice in the UK overall varies considerably from force to force. Where sub-contracting occurs it not only involves digital forensic analysis of devices but also other specialist services such as translation (for example, Russian into English).

The basic training of digital forensic staff in the UK usually follows College of Policing (CoP) recommended programmes (previously mainly the responsibility of the NPIA). These include 'Core Skills for Network Investigations' and 'Core Skills for Data Recovery and Analysis' as well as CoP training in the use of specialist software such as the EnCase suite (see Chapter 8). However, this too is in the process of change as forces appear to now favour recruiting staff who are already trained, having studied a formal education and training programme for example (with the obvious economic benefits to the force). It is widely acknowledged that many of these units are overworked with considerable backlogs. Sir Paul Stephenson, the former Metropolitan Police Commissioner, has stated that: 'My investigators tell me the expertise available to law enforcement is thin, compared to the skills they suspect are at the disposal of cyber criminals' (The Sunday Telegraph, 2010).

The Police Central e-Crime Unit (PCeU) was created in September 2008 and is a national resource. It is currently based at the Metropolitan Police Service (London's police force). The PCeU works both nationally and with international organisations on serious digital crimes. It is not responsible for (PCeU, 2012):

* routine digital crimes (local forces in most cases are responsible for these);
* frauds which fall under Action Fraud/National Fraud Authority (see below); or
* digital crimes which fall under the remit of CEOP (CEOP, 2012a).

Within the PCeU there is a Computer Crime Team (CCT) with the remit to investigate and prosecute, inter alia, 'Electronic attacks upon the Critical National Infrastructure, Significant Intrusions (Hacks), Denial of Service attacks (DDoS / BotNet attacks), Significant False Identity websites and large-scale successful Phishing' (PCeU, 2009). At the time of writing the PCeU employs approximately 100 staff, 15 per cent of whom are police staff, the remainder police officers. In terms of initial training, new PCeU staff undertake the same CoP programmes as local force digital investigators (see above), together with training in the use of the AccessData software suites EnCase 1 and 2, the FTK 'Bootcamp' programme (see Chapter 8 for more on EnCase and FTK) and the IACIS Programme. In 2013 the PCeU is expected to become part of a new National Cyber Crime Unit (NCCU) based within the National Crime Agency (the NCA), which is also likely to include units with parallel cybercrime investigation responsibilities and other national LEAs. Similar developments of specialist units have occurred elsewhere in Europe.

The responsibility for digital crime investigation is not restricted to the specialist units or indeed to the 'traditional' police alone. There are various reasons for this, for example, in the UK the police do not necessarily investigate all reported online credit and debit card offences resulting from phishing and pharming (for example, through a 'botnet') or some fraud committed by more traditional means. These types of crimes are effectively 'screened' to decide whether to conduct further investigations. Frauds are dealt with at a national level through the National Fraud Reporting Centre (including Action Fraud), the National Fraud Intelligence Bureau, the National Fraud Authority, and the Serious Fraud Office. There are also specialist units for Trading Standards and HM Revenue & Customs.

In the UK, under the National Intelligence Model (introduced as a consequence of Intelligence-led Policing, see Chapter 6), any Level 1 and Level 2 digital crimes (see Chapter 6) which are to be investigated are likely to be tackled by a force-based unit. In the future Level 3 crime is likely to be passed to the new National Crime Agency for investigation. However, in many cases the industry itself (for example banks) will conduct further enquiries and assume responsibility for attempting to counter the spread of certain digital crimes (for example, emerging malware threats). In the UK, legislation allows public authorities to share information with organisations such as CIFAS, the 'UK's Fraud Prevention Service' (CIFAS, 2012).

The National Technical Assistance Centre (NTAC) provides specialist help for local law enforcement agencies in relation to encrypted data and legally intercepted communications (under the Regulation of Investigatory Powers Act 2000 (RIPA)). However, in some cases the decryption can take a considerable length of time, and up to year is not uncommon in some cases. Legal obligations associated with RIPA also mean that many telecommunications companies, such as Internet Service Providers (ISPs), have computer forensics professionals working for them. Under this legislation the companies are responsible for ensuring '...a "reasonable" level of intercept capacity to enable interception warrants to be complied with' (ZDNet UK, 2002).

The UK's intelligence agency GCHQ ('Government Communication Headquarters') has a national remit for cyber-security in the UK, although unsurprisingly, it rarely describes its operational role in any detail. GCHQ hosts the Cyber Security Operations Centre (CSOC), administered by the Office of Cyber Security in the Cabinet Office (rather than GCHQ itself). The role of CSOC is described as 'primarily defensive' although it 'will also be capable of launching a cyber attack' (Aldrich, 2010). They have produced baseline assessments concerning various aspects of the cybercrime 'landscape' and regularly produce topic reports, to which the PCeU, SOCA and GCHQ contribute. The most recent example of these was concerned with the "Hacktivist" threat.

Within the US there are numerous organisations and bodies (both public and private) that share responsibility for the policing of digital crime. No single organisation provides the lead for investigating cybercrime in the US. At the Federal level the departments of Defence (DoD), Homeland Security (DHS), and Justice (DoJ), and the Federal Trade Commission (FTC) all have various roles in the response to cybercrime. The FBI (for the DoJ) and the US Secret Service (the USSS, for the DHS) are particularly active in attempting to prevent against, detect and investigate cybercrime. Given its Federal remit, the FBI's focus (primarily through its 'Cyber Division', but where necessary also involving other agencies) is naturally often on cybercrime committed by organised crime groups (particularly financially-oriented cybercrime). However, this might be at the expense of investigating 'lone actors including hackers, stalkers, and online child predators' (Finklea and Theohary, 2013, p. 7). The USSS has a 'Cyber Intelligence Unit', and a combined total of over 60 Financial Crimes Task Forces and Electronic Fraud Task Forces. Their main role is to protect the financial and payment systems of the US from cyber-theft and cyber-attack. The Internet Crime Complaint Centre (IC3) is a partnership between the FBI and the National White Collar Crime Centre (NW3C) and is essentially a means by which members of the public can report a suspected cybercrime. State and other local law enforcement agencies also investigate cybercrimes. Texas for example, established its Cyber Crimes Unit in 2003 (Office of the Attorney General of Texas, 2012). As in many other countries, both Federal and State agencies will work with private organisations, such as ISPs and software vendors (for example, Microsoft) when gathering intelligence on cybercrime or as part of a specific investigation.

Chapter 6
Investigating Digital Crime

Robin Bryant with Ian Kennedy

Introduction

In this chapter we examine how the investigation of digital crime fits within the wider context of criminal investigation, how investigation is modelled, and the place of digital evidence within the criminal justice system. We conclude the chapter with a discussion on digital forensic standards and accreditation. We focus primarily on investigating digital crime in the UK and Europe, with occasional reference to the US and other countries but despite this, much will also be relevance and interest to those involved with, or studying, the policing of digital crime in other jurisdictions.

Since the 1990s in many western countries (particularly those that employ the adversarial form of justice) there has been a move away from treating criminal investigation as primarily a 'case building' exercise against a suspect towards a more principled, but more nebulous, 'seeking after the truth'. This approach demands, for example, that a criminal investigator develops lines of enquiry that point towards the innocence of a suspect just as much as they explore and test those that suggest guilt. By the mid 1990s this 'new wave' in criminal investigation was manifested in the UK in legislation, for example through section 23(1)(a)) of the Criminal Procedures and Investigations Act 1996 (CPIA) that requires that all 'reasonable lines of enquiry' be pursued, whether they point towards or away from the suspect. Much of the legislation was enacted as a reaction to a number of miscarriages of justice in which the police had withheld important information, ignored exonerating facts, and simply constructed cases against individuals.

Intelligence and Intelligence-led Policing

The use of intelligence, the collection and use made of evidence, and most pertinently of all, the investigative process itself are all of importance to the policing of digital crime in many jurisdictions. Intelligence, in the investigative context, may be considered a form of information, but with a particular quality – that is, it is information which has taken on meaning. Within a criminal investigation there are likely to be three distinguishable forms of incoming data (Bryant and Bryant, 2013): information, intelligence and evidence (although these will not necessarily be distinguishable one from the other at the time and point of collection). Information is normally from a source with no confidentiality constraints or protection requirements. It is overt information, such as a message posted on Twitter. Intelligence is more difficult to define but is generally considered to be information derived from many sources (some confidential) that has been recorded, graded, and evaluated; in short, intelligence is information with meaning. Whitaker (1999, p. 5) defines intelligence as 'the systematic and purposeful acquisition, sorting, retrieval, analysis interpretation and protection of information'. For example, we might have information derived from a social networking site which uses a particular form of criminal argot. If we link this information to a particular group of criminal associates then we begin to derive intelligence from the information. Evidence on the other hand can be either information or intelligence, and is generally material that can be admitted in a court of law and abides by the 'rules of evidence' – that is to say, it is both admissible and carries probative weight (see below). Intelligence is thus not the same as evidence. Some intelligence may become evidence or suggest a means of obtaining evidence, but other intelligence will not be used as evidence in any circumstances.

One way of categorising intelligence is to typify it as either 'open' (overt) or 'closed' (covert). An example of open intelligence (sometimes referred to as 'OSINT') is so-called 'Internet Open Source Intelligence' – the use of social network sites such as Facebook to adduce gang membership would be a tangible example of online OSINT. Examples of covert forms of intelligence include police investigator use of 'key-loggers' to remotely monitor a suspect's use of a PC keyboard to capture intelligence on the websites visited or passwords the suspect has used to access sites and the 'dark web' (see Chapter 10 for more on the dark web). However, as Innes and Sheptychi (2004, p. 9) argue, imposing such a dichotomous definition ('open/closed') on intelligence gathering is inherently problematic, as it 'tells us nothing about how [intelligence] informs practice' (ibid.). In terms of intelligence and digital crime, police practice often demonstrates the limitations of imposing a false dichotomy. We can also add that a further problem is the attendant danger of underestimating the utility and importance of open forms of intelligence, and overestimating that of closed forms. There are probably a number of reasons for this, including the psychologically compelling nature of intelligence that appears to be 'secret' and difficult to come by, and the need to justify the often costly investment in time and people required to capture covert forms of intelligence.

Intelligence-led policing (ILP) methodologies can be discerned in a number of approaches to investigating digital crime, for example, the use of 'honeytraps' (or 'honeypots') to collect intelligence on offenders (see below) or police officers posing as casual users of social network sites. Urbas (2010) describes the legal context (in Singapore and Australia) that allows police officers to assume a 'false' identity to identify individuals intent upon online child grooming for sexual purposes. He notes that for a police investigator '[a]dopting a false or fictitious identity, as is commonplace in covert policing generally, is particularly easy to do online' (ibid., p. 412), and goes on to claim that the practice is frequently undertaken in many countries (ibid., p. 414). However, in some countries the legal issues around entrapment might well complicate such operations at best, or at worst prohibit them altogether. On a practical level, in some jurisdictions intelligence-led covert operations will be mounted by a national law enforcement unit, rather than a regional police force.

However there would appear to have been only a limited and piecemeal application of ILP approaches to countering digital crime, at least according to published sources, particularly in terms of targeting prolific online offenders. A further problem is that detection as a tactical operational approach to digital crime tends to be emphasised at the expense of disruption and dissuasion as alternative strategies. Hence, there would appear to be some scope for adopting a more intelligence-led approach to policing digital crime, particularly when, for example, in 2010 it was estimated that a single botnet (Rostock) was responsible for almost 40 per cent of all the world's spam (CNET, 2010).

In the UK there are three levels of criminal intelligence within 'National Intelligence Model' (NIM) employed by police forces:

- *Level 1*: relevant to local neighbourhood level crime and anti-social behaviour that can be addressed through local resources. Examples include those 'traditional' volume crimes such as illegal drug supply but with an added digital component (such as the recovery of digitally-based evidence).
- *Level 2*: relevant for more serious crime, or crime over wider geographical area (force, inter-force and regional criminal activity) which usually requires the use of additional resources. Examples include the illegal trading of counterfeit goods and products through electronic markets.
- *Level 3*: relevant at a national level for the most serious and organised crime, crime with a 'high impact and high spread' (Home Office, 2011a, p. 15). Examples include organised crime groups operating online fraud. In the future in the UK this is likely to involve the cybercrime unit of the National Crime Agency (the NCA).

However, in the UK police and Home Office rules and decisions regarding the recording crime might well inadvertently influence local approaches to countering digital crime. UK legislation does not formally define digital crime as an offence type although the Home Office has recently introduced new recording classifications that include malware, hacking and DDoS attacks. At the local police force level a DDoS attack for example is more likely to be reported in the UK as extortion demand rather than a 'digital crime' Further, Fafinski et al. (2010, p. 13) make the more general point (citing a House of Lords report) that many Level 2 and Level 3 cybercrimes may be 'slipping through the net' and going unreported and unrecorded.

One approach to gathering intelligence in some countries is the use of the 'honeypots' mentioned earlier. The term refers to a resource on a computing system that is designed to attract potential offenders to interact with it, but will have little attraction for others. As Spitzner explains, 'A honeypot is an information system resource whose value lies in unauthorised or illicit use of that resource' (Spitzner, 2003). Different types of honeypot have different purposes: some are designed and set up to waste the time of the purported attacker and hence keep them away from resources of value, while others capture information about cyber-criminals' tactics that can then be used to devise appropriate defences. Honeypots can also be used to gather information to facilitate the prosecution of intruders, although even after collecting data it is not always a straightforward matter to obtain convictions (Even, 2000). The typical honeypot sits inside an organisation's firewall. The route for accessing it clearly indicates that it is for authorised users only (although many cyber-criminals will in fact not pass through the 'authorised entrance' and hence may not see the 'authorised users only' message). Once inside the system, the activities of the cyber-criminal are monitored, and fake data is used to maintain the interest of the criminal to further capture information. Although most commentators do not believe that honeypot deployment is unlawful (for example, in terms of 'entrapment' - see Spitzner, 2010), other legal issues may apply, for example liability and privacy (by privacy we mean the issue of recording information about the users of the honeypot and whether this can be allowed under law). As yet however it appears that there has been no case law to clarify these legal issues. One view relating to the use of such methods has been put forward by Salgado, senior counsel for the US Department of Justice's computer crime unit (Poulsen, 2003). In his argument he does not argue honeypots are illegal, but rather that there are a number of legal issues to consider carefully when deploying them. In relation to liability, if the use of a honeypot by a criminal had a resultant harmful effect on others, could the 'owners' of the honeypot be open to a civil case for damages? For example a honeypot used by criminals to store and run pirated software might leave the owners open to prosecution by the original copyright holders for breach of copyright. These and other issues relating to the use of honeypots are discussed at length by Lakhani (Lakhani, 2003). The Honeynet Project (The Honeynet Project, 2012) has developed a number of software projects that enable organisations to develop their own honeypots and the associated tools to enable information capture and analysis about usage

General Models of Criminal Investigation

In the UK an influential model of a synthesised general criminal investigation is the ACPO Core Investigative Doctrine, first developed in 2003 by the National Centre for Policing Excellence. (This was subsumed within the National Police Improvement Agency, the NPIA, aspects of which are soon to become part of the new National Crime Agency). The doctrine 'articulates the principles' (McGory and Treacy, in Haberfeld et al., 2012, p. 124) underpinning criminal investigation in the UK.

The Doctrine covers six main areas, within the two broad themes (ACPO/ Centrex, 2005) as shown in Table 6.1. Further, the doctrine proposes conceptualising investigation in terms of Activities, Decisions and Outcomes.

Table 6.1   The ACPO Core Investigative Doctrine

Theme	Area	Description	Examples
Underlying Principles and Knowledge	Investigative knowledge	Characteristics of crime (victims, witnesses and offenders), national and force policies, principles of investigation	Modus operandi of offenders. Understanding the investigative process.
	Legal framework	Evidence, the CJS, key legislation	Admissibility of types of evidence. Understanding the adversarial system of justice. Knowledge of PACE 1984, CPIA 1996 etc.
Process of Investigation	The criminal investigation process	The generation of material, the stages of investigation, a standard model for investigation	Material gathered from locations. The 'Golden Hour' of forensic opportunity. Gathering intelligence. Reactive and proactive forms of investigation.
	Investigative decision-making	How decisions are made, the 'investigative mindset', investigative and evidential evaluation, the evaluation process, hypotheses and decision support	Verification bias and availability error. Planning, preparation, examination, recording and collation followed by evaluation. Developing and testing hypotheses.
	Investigative strategies	Including scene; forensic; search; suspect, victim and witness strategies; intelligence and data strategies. Trace/ interview/eliminate (TIE). Communication and covert policing strategies.	Securing crime scenes. Methods of searching. Conducting interviews. Gathering and analysing intelligence. Dealing with the media.
	Management	Managing resources, people, risk and actions. Record-keeping.	Exhibit management, briefing and de-briefing.

(Authors' interpretation and description, based on ACPO/Centrex, 2005).

Criminal Investigation in Practice

The notion of a 'criminal investigation' superficially suggests a process of police enquiry into a crime. However, an intrinsic part of all criminal investigation is also to establish whether indeed there is any case to be answered. In the UK for example, a criminal investigation is legally and formally defined by section 22 of the Criminal Procedure and Investigations Act 1996 as '[a]n investigation conducted by police officers with a view to it being ascertained whether a person should be charged with an offence, or whether a person charged with an offence is guilty of it'. The CPIA Codes of Practice also explain that this will include investigations begun in the belief that a crime is about to be committed as well as those reported as already having happened. As this implies therefore, criminal investigation can be either reactive (based for example, on the report of a suspected crime, or attendance by a police officer in uniform at an incident), or proactive, that is consequent to the acquisition of intelligence or following a covert police operation (see discussion on intelligence above).

In the UK the model of criminal investigation is currently based on the 2005 Core Investigative Doctrine (see above). The model consists of eight possible stages: instigation, initial investigation, investigative evaluation, suspect management, evidence assessment, charge, case management, and finally 'court' (ACPO/Centrex, 2005). The typical activities, decisions and outcomes at each stage are illustrated in Table 6.2.

Table 6.2　　Phases of an Investigation

Phase	Explanation
Instigation (activity)	Instigation of an investigation may occur reactively; for example reports from the public, re-opening of an old case in the light of more information or proactively; for example through an intelligence source.
Initial investigation (activity)	In the case of an emergency call this will include the 'first officer on the scene'. The crime scene is managed (if applicable) – there is particular emphasis on the 'golden hour' of forensic opportunity. Other 'fast track' actions may occur for example quickly collecting CCTV footage. 'Material' begins to be collected from places (including scenes of crime), witnesses, victims, suspects, databases (including intelligence databases), mobile phone records and so on. Specifically, initial interviews with witnesses, victims and suspects (if identified) will be conducted. An investigating officer may be appointed, a risk assessment of the case conducted, and information recorded. The investigation may be handed over to a more experienced officer.

Phase	Explanation
Investigative evaluation (decisions)	Material is evaluated for evidential relevance, reliability and admissibility. Decisions include whether further investigation is required, or no further investigation warranted (intelligence might still be collected and disseminated). In the case of further investigation a 'gap analysis' is conducted.
Suspect management (activity)	A number of investigative strategies may be employed for example to test the veracity of a suspect's claims.
Evidence evaluation (decisions)	Material is further evaluated for evidential relevance, reliability and admissibility. Decisions include 'charge' as well as 'no charge' or another form of resolving the enquiry (short of a court appearance by the suspect). On many occasions there will be further investigation before a final decision is made.
Charge (outcome)	Is there sufficient admissible evidence to charge the suspect?
Case management (activity)	Any new relevant lines of enquiry to be followed up, file preparation undertaken, forensic reports to be checked, exhibits, liaison with the defence (for example 'disclosure').
'Court'	In some cases this is the final outcome, for example a suspect (by this stage the 'defendant') attends a Magistrates' or Crown Court.

(Authors' interpretation and description, based on ACPO/Centrex, 2005)

Note that only a proportion of criminal investigations are likely to result in a court appearance by a suspect. In some cases a suspect will accept a formal caution, in others the investigation will be dropped (perhaps because there is no case to answer), in others the prosecuting authorities (such as the CPS in the UK) might decide not to go ahead with a prosecution, often because of insufficient evidence.

The activities in a criminal investigation as shown in the table in fact frequently overlap and are not necessarily distinct. The details of practice of criminal investigation will also vary, not only from country to country but also between different law enforcement agencies within the same country. Often some form of overarching process will be adopted, sometimes expressed in a way that enables an investigator to focus on the 'unknowns' of an investigation, establish hypotheses and test them. For example, in the UK a common way of doing this is for the investigator to consider the 'five Ws and the H' of the investigation: Who? What? When? Where? Why? and How?

Models for the Investigation of Digital Crime

Given the ubiquitous availability of digital devices it is inevitable that more and more criminal investigations, and not just those involving cybercrime, will also involve forms of digital forensic investigation. We discuss in Chapter 5 the organisational structures that have been established for digital investigation, but here we examine the models for the process itself. As for criminal investigation generally, there are a number of reasons why it is important to study the models of digital investigation employed by law enforcement agencies and others. However, perhaps the most important reason was given by Ó Ciardhuáin when he argued that 'A good model of cybercrime investigations is important, because it provides an abstract reference framework, independent of any particular technology or organisational environment, for the discussion of techniques and technology for supporting the work of investigators' (Ó Ciardhuáin, 2004, p. 1).

At the outset it is worth noting that as Yusoff et al. point out, the reader might encounter a variety of different terms for describing the process of digital investigation 'model, procedure, process, phase, tasks, etc' (Yusoff et al., 2011, p. 18). It is also unlikely that a universal model of digital criminal investigation could be formulated, because the definition of 'digital crime', and therefore what qualifies as such, is diverse, and specific technical challenges are likely to arise in different cases. In practice the model adopted for any one case might have to reflect by necessity the particular form of digital criminal investigation undertaken and the specific circumstances of the case. Finally, it is worth noting the distinction between models of digital criminal investigation and digital forensic investigation guidelines (such as the ACPO 2012 Guidelines): the latter are more concerned with the specific requirements around the collection and analysis of digital evidence.

Models of digital crime investigation, although subscribing to the basic principles of the more generalised models of criminal investigations described above, possess some unique features and are not simply subsets of criminal investigation (see for example Casey, 2004 and Hutton's 2009 'Cybercrime Investigation Framework'). Etoundi and Moyo (2012) discern three possible categories for models of digital investigation: proactive, active and reactive processes. But they also add that '[a]lthough several models exist within the digital forensic industries, they are essentially limited to reactive digital forensics' (ibid., p. 14).

An early model was outlined in 1984 by Pollitt who described a 'Computer Forensic Investigation Process' as consisting of acquisition (electronic evidence captured in a legally acceptable manner), identification (human recognition of the meaning of the data), evaluation (deciding whether the identified data is relevant to the investigation) and admission (presentation to the criminal justice system) (Pollitt, 1984). In 2001, the first Digital Forensics Research Workshop (Palmer, 2001) agreed a linear process model (known as the 'DFRWS model') with seven stages: 'identification' (for example, audit analysis), 'preservation' (chain of custody), 'collection' (recovery of data), 'examination' and 'analysis' (although described as separate stages these often converge, examples include the recovery of hidden data), 'Presentation' (for example, documentation) and 'Decision'. In 2002 Reith, Carr and Gunsch (2002) outlined a model which, although based in part on the DFRWS model, was somewhat more detailed and comprehensive:

'identification', 'preparation', 'approach strategy' (largely a reference to the need to make preparations before a seizure of digital forensic evidence), 'preservation', 'collection', 'examination', 'analysis', 'presentation' and 'returning evidence' (at the completion of an investigation).

In 2004 (but building on earlier work) Eoghan Casey set out a four stage model of digital (evidence) investigation: recognition; preservation, collection, and documentation; classification, comparison, and individualisation; and finally, reconstruction (Casey, 2004a).

One of the most theoretically-grounded models was proposed by Ó Ciardhuáin in 2004. His 'extended model of cybercrime investigations' was one of the first to move from a largely forensically-based model to one that conceptualised digital crime investigation in its own right. A novel feature was the emphasis on information-flow as an important aspect of digital criminal investigations. There are 13 activities in the model, and these are summarised in Table 6.3.

Table 6.3   Ó Ciardhuáin's 'Extended Model of Cybercrime Investigations'

Activity	Explanation
Awareness	Recognition that an investigation is needed e.g. validated report of hacking
Authorisation	For example, through the issuing of a warrant
Planning	Using information collected by the investigator
Notification	Informing the subject and other interested parties that an investigation is taking place
Search for and identify evidence	For example locating the PC used by a suspect
Collection of evidence	Potential evidence is taken possession of and then…
Transport of evidence	Transported to an appropriate location
Storage of evidence	Storage methods should reduce the risk of cross-contamination
Examination of evidence	The use of specialist techniques e.g. recovery of deleted data
Hypothesis	A tested formulation of what may of occurred
Presentation of hypothesis	For example to a jury
Proof/defence of hypothesis	Contrary hypotheses will also be considered
Dissemination of information	The information may influence investigations in the future

(Based on Ó Ciardhuáin, 2004 but authors' interpretation and description)

There are a number of distinct advantages of the Ó Ciardhuáin model, particularly its use of hypothesis testing to formalise the reasoning used in a digital criminal investigation, and that it has been 'field-tested' and evaluated in practice.

Further models have since been proposed, for example, the 'Enhanced Digital Investigation Process Model' (EDIP) from Baryamureeba and Tushabe (2004), the 'Computer Forensics Field Triage Process Model' (CFFTPM) in 2006 and in 2011, Ademu and Imafidon's 'Systematic Digital Forensic Investigation Model' (SRDHM). In the same year Yusoff et al. proposed a 'Generic Computer Forensic Investigation Model (GCFIM)' which was a synthesis of the various models they established through an inductive synthesis of all extant and previous models. In many cases the models described above were built upon earlier attempts and therefore became more detailed and involved.

A particularly active researcher of models of digital criminal investigation is Hunton (2009, 2010) who has proposed a 'Cybercrime Execution Stack' and the 'Stages of Cybercrime Investigation' and most recently a 'Cybercrime Investigation Framework'. The latter is based in part on the ACPO/Centrex Core Investigative Doctrine (see above) but also incorporates some of Hunton's earlier work. The Framework involves Investigation, Initiation, Modelling, Assessment, Impact/Risk Planning, Tools, Actions and Outcome. However, note that Hunton intends this to be a somewhat more cyclic process than its presentation as a mere list suggests.

Digital Crime Investigation in Practice

Despite the advent of intelligence-led policing (see above) most digital criminal investigations in most parts of the world will be begin in a traditional reactive manner: that is the report of a crime or suspected crime, involving data as either the target and/or as part of the potential evidence. Note that in the sections that follow references to the law are in the context of a digital criminal investigation: civil matters can be very different and are not covered here.

As we discussed earlier, a criminal investigation in the UK (and in many other parts of the world), when seen through to a prosecution, follows a more-or-less set pattern of activities, in seven phases from instigation to court. A digital crime investigation will usually be part of a more general criminal investigation, running alongside it. Depending on the nature of the offences being investigated it will occupy a greater or larger proportion of the overall investigation. So, for example, a homicide enquiry might involve the recovery of deleted SMS messages from a number of mobile phones, and the intelligence gathered could then influence the interview strategy of the underlying criminal investigation.

The digital criminal investigation will be used to test hypotheses both on the level of the digital information itself and also at the level of the criminal investigation it forms part of. A digital investigation can either support a hypothesis through inculpatory evidence, or refute it through exculpatory evidence): the terms 'proof' and 'disproof' are not normally used at this stage.

A digital criminal investigation may be instigated reactively through reports from the public or public agencies, or consequent to other investigations. Or it may be mounted proactively, for example based on open or closed intelligence. However, in common with most crime, many online crimes will not be reported to the police (and hence not recorded in police data), and this particularly applies with online fraud, which is often only reported to the banks and companies concerned. There is also a problem that in the UK at least, that local crime reporting and recording still tends follows geography, with the general 'rule' that crime is recorded where it took place – in the case of online auction-house fraud this poses obvious dilemmas. In response to these problems, by April 2013 all police forces in England and Wales are expected to use 'Action Fraud', for reporting allegations of 'fraud and cybercrime' (in this case defined as financially motivated internet crime). This centralised system is run by the National Fraud Authority working in partnership with the National Fraud Intelligence Bureau. Members of the public can also report suspected online crime to Action Fraud.

The procedures at a digital crime scene are described in Chapter 7 that follows. In many cases the first response to a serious crime with a digital dimension will be a police officer or police staff employee, the so-called 'First Officer on the Scene'. In the UK, sections 19 and 20 of the PACE Act 1984 provide the legal basis for the seizure of data at the scene. There are two issues here: first is the need of the police staff at the scene to be aware of where digital evidence might potentially reside; most police officers or police staff will understand the importance of a suspect's mobile(s) and computing equipment but may not appreciate that digital evidence can also be potentially located in games consoles, digital cameras and indeed any other device that can store data. (The ACPO e-crime Strategy has more to say on this issue; ACPO, 2009). Secondly, there is the need to eliminate or at least minimise the risk of digital contamination. For this reason, it is considered important in many jurisdictions for the first officer to keep careful notes of any actions that were taken (for example, turning off a PC as it appeared to be running a destructive routine). Many countries have detailed guidelines on the processes to be followed: for example, in the UK there is the 2012 ACPO Good Practice Guide for Digital Evidence and in the US the Department of Justice's 'Forensic Examination of Digital Evidence: A Guide for Law Enforcement'. If the seizure of a suspect's PC is planned, a police force Digital Forensics Unit (or Computer Crime Unit or similar, see Chapter 5) will be contacted by the investigating team in advance for advice and, if needed, requested to attend the scene. However, in at least some cases a generalist uniformed police officer will physically seize and package digital devices: this individual will probably have received basic initial police training, but will not be a specialist in digital crime. In the UK a police constable also has the legal power to seize and examine a mobile phone. However, this is normally only to establish the IMEI of the mobile and check it against the National Mobile Property Register (NMPR) rather than for purposes of digital forensic analysis.

Regardless of who may be seizing digital evidence, there remains the question of what should be seized. For example, when searching a suspect's home address there are likely to be many sources of digital data, not only the more obvious mobile phones, digital cameras, laptops and PCs, but also tablet devices, media servers, games consoles and satellite receivers. The temptation must be to seize everything that might possibly contain data, and copy all live data in situ but this has obvious problems not only in terms of practicality but also in terms of proportionality and respect for privacy and human rights. As ACPO argue, 'Digital devices and media should not be seized just because it is there' (sic) (ACPO, 2012, p. 30). The rule adopted is one of a reasonable expectation that the digital device or website is likely to hold information pertinent to an investigation. The process of selecting which devices to be seized, or live data to be copied, is often known as 'triage' (the term is also used when referring to choices made when analysing large amounts of data). The concept of triage originated in medical practice and refers to the process of sorting injured people into groups according to their need for, and likelihood to benefit from, immediate treatment. It is not simply 'first come, first served'. In terms of a digital crime scene the considerations for prioritisation are likely to include a consideration of which devices are most likely to contain relevant information and the volatility of the data. However, as Professor Peter Sommer notes, in the UK at least '[i]nsufficient thought has been given to how [triage] is executed – and by whom' (Sommer, 2012, p. 97).

In the UK there are particular issues concerning the 'disclosure' of unused digital material that has usually been gathered during an investigation (that is material that will not be used by the prosecution in court as evidence against the defendant or defendants). In essence the Criminal Procedure and Investigations Act 1996 (CPIA) requires the recording, retention, revelation and disclosure (to the defence) of unused material, and this includes electronic (digital) material. As noted at the outset, the CPIA Code of Practice also makes it the duty of the investigator to pursue all reasonable lines of enquiry. Both of these strictures have particular implications in the context of digital material which is often voluminous by its very nature, and analysed in ways where large amounts of data remain 'unused' (for example, a 2Tb hard drive might only contain a few Mb of data that are determined to be relevant to the case). In practical terms the responsibility for the digital criminal investigator is to ensure that all unused material is made known to the prosecutor for decisions to be made concerning disclosure.

The forensic analysis of digital evidence is described later in Chapter 8. During basic initial training a police constable in the UK will be taught about some aspects of digital forensics, for example trainers and speakers may provide input on the potential evidence that might be recovered from a website, examples of mobile phone traffic data, service use and subscriber information. A generalist criminal investigator in the UK will also be able and permitted to undertake some of the more common digital forensic techniques, such as identifying and retrieving an email header, printing off a screen-shot of a PC, checking eBay for suspicious activity, and how to access electronic open sources of intelligence (see above) from social network sites. The UK government has also created a new form of 'Special Constable' (a volunteer part-time police officer) based with the new National Cyber Crime Unit within the

National Crime Agency, with specific responsibility to assist in the investigation of digital crime, and from time to time there are also calls to create a new specialist post of 'Digital Scene of Crimes Officer'. However, in many countries much of the expertise required to undertake an initial digital crime investigation is not found within the conventional law enforcement agencies and resides instead in industry, the private sector and the security and intelligence agencies.

Irrespective of the agency involved, or role of the person carrying out the forensic analysis, there is normally a requirement to communicate to others the on-going and final results of any examinations and analysis. This is normally given verbally by the analyst on a regular basis throughout the enquiry, although it is often considered good practice for the analysts to back up the verbal report soon after with a written report (perhaps in an email), and to keep their own notes of the verbal report. In the UK this practice is considered particularly important given the requirements of 'disclosure'. Most jurisdictions require some form of formal written statement from the analysts at the conclusion of the enquiry, which normally includes a discussion of the reliability, validity and confidence in the conclusions, with 'opinion' clearly identified as such.

A key stage of an enquiry will be the charging of the suspect or a decision not to continue with a prosecution. Where charges are laid, specific cybercrime legislation is likely to be cited such as the UK's Computer Misuse Act 1990 in the case of allegations of hacking or virus attacks. Note however, as we discussed in Chapter 4, in many jurisdictions a crime committed online is likely to be prosecuted under 'terrestrial' legislation (such as fraud or communications legislation) rather than specific digital crime legislation.

During a prosecution a digital forensic analyst may be required to give evidence in court, and is likely to be asked to give details concerning their qualifications and experience, and in the UK and many other jurisdictions will be mindful of the important distinction between 'opinion' and 'facts' when giving evidence. However, there are a number of problematic issues surrounding expert witnesses and these are discussed in Chapters 4 and 10.

Cooperation with ISPs, other Service Providers and ICANN

During a digital criminal investigation, cooperation with Internet Service Providers (ISPs), other service providers (such as Microsoft, Google, Twitter and Skype) and internet 'backbone' companies such as ICANN might be necessary. ISPs are normally private companies (such as Comcast in the US and Virgin Media in the UK) which provide individuals and companies with the means to gain access to the internet. So, for example, a person sowing malware will use an ISP to attempt to upload and distribute it, and no doubt many offenders will also take steps to try to hide their identity, through for example using public wifi or 'anonymising' web-services. However, in some cases naive individuals have employed their usual 'home' ISP to facilitate and enact the crime, and the ISP concerned might be able to provide data to support such a hypothesis. Indeed, in many digital crime cases an ISP might hold information that could potentially be of great importance to an investigation. In an investigation, the issue then becomes one of gaining lawful access to this information. In principle, a suspect could request information themselves from an ISP to pass to an investigator but such cooperation is unlikely to be forthcoming, or even desirable. In the UK authorisation is needed (usually in the form of a court order) to require an ISP to hand over data such as weblogs to an investigator. The authorisation would be provided under the Regulation of Investigatory Powers Act 2000 (RIPA). The ISP might also be able to provide evidence or intelligence from emails sent or received by a suspect or others, although this type of evidence can also be recovered from PCs and other similar devices. RIPA will also apply for data concerning traffic (for example, email recipients and senders and the amount of data transferred, rather than the actual content of emails). Authorisation is provided under RIPA Chapter II, but for access to content (see below) a warrant signed by the Home Secretary is required. In many other countries there are similar legal requirements, for example in the US the Communications Assistance for Law Enforcement Act (CALEA) provides for the monitoring of broadband traffic through ISPs.

A number of major corporations and companies such as Microsoft, Google and Yahoo! provide web-based email (for example, Microsoft's 'Outlook.com' and Google's 'Gmail') and online data storage to the public and organisations. Gmail alone had 425 million monthly active users during 2012 (Google, 2012). The data requested by law enforcement agencies from these providers is usually of the form of 'non-content data' and/or 'content data'. Non-content data consists of information such as an account holder's first and second name, age, sex and country of residence (these are declared by the user during the sign-up and hence are not necessarily reliable), his or her email address, allocated IP address (at the time of registration), dates and times of communication traffic and last login IP. There may also be non-content data specific to a particular service provider – for example, in the case of Microsoft, an Xbox gamer profile. Content data includes (in addition to all available non-content data) the full content of an email or an image stored on a Cloud service (see Chapter 10). Microsoft, Google and other companies will require authorisation from the law enforcement agency concerned; in the case of Microsoft non-content data requires 'a valid subpoena or legal equivalent' and content data 'a court order or warrant' (Smith, 2013). Microsoft's stated policy is only to disclose data to law enforcement agencies from countries where Microsoft has the 'ability to validate the lawfulness of the request' (Microsoft, 2013c). In 2012 Microsoft received 75,378 law enforcement requests for customer information from around the world, which affected up to c. 137,000 accounts (Microsoft, 2013d). The number of user requests (excluding Skype) ranged from just a single request from Slovenia to 14,301 requests from the UK and 24,565 from the US (ibid.). In 2012 Microsoft granted 82 per cent of all requests from law enforcement, of which 96.6 per cent was non-content data and 3.4 per cent content data (percentages derived from Microsoft, 2013d). However, many countries are not listed on the Microsoft (non-Skype) law enforcement requests report – for example, there are no requests from China or Russian Federation reported. In 2012 China made 50 requests for Skype user account data from Microsoft but, as of December 2012, none had resulted in Microsoft giving 'guidance to law enforcement' (derived from Microsoft, 2013d).

A number of digital crimes (such as the distribution of malware or the provision of illegal online services) will exploit the relative ease of creating and changing domain names. The registrars of domain names generally make little attempt to validate the details of customer registrations. Law enforcement agencies in a number of countries have been lobbying ICANN (the Internet Corporation for Assigned Names and Numbers) to improve the validity of domain name information, for example to ensure that the name and address of registrants are genuine. This would improve the reliability of WHOIS searches, a valuable technique for digital criminal investigation.

Covert Techniques

A digital crime investigator will sometimes need to employ covert investigatory techniques, for example to identify suspects who are grooming for sexual purposes or participating in online organised criminal activity. The adoption of a 'false' identity might also be required for other aspects of an investigation, otherwise simply accessing a website for example, could alert its controller that a police investigation is underway. However, even if the information gained is to be used as intelligence rather than as evidence (see above), in the UK the requirements of RIPA and PACE (the Police and Criminal Evidence Act 1984) still need to be met.

The police will also use Social Network Services (SNSs, such as Facebook) as part of an investigation, sometimes by first creating a false profile (for example, masquerading as a child) and then collecting information if contacted by those individuals apparently intent on sexual grooming. However, there may be legal problems associated with this. As O'Floinn and Ormerod note (2011, p. 4) in their conclusion, 'in all but the most passive activities, such as monitoring public profiles, there is a risk that SNS policing using fake profiles might be criminal'. Their argument is that an SNS is a 'private telecommunication system' under section 2(1) of RIPA 2000, and that the monitoring of communications on a SNS by investigating officers could be an interception offence under section 1(2) of RIPA.

Covert monitoring of a suspect's PC via a network or the internet is sometimes carried out by investigators. Indeed, software for this very purpose is available to law enforcement authorities, for example Encase's Field Intelligence software allows the remote forensic imaging of a PC's hard drive, the recovery of deleted data, and even the capture of volatile data from running processes (Encase 2012). However, as with many covert techniques, the investigator needs to be mindful of the legal context in order to avoid falling foul of the law, for such activities a warrant under section 26(3) of RIPA is required (which in turn refers to section 32(3) of RIPA which sets out the tests of necessity and proportionality). There are a number of potential problems, for example the covert monitoring could be noticed by the user of the target machine (for example, being identified by a virus checker), and the reliability of any evidence gained through these techniques could be challenged because covert entry onto a suspect's PC will give rise to a change in data in the target machine (in apparent contradiction of the ACPO principles). Software is also available to allow law enforcement authorities to monitor traffic on a suspect's machine to capture usernames and passwords (this is particularly useful where a suspect is using encryption, see below) but RIPA also applies to this kind of activity.

Another possible covert tactic for the police digital crime investigator is the use of key-loggers to gather intelligence and evidence. There are two possible forms of key-logger: physically installed hardware on the target machine, and software covertly run on a target machine (either directly or remotely via the internet). Using covertly installed hardware key-loggers would appear to fall under Part 3 of the Police Act 1997 but again investigators need to be mindful of the RIPA requirements (in this case section 1).

Dealing with Encrypted Data

Investigators may encounter encrypted data as part of an investigation. There could be 'innocent' reasons for why the data has been encrypted: for example, it might be company policy. However, some suspects may have taken deliberate and careful steps to encrypt data, either because it could incriminate them, or to inhibit a future police investigation. Some countries have a national resource to support investigators in dealing with encrypted data: for example the National Technical Assistance Centre (NTAC) in the UK (see Chapter 5). It is also worth noting that the legislation relating to investigations where suspects have used encryption often employs a specific language. For example, in the UK, RIPA 2000 uses the terms 'Protected Information', 'Data key ' and 'Intelligible form'.

An early step in de-crypting a suspect's encrypted material is to attempt to identify the form of encryption used (for example, symmetric or asymmetric) and the software employed, for example 'Kruptos'. As described in Chapter 10, encryption is a potentially very difficult hurdle to overcome, and 'industrial-strength' encryption is available to anybody via the internet. A password will usually be required to decrypt the data (see below). It may sometimes be possible to exploit an inherent weakness in the method of encryption used. This is unlikely, but some encryption software does have 'back door' entry points.

In the UK, section 50(3)(c) of RIPA 2000 provides the authorities with a power 'to require disclosure of the means to access protected information or the means to put it into intelligible form' with failure to do so an offence. There have been a number of successful prosecutions under this legislation but some of these are likely to have involved offenders who have weighed up the likelihood of prosecution under RIPA against the potentially more serious repercussions of facilitating access to incriminating material (for example, child sexual abuse imagery).

Password Cracking

Passwords are important to the forensic digital investigation for two main reasons: to gain access to password protected but intelligible material and (often more demanding) as the key required for decryption (see above).

Passwords can be obtained by:

1. Asking the suspect for the password. Social engineering could also be used to guess a suspect's password, using information from a social networking site about his or her interests, biographical details, family, friends, pet's name, and other names and numbers that might be important (such as DoB or a mobile number).
2. Using 'key-logger' software (recording any input via a keyboard) to covertly obtain passwords.
3. Conducting a physical search for the password, for example locating a 'post it' note on the reverse of the keyboard, behind monitors or an entry in a mobile phone.
4. Conducting an electronic search of the suspect's PC and other devices for a plaintext version (or fragment) of the password.
5. A 'dictionary attack', in both English and the language of the suspect (for example, Polish in the case of a Polish-speaking suspect), where words from a dictionary (together with numbers and other symbols) are checked against the encryption software. There are automated password cracking systems, including online dictionaries which can very quickly cycle through a list of known words and words with common alterations such as replacing 'l' with '1' (e.g. paypa1). If a suspect's personal information is available then dedicated software can be used to generate likely passwords based for example on his or her place or date of birth. The exhaustive checking of passwords is known as a Brute Force Attack (BFA). The security of a password in terms of its vulnerability to cracking depends on a number of factors, the most obvious being the length of the password and the character set used. For example if a system constrains the choice of the characters to the lower and upper case letters in the English alphabet and the digits 0 to 9, then there are 62 possibilities for each character of the password (26 lower case letters, 26 upper case letters and 10 digits). And if the password must consist of six characters (drawn from the set of 62) there will be 62^6 or nearly 57 billion possible passwords. Although this is a large number, it is entirely feasible to check 57 billion possibilities by using automated software. If a thousand passwords could be tried in one second, it would take approximately 657 days to check all possibilities. Obviously, in the case of password-controlled services and resources there are often systems which limit the number of password 'guesses' and this would limit the feasibility of such attacks. However, the method is often used against databases of stolen usernames and passwords which are then attacked

offline, and can also be used by law enforcement agencies. In reality very few systems however limit the password length to six characters, and for a seven character password, an additional 40,759 days would be needed to check all possibilities. If a further ten characters such as '&' are included in the character set, the time required to check the passwords becomes 1,612 days for 6-character passwords and 116,096 days for 7 characters. Of course not all passwords would need to be searched; on average only half the entire possibilities would need to be tested before a match was found. Where the password has been encrypted then a variation of the BFA is to use a 'rainbow table' consisting of all possible combinations of hash values derived from a set of characters and symbols.

6. A 'frequency attack' (but only in the case of some particular forms of encryption), which exploits the fact that letters of the alphabet occur with variable frequencies.

The CJS and Digital Evidence

In this section we examine how investigation of digital crime sits within the Criminal Justice System, and in particular, the legal issues surrounding digital evidence. Our focus here is mainly on the criminal law rather than the civil law, and on the UK in particular, however, much of what follows will also apply in other jurisdictions, particularly those that employ the adversarial system of justice.

As we described earlier, a digital crime investigation takes place within the framework for criminal investigation in general, and hence a broad understanding of the Criminal Justice System (the CJS), the forms and legal standing of digital evidence would seem appropriate. Digital evidence is certainly of growing importance as we witness the 'emergence of digital evidence not only featuring in computer specific criminal cases such as hacking and malware attacks, but becoming a more common element in almost any type of crime' (Grobler, 2012, p. 1).

The CJS encompasses a number of procedures and institutions, for example the law itself, law enforcement, and dealing with transgressions of the law in a particular country. So for example, the CJS in England and Wales includes the police, the Courts of law, the National Offenders Management Service (NOMS), the Youth Justice Board, and the Crown Prosecution Service (CPS).

In order to determine the guilt or otherwise of a defendant a Court will consider the evidence. During many criminal investigations, particularly complex ones, a large amount of material will be generated by the crime itself, a subset of which will be gathered by the police (for example, a witness statement) but only a proportion of this will be admissible as evidence in any prosecution (ACPO/Centrex 2005, p. 45). In the UK evidence is usually regarded as consisting of four kinds: oral (also called verbal or spoken); real (an article, object, or thing with material existence that can be produced as such in court); documentary (a document, paper, or record, which can be electronic); or hearsay. As far as we can tell (research is by necessity limited) the courts (and juries in particular) are most comfortable with oral evidence (that is, evidence given by a person describing their direct experience of what they saw, heard, felt and so on), and with real evidence such as a knife.

Carrier and Spafford (2006) defined digital evidence as digital data that supports or refutes a hypothesis about digital events or the state of digital data. However, digital data as evidence within the CJS is unusual because it is virtual rather than actual, and its meaning has to be inferred. (The device that produced the digital evidence is real but the data it produced is not). Digital evidence has to be represented at some more abstract level than the bits and bytes of its actuality. For example, a prosecutor could simply print out a long list of the hexadecimal code that related to a particular deleted document on a PC, but this would 'prove' nothing. Hence the decision instead is always to show an interpretation in the form of file structures, images within folders and so on and to present this as documentary evidence rather than as 'real' data. However, there are few if any, uniform standards in place for the interpretation and presentation of this digital data, but accepted custom and practice have gradually developed since the inception of digital evidence. By and large in the UK the documentary digital evidence realised from the actions of a PC is admissible, under a presumption that it was reliably produced. The person making the interpretation will give a witness statement and also be present in court to give oral evidence and to be available for cross-examination. The reliability of the record may however be called into question. Expert witness evidence is discussed further in Chapter 10.

We can identity a number of categories of digital evidence, which are summarised in Table 6.4. The categories are neither mutually exclusive nor exhaustive.

In the UK evidence generally only features within the deliberations of a court if it satisfies the tests of relevance, admissibility and weight. (It is likely that these considerations will feature throughout many stages of a digital criminal investigation, and not simply at the stages of formal prosecution, when it might be rather too late.) Evidence is relevant if it has some bearing on proving or disproving some point in dispute in a prosecution and trial. Admissibility is closely related to relevance and simply refers (in a rather circular fashion) to evidence which can be properly received and heard by the court. Evidence is considered inadmissible if it has been 'unfairly acquired', if for example it has been obtained in violation of codes of conduct such as the PACE Codes in the UK. In many European countries with an inquisitorial system of justice (with an examining magistrate) there are no formal rules of admissibility but instead the single test of 'relevancy'. In the US admissibility is determined by the Federal Rules of Evidence.

If the digital evidence is deemed admissible, it is then further considered in terms of what 'weight' of fact it might carry – that is its 'probative value'. Digital evidence is likely to have greater weight if it is authentic, accurate and complete. The degree of authenticity depends on how explicitly the evidence is connected to the suspect or others, and the circumstances of the alleged crime. For example, the authenticity of a print out of an email would be high if it was shown that the

Table 6.4   Categories of Digital Evidence

Type of digital evidence	Description
Content data	Words, sentences, numbers, images etc from PC hard drives, emails, websites, mobile phone memory dumps and so on.
Recovered data	Data which has been (apparently) deleted by the suspect but then recovered by an investigator, for example recovered deleted instant messaging logs on a mobile phone.
Hidden data	Data which has been deliberately hidden such as using steganography to hide an image portraying child sexual abuse.
Event and location data	Data which includes information about events and location for example from a satnav device giving details of places, times, duration of stops, or Android location cache files and likewise.
Metadata	Information about data – for example, when an MS Excel spreadsheet file was created, edited; Android YAFFS2 (moving to Ext4) metadata.
Ambient data	The Windows page file, fragments of data.
File and folder data	Windows registry data, time-stamps – for example, Nokia S40 format dates.
Back up data	Data backed up, for example to a Cloud service.
Network communication data	For example, email traffic data collected from an ISP or by covert means (for example by using a 'sniffer'), or GPRS data from communications service provider(CSP).

email was sent using the account controlled by the suspect from the IP address of a networked PC under his or her control and regular use, and the email content related to the alleged offence. Likewise, the simple existence of an indecent image of a child on a person's PC would not in itself carry sufficient weight to prove possession in a court of law, but the existence of the image together with date stamps showing when the image had been accessed, the creation of a folder to store the image and so on would significantly add to the weight in terms of authenticity (see Chapter 6).

The weight of the accuracy of the digital evidence also partly depends on the reliability of the methods that have been used to collect, analyse and interpret the data. Hence it includes considerations of the likelihood of the 'contamination' of the evidence (for example, undocumented change to the data), and the scientific standing of the techniques used. For example, digital evidence that has been produced by a person with recognised professional standing, and who has used a suite of recognisable and reliable forensic software according to professional guidelines (such as, in the UK, the ACPO Good Practice guidelines for Digital Evidence, ACPO 2012), is more likely to carry significant weight in terms of its accuracy (but see below). Finally, the more complete the digital evidence is, the more weight it carries. Completeness is a reference to the quality of the 'narrative' of the digital evidence: does it hang together as a coherent account confirmed by cross referencing?

There are a however, number of issues surrounding digital evidence and the CJS. One concern is that legal practitioners are not able to fully appreciate the potential weight of digital evidence (Boddington et al., 2008). The volatility, complexity and at times large quantity of digital evidence be challenging for legal practitioners. There may be doubts about the authenticity and completeness of electronic records because they are much easier to fabricate than physical evidence, and this can impact, they argue, on the admissibility and weight of the evidence.

Moves by the Forensic Regulator (Home Office, 2010) to improve the quality of forensic practice in the UK refer to scientific concepts such as 'reliability' and 'validation'. Unlike professional scientists, most forensic investigators do not necessarily have the skills or training required for conducting authoritative scientific research (Beckett and Slay, 2007). The House of Commons Science and Technology Committee have previously expressed concerns over the lack of an established protocol for admitting expert evidence (House of Commons, 2005). In the same report, the admissibility systems of Frye and Daubert in the US are cited as an 'interesting development', suggesting there may be moves in the future towards a similar gate-keeping system for expert evidence in the UK (and not just for digital evidence). This is also discussed in Chapter 10.

Furthermore, the probative value of at least some digital evidence is subject to a number of possible 'defences', particularly within adversarial systems of justice. For example, the separation of user actions from events caused by malicious software is the basis of the so-called 'malware defence', often also referred to colloquially as the 'Trojan defence'. In the UK the cases of *R* v *Caffrey* (2003), *R* v *Green* (2003), *R* v *Gray* (2009), *R* v *Schofield* (2003), *Amero* (Rasch, 2007) and *Fiola* (Leyden, 2009) all involved a defence that cited malware as the cause of all or part of their alleged actions. Typically, the Defence (in an adversarial system) will argue in terms of possibilities (and hence introduce reasonable doubt), while the Prosecution focus on likelihoods (and how unlikely they claim such events are). Unfortunately, neither side usually present anything other than anecdotal evidence to support their stance.

From a sceptic's perspective, the malware defence is not an issue. Conventional artefacts are sufficient to determine if the identified actions were performed by malware, or intentionally by the user (Carvey, 2009). However, anti-forensic measures (which are common with malware) are cited as a risk to the practice of using conventional artefacts in this manner (Kessler, 2007). Anti-forensic measures include packers (Desfossez et al., 2009), virtual machine (VM) protectors (Sharif et al., 2009) and RAM based malware that does not touch the disk (Miller, 2004, Wallisch, 2009) – but instead uses techniques such as 'Reflective DLL injection' (Fewer, 2008).

There may be anecdotal arguments of certain behaviours having not been witnessed (McLinden, 2002; Douglas, 2007) and this can be convincing, but according to the principles of 'falsifiability' proposed by Popper (1968) the arguments are insufficient. Simply because something has not been observed, it cannot be discounted as a possible explanation, and offenders may attempt to exploit this. It may be argued that anecdotal arguments are accepted by courts and are therefore sufficient, but some see this simply as the result of the court's naivety in the area of science (Saks and Faigman, 2008).

The use and interpretation of statistical values is yet another area where problems arise, for example five different schools of thought on interpreting probabilities in a legal context have been identified (Schum, 1986). The Prosecutor's Fallacy (House of Commons, 2005; Garrett and Neufeld, 2009) and the Ecological Fallacy (Beach, 2010) are well-documented examples of inappropriately cited statistics.

Digital Forensic Standards and Accreditation

The office of Forensic Regulator was formed in the UK in 2008 with a remit to 'establish and monitor compliance with quality standards for the provision of forensic science services to the police and wider criminal justice system' (Forensic Science Regulator, 2009). The events and concerns leading up to this are set out in Chapter 10. The Regulator's 'Codes of Practice and Conduct' (Home Office, 2011) are aligned to BS EN ISO/IEC 17025:2005 (ISO, 2005). Forensic service providers now face an emerging regulatory requirement to demonstrate that their working practices meet with minimum standards.

The draft Codes of Practice produced by the Forensic Regulator for forensic service providers and practitioners seek to provide greater 'confidence in the reliability of forensic science evidence' (Home Office, 2010). The standard is designed for the testing and calibration of laboratory equipment. It makes reference to procedures that incorporate concepts such as validation, reproducibility, and objectivity. The standard also makes provision for the use of non-standard methods, such as might be applied to the extraction and interpretation of data from an unfamiliar file format. The requirements are explicitly set out and provide a clear indication of the scientific approach that underpins the standard as a whole. The techniques for non-standard methods are required to include at least one of the following:

- calibration using reference standards or reference materials;
- comparison of results achieved with other methods;
- inter-laboratory comparisons;
- systematic assessment of the factors influencing the result;
- assessment of the uncertainty of the results based on scientific understanding of the theoretical principles of the method and practical experience.

Given these concepts and requirements, the ISO 17025 standard (and hence the Forensic Regulator's draft Codes of Practice) demonstrate a significant commitment to scientific principles.

Applying the ISO 17025 standard to malware forensics presents a number of challenges, such as the lack of science, the inherent conflict between scientific and legal requirements for truth (see Chapter 10), testing methodologies, and the skill needs of both forensic and legal practitioners with respect to malware forensics. For example, section 5.4.6 outlines the requirement for an estimation of the uncertainty of measurement. A measurement is a property comprising of both a quantity and the associated units of measurement (Bell, 2001), and the International Vocabulary of Metrology from which the ISO 17025 standard takes its definitions also defines a measurement in terms of a quantity and unit of measurement. Many of the artefacts obtained from a computer investigation cannot be quantified in terms of physical units of measurement: for example, registry values, internet history records, chat-logs and even file sizes in kilobytes. The standard is therefore more readily applicable to physical science than to computer science laboratories. ILAC-G19 and the newly emerging ISO 27041 standard are however now addressing these particular difficulties.

Chapter 7
Procedures at Digital Crime Scenes

Ian Kennedy with Ed Day

Introduction

Many readers will be familiar with the role of the 'crime scene investigator' (CSI), previously known as the 'Scene of Crime Officer', or erroneously as the 'Forensic Scientist'. CSIs specialise in locating and preserving evidence such as fibres, DNA and fingerprints at a crime scene. In principle, their training and experience allows them to identify the best places to look for, retrieve and (to a lesser extent – see Chapter 8) analyse and interpret traditional forensic evidence. However, for criminal investigations in the UK that involve digitally-based evidence, this role is performed by what is typically termed a 'first responder' (or 'digital evidence first responder', DEFR) from a police force Digital Forensics Unit (DFU), or a unit with a similar title. The first responder has the key responsibility for recognising the sources of digital evidence that may be relevant to the subject under investigation. In the UK, police officers receive training to act as first responders as part of their initial training (see Chapter 6 and Bryant and Bryant, 2013), but in practice this role is often performed by other police staff. The forensic investigators (or 'digital evidence specialists', DESs) and the first responders are collectively known within a DFU as 'forensic practitioners'. The forensic practitioners may be warranted police officers or other police staff; the balance varies between forces. In some forces the investigators might also on occasions act as first responders.

As for any crime scene, an entry plan is likely to be created before arrival, if time permits. The plan often includes an assessment of any potential disruption caused by search, seizure and other activities, for example consideration could be given to the extent to which the seizure of a company's server would damage its business. Any relevant warrants must be obtained prior to arrival at the scene (Britz, 2004). In the UK a lawful search for evidence is typically performed under s 18 of the Police and Criminal Evidence Act 1984 (PACE), and evidence is typically seized under s 19. In addition, the PACE Codes of Practice also apply to searches and seizures. The types of digital evidence that first responders are likely to encounter are very varied, and any location or device with the capability for storage or communication of digital data will be of interest (see below). The procedures to be followed at digital crime scenes are in part related to a subsequent analysis of digital information and evidence, which is examined in Chapter 8.

Principles and Guidelines for Attending Digital Crime Scenes and Collecting Evidence

There are a number of sets of national guidelines and developing international standards that relate to attending digital crime scenes and collecting of digital or electronic evidence. Perhaps one of the better known of these are the ACPO guidelines those from the Association of Chief Police Officers (ACPO) for England and Wales. There have been a number of iterations of the ACPO guidelines (although the underpinning principles have remained largely unchanged), and the latest edition of the guidelines ('the ACPO Good Practice Guide for Digital Evidence') was issued in March 2012. It outlines four overarching principles that should be followed in any digital investigation (ACPO, 2012, p.6) and the principles are worth quoting in full:

Principle 1:   No action taken by law enforcement agencies or their agents should change data held on a computer or storage media which may subsequently be relied upon in court.

Principle 2:   In circumstances where a person finds it necessary to access original data held on a computer or on storage media, that person must be competent to do so and be able to give evidence explaining the relevance and the implications of their actions.

Principle 3:   An audit trail or other record of all processes applied to computer-based electronic evidence should be created and preserved. An independent third party should be able to examine those processes and achieve the same result.

Principle 4:   The person in charge of the investigation has overall responsibility for ensuring that the law and these principles are adhered to.

In most circumstances these are sound principles to follow when dealing with digital devices and data, and we will see how they can be applied to investigations in this chapter and in Chapter 8. There is however, some debate concerning the applicability of the principles to solid-state drives and similar media, and this is discussed further in Chapter 10.

There may at first sight appear to be a conflict between the first and second principles; the first principle requires that original data must not be altered, whereas the second principle refers to accessing the original data. The problem arises because unless certain precautions are taken, it is highly likely that the original data will be altered in some way when accessed. For example, the process of logging on to a windows-based PC will change the data because a record of the log-on will be recorded in the Windows' registry (amongst other places). So if an investigator is unable to adhere to the first principle (because the data is probably being altered when it is accessed) then the second principle must be followed – the person must be competent and able to give evidence concerning the consequences of their actions.

In the US the Department of Justice (DoJ) produced a guide (in 2004) for law enforcement agencies on the forensic examination of digital evidence, which includes recommended actions at a digital crime scene. The guidelines are similar in nature to the ACPO principles cited above, for example, the DoJ requires that:

> [a]ctions taken to secure and collect digital evidence should not affect the integrity of that evidence'; that '[p]ersons conducting an examination of digital evidence should be trained for that purpose' and that '[a]ctivity relating to the seizure, examination, storage, or transfer of digital evidence should be documented, preserved, and available for review. (National Institute of Justice, 2004)

The Federal Rules of Evidence in the US apply to digital evidence in the same way as to more traditional forms of evidence (particularly 'Rule 702: Testimony by Expert Witnesses', much of 'Article IX: Authentication and Identification', and some of Article X: Contents of Writings, Recordings and Photographs'). Hence in effect the Rules provide a set of underpinning principles to guide the actions of responders and investigators at digital crime scenes.

In 2002 the International Organization on Computer Evidence (the IOCE) working in consultation with the G8 nations produced their own digital forensics guidelines ('Guidelines for Best Practice in the Forensic Examination of Digital Technology', (IOCE/G8, 2002)). Section 7 describes best practice in location and recovery of digital evidence at the scene, including anti-contamination precautions, searching the scene, collecting the evidence, and packaging, labelling and documentation.

Finally, in 2012 a new ISO standard (ISO/IEC 27037:2012) was published dealing with '[i]nformation technology – security techniques – guidelines for identification, collection, acquisition, and preservation of digital evidence' (ISO, 2012a). Sections 5 and 6 will be of particular importance to countries implementing these standards. Section 5 provides an outline of the principles, and section 6 describes the key components of identification, collection, acquisition and preservation of digital evidence (including chain of custody), the precautions to be taken at the site of the incident, the required competency, roles and responsibilities of the personnel involved and what documentation is required (ISO, 2012b).

Possible Locations for Evidence

The digital information of interest to a first responder and an investigator may be present wherever data is stored and processed, for example in any device with a microcontroller. The hard drives of PCs and the solid-state devices within some laptops and mobile and smartphones, are obviously locations where a digital forensic investigator might locate relevant information, for example concerning preparations for committing a crime. Less obvious examples include modern washing machines whose programmable cycles use solid-state memory, and which might for example be analysed during an investigation into sexual assault. It is vitally important that first responders keep abreast of a rapidly developing field in which the products of new technologies may be smaller or simply unrecognisable as sources of digital evidence. Digital forensics can also be used to access volatile data of the kind normally encountered when investigating computer networks.

Locations include (but are not limited to) digital storage media used in PCs, Macs, tablet computers (hard drives, solid-state drives), memory cards, USB pen drives, optical and magneto optical disks (CDs, DVDs, DRAM, Blu-ray), smartphones and mobile phones, Personal Digital Assistants (PDAs), games consoles, mobile navigation systems (Satnavs), photocopiers and fax machines, digital video cameras (including CCTV) and networks (see Chapter 9).

Together with a time-stamp and in some cases geo-location, data from a device could corroborate or challenge any defence offered by a suspect. Figure 7.1 shows an example of how mobile phone data was used in an investigation conducted with Dutch authorities. Time-stamp evidence is discussed further in Chapter 8.

Other sources of evidence include router and modem logs, together with any logs kept by an Internet Service Provider (ISP). These can corroborate when an internet connection was made, and possibly to what location.

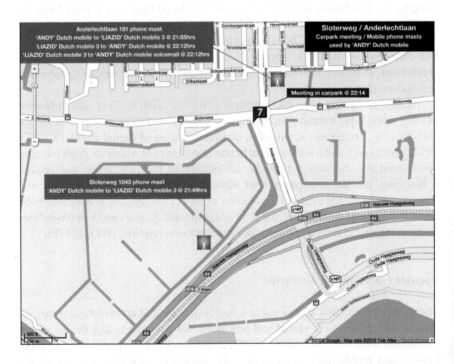

Figure 7.1   Using Mobile Phone Data with a Time-stamp (Google and the Google logo are registered trademarks of Google Inc., used with permission; map data: Google, TeleAtlas)

The increasing availability of cloud-based data services such as DropBox (2007) and Apple's iCloud means that not all the relevant data may be held at the location being searched. Although a court order may be issued to secure such online data, timing is crucial as the subject of the investigation may promptly arrange for a third-party to erase the data remotely. The challenge to digital forensic investigation provided by cloud storage is discussed further in Chapter 10. As well as cloud-based data, digital forensic investigators are increasingly being asked to also examine the volatile data from the memory (RAM) of a powered-on computer.

Having identified the sources of evidence to be examined, the next step is to secure a copy of this data in a forensically secure manner, and initially this typically concerns the preservation of evidence. As noted earlier, guidelines on the preservation of evidence have been produced in the US (National Institute of Justice, 2004) and the UK (ACPO, 2012), as well as in other jurisdictions. However, the guidelines inevitably cannot cover every eventuality and hence there are times when knowledge and experience requires a judgment call on the part of the first responder. For example, it will have to be decided whether to seize the computers concerned (including servers if necessary), or leave the hardware in situ and 'copy' or 'image' (see below) the hard drives and other forms of digital storage. This decision is particularly important when data is being secured at a business address; it is common practice to produce a forensic 'copy' onsite to minimise any disruption to the business. It is possible to copy a 1TB hard disk on-site in around two hours under certain conditions. This is preferable to taking the whole system away for around 24–48 hours for it to be processed and subsequently returned (which might require further permission). In most countries the first responder is required to make a careful note of the decision taken and the justification.

Managing Suspects

Many national guidelines advise that on arrival at the scene any suspects should be removed from the location and kept separately. Any 'advice' suspects provide should generally not be followed since it could be requesting investigators to perform actions that could potentially lead to the destruction of evidence. For example, if a suspect is asked for a password to log on to a live PC, the 'password' may in fact be nothing of the sort, and when entered by the investigator it could cause the machine to run a script that destroys potential evidence stored on its hard drive. The suspect should be questioned when appropriate (in most cases under caution at a police station), and asked for any passwords necessary to access any data seized. It may also be possible to obtain passwords from the scene, on 'post-it' notes for example (ACPO, 2012). Issues relating to passwords are covered in more detail in Chapter 3, and password cracking is covered in Chapter 6.

Powered-on Computers

When digital devices are encountered they may be either powered-on or off, and is important that the correct actions are carried out in each case. This will depend on the exact situation, for example a PC that is in the process of downloading indecent images might well need to be left on by investigators, but a PC involved in a distributed denial of service attack (DDoS) should probably be shut down as soon as possible. The ACPO guidelines (2012) provide some general rules to follow depending on the kind of device encountered and whether it is on or off.

For a PC that is powered-off, under no circumstances should it be switched on since this would alter the machine's contents and could for example start up self-destruct scripts to wipe its hard drive. The power cable from a desktop PC that appears to be powered-off should be removed, because it might only be in hibernate mode, with an uninterruptible power source (UPS) supplied through the cable. ACPO (2012) advise that the battery of a laptop should be removed, but without opening the lid as this can sometimes cause it to switch on. (However, a laptop with a closed lid is not necessarily powered-off as many operating systems allow users to determine the results of closing the lid).

If the PC is already powered-on then the situation is more complex. A simple step that can be taken in most circumstances is to photograph the image on the screen of the PC. If no specialist advice is available and it is thought that no vital evidence will be lost by terminating any running processes, then again the power cable should be removed (ACPO, 2012). However networks are commonly found to be involved in investigations, and this will frequently be via the internet, but other internal and external computer networks may also be present. An example of this would be an investigation involving the distribution of child sexual abuse imagery over the internet involving a number of networked PCs in a suspect's home or work environment. In these types of investigations 'pulling the (power) plug' may destroy vital information including any running processes, network connections, and any dynamically stored data in the RAM (ACPO, 2012). Dedicated software can be used to investigate live systems but it must be forensically sound, and it will also 'leave a footprint', ie cause changes to data on running systems. Obviously this would have to be taken into account in evidential terms (ACPO's second principle). Note that it may be possible to retrieve plaintext encryption keys (Marshall, 2008) from machines left in a live state (if they are not running destructive processes).

When securing volatile data, it is not sufficient to simply obtain a copy of the computer's RAM and analyse it. A computer's memory typically exists as a virtual block spanning both the physical RAM and the 'paged' areas on the disk. Ideally both these elements should be examined together as a single entity. Furthermore, historical copies of RAM exist in hibernation files on laptops (from when the laptop has 'gone to sleep'), and in crash dumps produced as a result of a Windows 'Blue Screen of Death'.

It should be acknowledged that RAM analysis is still in its infancy, and hence it is often the case that findings from the RAM will be corroborated with other results achieved independently. For example, securing metadata about the live system (and other information from running processes and open ports or files) is a useful means to for acquiring data for comparing with any results obtained from RAM images. When working with live systems, consideration should also be given to the order of volatility of data. A suggested approach (together with a study on the footprint of volatile data collection tools) is provided by Sutherland et al., (2008). For situations involving malware analysis, more detailed advice is available from Malin et al., (2008), including suggestions for suitable tools.

Preserving the Evidence

Preservation of digital evidence typically involves the creation of a forensic copy (or 'image') of the evidence. This copy is then much more transportable and can be readily copied to produce working copies. At all times it is normally considered essential that any change to the original evidence is kept to a minimum. Under certain circumstances however (volatile data acquisition, see below) changing the original evidence is unavoidable; it is necessary to perform an action that will make a change to the original data. In keeping with ACPO guidelines and similar principles in other jurisdictions, when such actions are performed, there is usually a requirement to record the reasons for the actions and their expected impact. Many professional commentators suggest that in terms of recording the scene and the investigators' activities, the more the better, and at a minimum the scene should be sketched, photographed and if possible videoed (Britz, 2004).

Copying, Imaging and Write-blocking Non-volatile Data

In many countries (but not all) it is standard practice to make a 'copy' of seized data for analysis, with the general proviso that the copied data must be exactly the same as the original data. However a simple tool such as Windows Explorer cannot be used to make a full copy of a hard drive (for example) as this only *appears* to make exact copies. Certain parts of the hard drive (such as files that have been deleted and emptied from the Recycle Bin) are not generally retrievable by tools such as Windows Explorer. Instead, a specialist tool (often a combination of hardware and software) that performs a bit-by-bit copy is required; this creates what is known as an 'image' (Sammes and Jenkinson, 2007).

Great care should be taken in relation to solid-state drives (SSDs) as the data on these is often being rearranged when powered-on. This can lead to the loss of hidden data (for example remnants of files that have been previously deleted by the user), as explained in more detail in Chapter 10.

Figure 7.2   Hard Disk Imaging Begins (image copyright Ian Kennedy)

The capture of data present on hard drives can take hours to complete. This may not always be a problem, but there is a finite amount of time a suspect can be held prior to a charging decision being made. Alternatively, it may be that the data capture is taking place under warrant at a business premises and again time will be limited by the warrant. Under both these circumstances, the forensic data capture must be completed as quickly as possible.

Forensic practitioners should always check the 'clock-time' on the PC containing the hard drive to be copied. All PCs have a BIOS clock on the motherboard, which many applications running through the operating system will use to determine the date and time (some however will use an 'internet-time' instead). Crucially, the BIOS clock cannot be assumed to be the correct date and time, and any difference will need to be determined and recorded (see Chapter 8 on *metadata* for further details).

For rapid data capture, hardware-based solutions are preferable as these can provide data transfer rates of up to 9GB per minute, so a 500GB disk could theoretically be copied in just under an hour. In practice however, the copying speed is highly dependent on the characteristics of the disk being copied, so the copying may take significantly longer. Examples of hardware solutions for data capture include the Forensic Dossier (Figure 7.2) and the older Forensic Talon (Figure 7.3) (Logicube 2011).

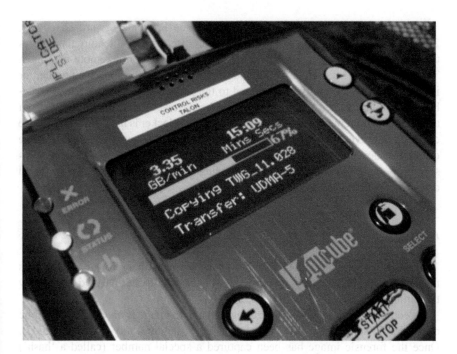

Figure 7.3   Data Imaging in Progress (image copyright of Ian Kennedy)

Live Forensic Discs

A live forensic disc is a software-based imaging solution on a CD, DVD or USB pen drive. Some solutions provide a bootable operating system, typically Linux based, which allows a computer to be booted in a forensically sound manner, without the internal disk(s) being automatically mounted. Other solutions, such as the free tool FTK Imager for Windows (AccessData, 2010) are not bootable, but enable a first responder to capture live data, for example from a server that would not normally be taken offline. It is possible to create an image from a live and mounted disk, but the integrity of this copy is not as pure as an offline, forensic copy. This is because the files on a live disc are subject to on-going changes by users or the operating system during the imaging process. Furthermore, it is not a repeatable process, which has disadvantages in terms of evidential requirements.

Some solutions, such as the Helix disc (e-fense, 2013), provide the relevant software for both approaches on the same disc, which has the advantage that the first responder does not need to decide in advance which approach to take. Many first responders will in fact carry a few different versions and types of 'live forensic' discs in their toolkit. They can be used in parallel if there is a need to copy several disks simultaneously, or if the source hard disk does not work with the solution of first choice.

Other examples of live forensic discs include Raptor (Forward Discovery, 2011) and Paladin (Sumuri, 2011). The Paladin disc also has a feature that allows the copy to be sent over a network to a network share on a remote computer. This can be useful if there are not enough USB ports on the source computer, or if the USB ports are faulty or restricted to the slower USB1.1 standard. A write-blocker should be used when copying or otherwise accessing the hard disk from an original exhibit held as 'best evidence'. A write-blocker is hardware or software designed to prevent any writing to the target device, and is used to ensure that the original evidence is kept pristine. It is necessary to take such precautions as even seemingly unobtrusive actions such as reading a hard drive may change its stored data (Knetzger and Muraski, 2008).

Hashing

The authentication aspect of ACPO's first principle means that forensic practitioners must be able to show that any image that may subsequently be analysed is precisely the same as the original data (ACPO, 2012).

A common method of demonstrating that a data image is an exact copy of the data initially seized is by the use of 'hashing' (Sammes and Jenkinson, 2007). Once the forensic image has been captured a special number (called a 'hash') is calculated from both the source disk and the forensic image. If both produce exactly the same number, then the copy is an exact copy of the original data. A hash function is a mathematical algorithm (there are a number of such algorithms, two of the most popular are MD5 and SHA1) that takes an input and uses it to generate a much smaller 'digest'. The digest will always be the same for the same input, and any even slightly different inputs will generate very different digests.

As an example of a hash, consider the contents of this paragraph preceding this sentence ('The digest will ... very different digests.'). This would have an MD5 hash of

94696e913ca9198643a718276cd7d9df.

However the hash is very different for the same sentence with a single space added after its final full-stop. The hash becomes:

4924a5ecb7592543cc3dbaf87112ac1e.

Hashing has the additional useful property that hash functions are a one-way operation: the original input cannot be ascertained from a digest (Stallings, 2010). Note that 'collisions' (ie false matches) have been discovered in hash functions but these are so unlikely that in practice the system works as intended. (There is in fact a 1 in 2^{128} chance of two different forensic images having the same hash value. Put another way, on average 340,282,366,920,938,463,463,374,607,431,768,211,

456 images would need to be produced before the next would have the same hash as one of the proceeding images.) A hash number can be recalculated at any time subsequent to the original data capture to confirm that neither the original disks nor the forensic copy have been changed.

Volatile Data

In addition to the traditional hard disk imaging process, live (otherwise known as 'volatile') data can now be acquired from running systems. This can provides valuable potential evidence because some information may only exist in the Random Access Memory (RAM) of a computer whilst it is running. An analysis of RAM data can provide (AccessData, 2009) information such as:

- a list of all the processes running and terminated on the computer;
- the path to where a program is located;
- command line arguments used;
- network connections (both idle and active);
- content from encrypted files that have been opened; and
- passwords entered by the user.

Network-based data (called 'IP packets') containing IP addresses, and hardware identifying data known as Media Access Controller (or 'MAC') addresses have been recovered by Beverly et al. (2011). This type of data can corroborate a hypothesis that two devices have communicated with each other over a network, (see Chapter 9 for further details).

In 2005 a challenge was set by the organisers of the conference DFRWS 2005 to develop a tool for acquiring RAM from a running computer (DFRWS, 2005), with two joint winners (Garner, 2005; Betz, 2005). There has since been an explosion of research in this area of data acquisition (Savoldi and Gubian, 2008; Simon and Slay, 2009; Walters, 2006; Kornblum 2007). One of the most versatile tools currently available to analyse RAM from Windows computers is probably 'Volatility' (Volatile Systems, 2007).

Referring back to the ACPO principles, there are two main considerations when acquiring volatile data. The first is the unavoidable fact that running a tool on a live computer system will change some of its memory (to allow the tool to be executed). Understanding the impact of this action, particularly how much memory is changed (the 'footprint') is crucial to abiding by the second principle of the ACPO guidelines. The second consideration is that the memory of a live computer system is constantly undergoing change as a normal part of its operation. Consequently, current techniques to capture memory are unable to obtain a 'snapshot' of memory, because it changes more quickly than it can be written to a file. Hargreaves (2009) observed that the output obtained from such attempts is more akin to a 'smear'.

Table 7.1   Methods for Isolating a Mobile Phone

Isolation Method	Benefits	Drawbacks
Switch the phone or device off	Simple, cheap, immediate.	A PIN or password may be required to access the device when it is switched back on.
Place the device in a Faraday bag such bags allow no electromagnetic signals to enter.	Simple, relatively cheap, immediate.	Only suitable to transport the device since the phone will continuously try and connect to a network when placed in such a bag thus draining the battery. Switching the phone to 'airplane mode' may avoid this but will alter data on the device.
Use of a jamming device	Stops any alteration of the device and requires no software or hardware access to the device.	Illegal in the UK and other jurisdictions and may interfere with other devices/ networks nearby.
Use of a Faraday tent – similar to a Faraday bag but a larger temporary structure.	Portable and allows room for examination.	Relatively expensive and requires time for setup. Any power cable entering the tent needs to be screened to prevent it acting as an antenna.
Use of a Faraday room – similar to Faraday tent but at a fixed location and permanent.	Provides ideal conditions for examination, since it allows for use of dedicated equipment that is either too heavy or fragile to be used in the field. Devices can be charged within the room.	Expensive, requires a lot of upfront costs and planning and not portable.
'Access card' type SIM. This is copied from the original SIM and thus has matching subscriber information, but the details required to access the network are removed.	Prevents the phone connecting to the mobile phone network.	Requires removal of the original SIM, which normally means battery removal hence the phone switches off. Requires a machine that can create such SIMs. When the access SIM is inserted, data will change on the phone.
Contact Network Service Provider (NSP) to block subscriber account.		Slow: requires NSP cooperation and may require warrants. May result in future voice mails not being saved.

Volatile data is not only found in RAM. Data stored online in what is termed the 'Cloud' can also be considered as volatile (see Chapter 10). Although it is accessible through the internet, the data itself is physically stored on a server that can be anywhere in the world. For a server located in the UK a warrant can be exercised to access a specified server in order to secure a forensic copy of the data, but for criminal investigations it is unusual for the server to be in the UK. Such a server is far more likely to be located in a jurisdiction where there is little or no means for gaining lawful access. Part of the problem is the 'chain of richness creation' problem, common to developing countries (Lovet 2009), for example money laundering can benefit a local economy, which would tend to undermine any political will to address the issue.

For civil investigations, physical access can be gained through the co-operation of the owners of the server. This could occur in the course of an investigation initiated by the owners or as part of a due diligence exercise. However, it may be impractical or unacceptable for a server to be taken offline to carry out a forensic imaging process of the internal disks. Under these circumstances software such as FTK Imager (AccessData, 2011) can be executed from a USB pen drive to create a forensic copy of selected files and/or folders. As discussed above, the second ACPO principle must be taken into account when assessing the possible unwanted effects of using this method.

PDAs and Mobile Phones at Crime Scenes

Any powered-off PDA encountered at a crime scene should be left as such. However if a PDA is found to be powered-on then consideration should be given to its battery life; it should be placed on charge as soon as possible. This is because after any loss of power or switching it off a password could be required to access it when it is switched back on again. The same is true for smartphones and mobile phones, however these have the added complexity that in order to follow ACPO's first principle, a wifi-enabled phone must be shielded from mobile phone networks and wireless networks (ACPO, 2012). Indeed, rapid isolation of PDAs, mobile phones and tablets from networks (including mobile data networks) is important for a number of reasons, not least of which is the ability of some devices to be 'remotely wiped'.

Isolation of a device can be performed in a number of ways as shown in Table 7.1.

Seizure and Packaging

In the UK the power to seize evidence after a section 18 PACE search is provided under section 19 PACE. If the forensic practitioner is not a police officer, his or her name will usually appear on the search warrant.

When handling any electronic equipment care should be taken since electrostatic charge can damage it. Grease, oil and other substances can also damage or contaminate equipment which could result in items becoming inadmissible as evidence. Therefore electronic equipment should be carefully packaged, avoiding materials such as plastic which may generate electrostatic charge (Britz, 2004; Bryant and Bryant, 2013).

Chapter 8
Digital Forensic Analysis

Ian Kennedy with Ed Day

Introduction

The definition of digital forensic analysis will vary, but it generally includes aspects of the preservation, identification, examination and interpretation of digital information, intelligence and evidence. It is normally considered a 'high level' process (Carrier, 2003, p. 1) – that is it involves deriving meaning from data rather than being simply descriptive. Such an analysis is often a stage within a digital criminal investigation which itself might be part of a wider investigation into a non-digital crime (see Chapter 6), often following the recovery of data from a crime scene (see Chapter 7). With detailed knowledge of the investigative requirements, the officer in charge of the investigation (OIC) normally provides guidance on what is sought from the forensic analysis. This guidance should obviously be as detailed as possible to correctly steer the form of the analysis to be employed. Establishing the 'five Ws and the H' (the Who? What? When? Where? Why? and How?) of a criminal investigation will be at the forefront of the OIC's concerns (see Chapter 6). Note that this chapter also includes explanations about how digital data is stored, and what sort of information is stored, mainly with respect to PCs. The level of detail provided is necessary for understanding how such features can be used in the process of digital forensic analysis.

In practice digital forensic analysis is usually performed with various dedicated software suites. Any hardware used (such as portable hard drives) tends to be either more rugged or more powerful versions of consumer hardware, or specialist hardware such as write-blockers. The processing and analysis of digital forensic evidence is typically performed on high specification PCs to cope with the large amounts of data that need to be indexed, searched or otherwise processed. Cellebrite's UFED device is often used for the analysis of mobile devices (Cellebrite is a fully-owned subsidiary of the Sun Corporation, a listed Japanese company). Guidance Software's EnCase is widely used for computer forensics cases in the UK as it allows for the automation of many of the processes, (Guidance Software Inc. is a US-based and NASDAQ listed company). Prior to the release of EnCase, law enforcement in the UK employed various tools including DOS utilities, Norton Disk Edit, Disk Image and Back-up System (DIBS), and Vogon tools (Jones, 2009).

However, many UK police forces now require dual tool verification in cases involving computers (that is, ensuring that the results obtained with one tool can be verified using another). This is in part due to problems associated with the use of EnCase, such as the proprietary nature of its code preventing independent 'white box' testing, and its frequent software updates making verification difficult and costly. (A further reason is that the police have made widespread use of EnCase, and it has been noticed that suspects are beginning to deploy a number of anti-forensics techniques). In the UK, AccessData's Forensic ToolKit (FTK) is now commonly used (the AccessData Group is a US-based company). Other commercial tools are also available, their popularity varying between countries, for example X-Ways Forensics is commonly used by German investigators. Free and open-source digital forensic software is also available such as The Sleuth Kit and Autopsy. Other tools for specific technologies have also been developed and are widely used by law enforcement, for example Digital Detective's NetAnalysis for internet forensics, and products from RTL Micro Systemation and others are also used for the examination of mobile devices (in addition to the Cellebrite tools mentioned earlier).

The location of potential digital evidence within a particular device will naturally depend in part on the type of device (see Chapter 7 above). The data of interest will depend on the investigation and may include image files, videos, document files, swap files, registry settings, event logs, print spooler files, temporary files, software and apps data, call information, address books, SMSs, location data, browser history and chat logs. Data may be easy to recover, but it may also be hidden, either deliberately or as a function of the operating system. An image file might be easily recoverable from a 'Pictures' folder, it might have been innocently deleted by a user yet still be recoverable, or a user might be deliberately hiding it via a variety of means, a simple one being renaming the file. Alternatively a suspect might have employed degaussing (exposing magnetic media to a powerful magnetic field) or used software in an attempt to erase data (Kissel et al., 2006), and it should be noted that not all software reliably removes all data. The increasing popularity of solid-state drives (SSDs) is a disadvantage for investigators in that file erasure is much quicker and certain (than for magnetic hard drives), and there is therefore much less chance of being able to recover deleted files from SSDs (Bell and Boddington, 2010). This is discussed in more detail in Chapter 10.

After it has been discovered, digital evidence must be authenticated, documented and preserved. In the UK, the first ACPO principle (see Chapter 7) should be followed: a 'copy' must be made of the original data, and it is the copy that is analysed, while the original is securely stored. The analysis of a hard drive is explained in detail below. We describe general and specific procedures that may be carried out on an entire hard drive image but the copy received by the analyst might be a subset of a drive, perhaps as small as a single file, in which case not all the procedures described here would be relevant.

Analysis of PCs

A forensically important component of a PC is likely to be its hard drive (sometimes known as a 'hard disc drive' or HDD). Digital forensic analysis of the hard drive is always undertaken at the 'logical' level and sometimes also at the 'physical' level (although the distinction between the two forensic processes is somewhat artificial). The data contents of a hard drive are physically scattered throughout the drive but are presented to the user as a logical structure, consisting of drive letters and folder and file names.

A typical initial step in a logical hard drive analysis is to identify the 'operating system' (OS), for example, the Microsoft Windows 8 OS. The OS is run by the PC and sits between application programs and the low level software and firmware on the machine. (Note that here we are using 'PC' as a general term, but it is sometimes used when referring to a personal computer running a Windows-based OS as distinct from an alternative OS). The OS controls the overall operation and resource management for the PC. There are a number of different OSs, for example Windows, Linux, Mac OS, iOS, Android and Java ME, but most PCs run one form or another of the Microsoft Windows OS (netmarketshare.com, 2011). More recently the so-called tablet PCs are becoming more popular and these predominantly run versions of Apple's iOS and Google's Android. Here we will focus on Windows as it is the OS most often encountered by investigators (as a result of its popularity), but much of what is described here also applies or is at least similar for other OSs.

A frequently overlooked aspect of a PC investigation is the internals of the PC itself. If a suspect has opened the machine in order to upgrade it, or for another reason, their fingerprints or traces of their DNA may be found on surfaces inside the case. The serial numbers of components such as the RAM may also provide evidence that the machine has been upgraded, similarly for the CPU, motherboard and any other components. If the internals are generally dusty but a particular connector is clean this might suggest that something has recently been removed. The replacement of internal components (if shown to have been performed by the user) would suggest that a user had a certain level of IT skills which might counter a defence that the user 'did not know what he was doing' (Bryant and Bryant, 2013).

The Registry

The Windows registry (to be found in Windows XP, Windows 7 and now Windows 8) is a storehouse of information, much of which can be of use to the digital forensic investigator. It is a special database that lists the computer's OS and other system configuration details and this information can be visualised using a tool called Registry Viewer. Figure 8.1 shows a screen shot (AccessData, 2011), with the installed operating system listed against 'ProductName', and the name of the 'RegisteredOwner', (redacted for privacy).

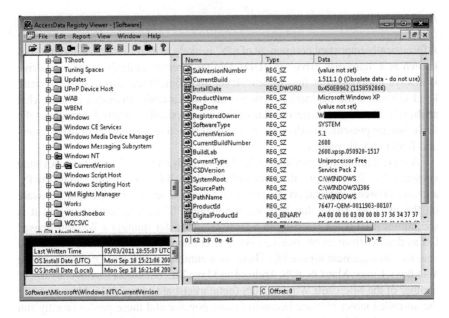

Figure 8.1   AccessData's Registry Viewer (reproduced with the permission of AccessData)

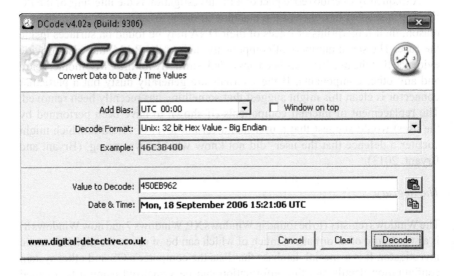

Figure 8.2   Converting Raw Data to Time-stamp Values (image reproduced with the permission of Digital Detective)

The date the operating system was installed on the computer is shown as the 'InstallDate'. In this example the date is stored as a 32-bit number, 0x450EB962, which the Registry Viewer tool helpfully translates to a date. As a means to verify this translation, the digital forensic analyst can use a second tool such as DCode (Digital Detective, 2011) to corroborate the time-stamp (see Figure 8.2). The procedure and the findings should be duly noted in contemporaneous notes.

In addition to details concerning the machine's configuration and application information, the registry also shows a list of all the users, and also the time each user most recently logged on and if a password was required (see Figure 8.3).

Other useful information in the registry includes the default number of days Internet Explorer retains internet history records for prior to deletion, the user's wallpaper settings, an historical record of USB devices that have been attached to the computer (including the assigned drive letter and serial number in many cases) and recently saved files (see Figure 8.4 below).

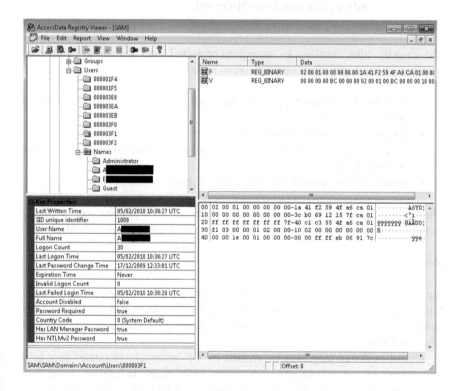

Figure 8.3 **Registry Information about Users (reproduced with the permission of AccessData)**

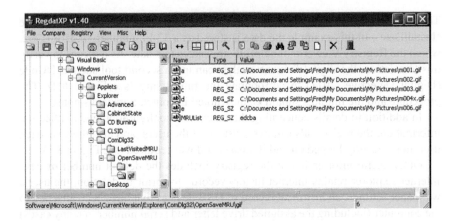

Figure 8.4   Registry Information – five files recently saved by the User (used with permission from Microsoft)

The registry also contains an encrypted/protected area known as 'Protected Storage' which stores sensitive information such as:

- data which has been typed for completing online forms (AutoComplete on Internet Explorer);
- passwords for protected websites;
- account identity information and passwords (including dial-up user accounts); and
- search criteria entered into web search engines.

The 'TypedURLs' area of the registry can also be useful it contains records of any website address that has been manually typed into the Internet Explorer address box.

Records kept by PCs

Various actions can be performed on a file from its creation through to deletion, and this information is all stored (see Figure 8.5). The Windows operating system is a comparatively diligent keeper of records, monitoring which log-on has accessed what, and when.

Useful evidence may also be created by OS automatic processes (not as a direct result of user action), and such evidence may reside in locations other than user-created folders. Windows XP and Windows 7 both allow the contents of a folder to be displayed in different ways, for example the 'thumbnail' view. This is often used for folders containing pictures, as shown in Figure 8.6.

When the thumbnail option is selected both Windows XP and Windows 7 create and save a separate and hidden file containing the small thumbnail sized

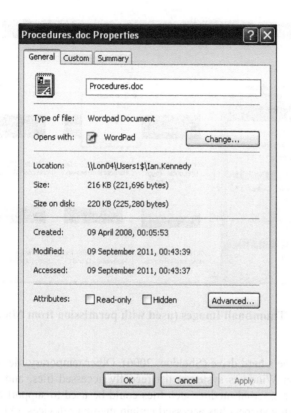

Figure 8.5 **Some of the File Information stored by Windows (used with permission from Microsoft)**

versions of each picture. This will remain on the drive even if the main image files have been deleted, and most users are unaware of this.

Another aspect of the Windows OS that allows for evidence recovery is the fact that Windows writes to what is known as a 'swap file'. The swap file is typically used when RAM memory is getting low: data that has not been recently used is 'swapped out' to the hard drive thus freeing up RAM. The swapped out data is stored in a very large file, and it may contain useful data for an investigation, such as plain text passwords or file fragments. In modern Windows OSs, this file is named Pagefile.sys and normally resides in the root of the C: drive. There may also be a file hiberfil.sys in the same location, which stores the data required for a 'hibernating' PC to resume function, and this may also contain forensically useful data (Ruff, 2008).

A number of processes on a PC create temporary files, which often remain on the hard drive after the process has completed, and these may contain forensically interesting information. This occurs for example when a user requests a file to be printed (in a process called spooling), and the temporary files may be retrievable

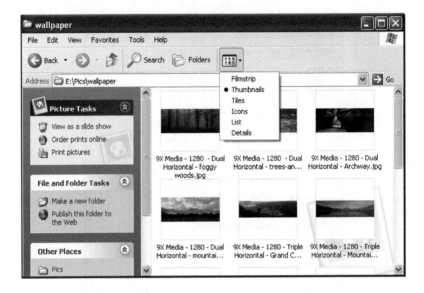

Figure 8.6   Thumbnail Images (used with permission from Microsoft)

from a machine's hard drive (Sheldon, 2006). Other temporary files that may be of interest (on Windows systems) list recently accessed files, and shortcuts to files, drives or external media. Such files could be used to support or refute the hypothesis that a suspect has accessed certain media or devices. Other processes such as the installation of software may also result in a tell-tale trail of temporary files, and again these can be used for hypothesis testing. For example if a suspect has removed a particular program that aids illegal file-sharing there may still be traces of the program on his or her machine.

Hiding of Data

Deliberate hiding of data may occur by either altering data or placing it in a location hidden in some way, or both. A suspect may alter OS-created data in order to hide the provenance or function of a file; for example an image file might be renamed by changing its file extension so it appears to be a Word document. A suspect could also change a Word document's 'metadata' (see below) to make it appear that the file was created by someone else.

During digital forensic analysis, these forms of hiding of data can be recognised by the use of known file filters (KFFs). These are available in some forensic software such as AccessData's Forensic Toolkit (FTK), mentioned earlier. KFFs are databases of known files, either benign (such as Winword.exe), or of forensic interest (such as known child sex abuse images), along with hash values that identify the files (see Chapter 7 for an explanation of hash values). The hash values are necessary since it is possible for a user to rename an illegal file as 'winword.exe.' for example. When FTK searches for illegal files it would consult its KFF when it encounters 'winword.exe' and check that the hash values match, and if they do not the file would be flagged as suspect. The KFF allows searches to be performed more quickly since benign files on the KFF can be ignored by the searching software (Davis et al., 2006). Other more recent developments for speeding up digital forensic analysis are discussed in Chapter 10.

Data can also be concealed within partitions of hard drives, by for example saving data onto the D: drive then de-allocating the partition, thus hiding it. When the user wants to retrieve the data the partition is simply reallocated. Two specific areas on a hard drive can be used for hiding data: the 'Device Configuration Overlay' and the 'Host Protected Area' that Windows cannot 'see', but specialist low-level software is needed to write data to these areas (Battula et al., 2009).

Data can also be hidden using certain file formats such as zipped containers for Office 2007, rather than the single document system found on pre-2007 versions of Office. The zipped container holds a number of folders and documents, some of which can be edited in order to conceal data (Park et al., 2009).

Metadata

Some file types, such as Microsoft Office files, also contain 'metadata'. This is data about the file (the 'author' and when the file was created) as distinct from the file's actual content. An example of file metadata is shown in Figure 8.7 (below). Note that the 'Edit time' value is recorded here as 4th January 1601 13:13. This means the total edit time for this document is zero years, three days, 13 hours and 13 minutes (starting from the epoch 1601 date). In fact Windows stores this value as the number of 100 nanosecond periods that have elapsed since 1 January 1601 00:00:00.

A file's time-stamp may allow investigators to ascertain the temporal order of certain actions in relation to a file. This can be very important when determining who was likely to have been responsible for particular actions. For example, if according to its time-stamp a file was created at a certain time then that can be checked against an event log in the registry (see above) to see who was apparently logged on to the machine at the time. This could provide information supporting the hypothesis that a particular user downloaded a particular file.

However the accuracy of any time-stamps depends on a machine's clock, which will depend on the time and the time zone set by the user, both of which may not be accurate. In addition, as for any clock the computer's clock may run fast or slow (Willassen, 2008a). It should also be noted that it is relatively easy to alter time-stamps using hex editing software.

In addition to the computer's clock, a file's time-stamp can also be affected by the file system (the methodology for storing, accessing and otherwise managing files on a partition). Most modern OSs provide support for more than one file system, but not all file systems store the same time-stamps. For example, the New Technology File System (NTFS) records the date and time the file was last accessed as well as

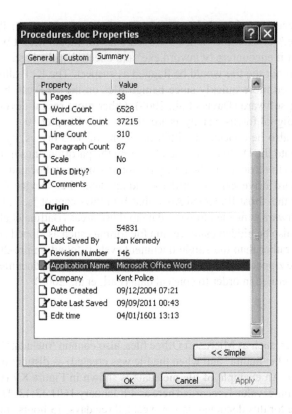

Figure 8.7   Some of the Metadata for a Word Document (used with permission from Microsoft)

the date and time any of the file's properties were changed (Access Modified), but neither of these time-stamps are supported by the FAT32 file system. Therefore it is not uncommon for time-stamps to be discarded when files are copied from a computer (using NTFS) to a USB pen drive (using FAT32). Files copied from a USB pen drive back to the hard disk in this scenario would bear a 'zero' time-stamp.

The OS can also affect time-stamps. A Windows 7 computer running NTFS, for example, will stamp a file with a created date, modified date, and last accessed date. As in the examples we show here, there can be a difference between the 'Created' date (see Figure 8.5) and the metadata 'Date Created' values (see Figure 8.7). When a file is copied to another device (such as a USB pen drive) the 'Created' date shown in Figure 8.5 will show the date the file was copied to the device. However the file's metadata is not automatically modified, and this includes the 'Date created' (as in Figure 8.7). The most likely reason for the discrepancy in this example is that the document was first created in 2004 and subsequently copied to another storage device in 2008.

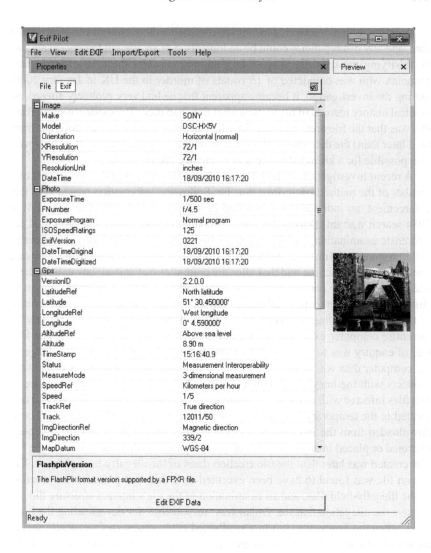

Figure 8.8   Metadata for a Photograph (reproduced with permission of Two Pilots)

Files containing digital camera or mobile phone generated pictures can also contain metadata. This can be read using a mainstream forensic tool such as EnCase, or specialist dedicated tools such as Exif Pilot which will present the information in a form more suitable for inclusion in a forensic report. Figure 8.8 shows that the camera that was used to take the digital photo is recorded as a Sony 'DSC-HXV5', and also shows the date and time the photo was taken ('DateTimeDigitized').

A digital forensic analysis can involve comparing the various levels of recorded data, and any discrepancies could be an indication of an attempt to conceal actions by falsifying the data. By way of an example, consider the case of Dr Harold Shipman who was convicted of 15 counts of murder in the UK in January 2000. During the investigation, it became apparent that he had very probably altered the medical history records of his victims after they had died. The evidence supporting this was that the file metadata date for when an entry was made was different from (and later than) the date entered by the user on the document itself. (It is, however, also possible for a knowledgeable user to change file metadata.)

A recent investigation in the UK provides an illustration of the application of a number of the methods described thus far. Following information provided to law enforcement, an individual was arrested in a dawn raid, executed under a PACE 1984 search warrant. During the search a computer was seized and submitted for a forensic examination, and this revealed that more than 5,000 indecent images of children were stored on the computer. In his defence, the suspect alleged that malware had infected his machine and that after the computer was seized, law enforcement had powered-on the computer, thereby downloading additional indecent images of children. If law enforcement had committed such an act, it would be a serious breach of the ACPO guidelines on handling digital evidence, and would have resulted in the entire computer exhibit being inadmissible in court (see Chapter 7). The first line of enquiry was to examine the computer for malware. The forensic image of the computer data was scanned for traces of malware using multiple anti-malware products with the latest virus definitions installed. This identified the presence of two files infected with malware; a Trojan and a key-logger. The key-logger file was located in the temporary internet files area of the computer, indicating it had been downloaded from the internet. No evidence was found to show this file had been executed or placed in any other area of the computer. Furthermore, the date the file was created was later than the file creation dates of the illegally-held pictures. The Trojan file was found to have been executed on a date that preceded the creation of the illegally-held files, and an examination of the file's internal structure did not support the allegation that the Trojan was 'responsible' for downloading the files. Also, when the Trojan was run in a sandboxed environment (a forensically secure means of running software and programs) no downloading activity was noted. An additional step was to restore the forensic image held to a clean hard disk and use this to boot the original computer, and monitoring the network activity of this machine demonstrated the Trojan in action, and again, no activity surrounding the alleged downloading of files was observed.

Turning to the allegation of the computer being powered-on when in police custody, examination of the computer revealed that the date the computer was recorded as last being shut down did in fact fall after the date it was seized by police. System logs kept by the Windows OS were found to be corrupted and unreadable, but manually editing the file at a low level rendered these files readable once more. Examination of the logs then revealed two entries recorded as taking place a week before law enforcement seized the computer. The first entry showed the computer's clock being set forward by one month and the other showed it being set back by one month. Both of these actions are very unusual and typically require user action, and all of the recorded illegally activity had occurred during this one month period.

This evidence did not support the claim that law enforcement personnel powered-on the computer whilst in their possession. As a direct result of work undertaken by the digital forensic analyst, the suspect was found guilty of these and related charges. He was subsequently convicted and sentenced to 12 years imprisonment. Furthermore, the allegations against the law enforcement agency were dropped and the defence expert concerned was warned against making such strong and unfounded allegations in the future.

Traces Left by Users

From a legal standpoint in the UK, it is usually not enough to find an incriminating file on a computer because this only demonstrates the guilty act (*'actus reus'*). To evidence a guilty mind (*'mens rea'*) it is usually necessary to demonstrate that a user had knowledge of an incriminating file, so the actions the user performed in relation to the file are of key importance. Chapter 4 covers *actus reus* and *mens rea* in more detail.

An appropriate place to start with this line of inquiry is the 'Recent' folder (on some versions of Windows) which shows the most recently opened files for a given user, the last 15 of which are presented to the user in the 'Recent Documents' menu shown in Figure 8.9. (The user may choose to delete the list of recent files, so it may be incomplete or empty). The records in the list are actually small files known as 'shortcuts' or 'link files'. These contain a record of when a corresponding file was opened, together with a copy of the file's own creation, modified and last accessed dates, and so can help to corroborate (or challenge) other dates stored elsewhere about a particular file.

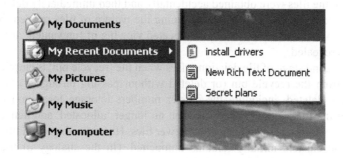

Figure 8.9   The Recent Documents Folder (used with permission from Microsoft)

Furthermore, an independent record is kept of files that are opened with a 'double-click' action (such as Microsoft Word documents). This can be used to corroborate previously identified records and help to identify any attempts to falsify dates and times, as described above. Other software may also provide useful information in this regard, for example Windows Media Player may contain a list of recently played media. Such a list could provide evidence supporting the points to prove in an indictment, for example, it could show that an individual has (a) knowledge of; and (b) has 'made' (that is, cause to be displayed) an indecent image of a child on the computer.

As well as user-based files, it is also possible to demonstrate that a user had knowledge of and executed a particular application. When a user executes an application (such as a hacking tool) Windows will create a special copy of the program called a 'pre-fetch' file, a copy of which is stored in such a way that it speeds up the loading of the program the next time it is run (in much the same way as the internet cache is used to speed up internet browsing). By reviewing the pre-fetch files it is possible to determine if, and when, an application was executed. The deletion of files by a user can also be traced owing to the way the Windows OS stores and deletes files. Windows stores a file by first dividing it into 'chunks' which are then typically written onto the hard drive in separate storage locations called 'clusters' (generally 4kB in size). A typical file will occupy several clusters, which are then said to be 'allocated'. When a file is written to a hard disk, there is no guarantee that it will physically occupy consecutive clusters. (This is a bit like a family trying to check in on a flight with seats together; they might not all be allocated adjacent seats). The locations of the clusters for each file are stored in either a File Allocation Table (FAT-based systems) or Master File Table (NTFS systems).

When a file is deleted on a PC using the Windows OS it is deleted in up to three stages. The first stage (which is optional) arises when a file is 'deleted' to the recycle bin (a special folder where the file is kept ready for 'permanent' deletion). All the dates and times together with the original location associated with the file are preserved by the OS, and a simple 'Restore' action by the user will bring the file back. Incriminating files are often found within this folder, and suspects typically claim that the files were obtained accidentally and then immediately deleted. This could be corroborated in part by examining the pattern of files opened; but such a defence would be undermined if a repeated viewing of 'unwanted' and deleted files was revealed.

The second stage of file deletion arises when the 'recycle bin' is emptied. Files deleted from the recycle bin (or deleted without passing through it) have their references deleted, including the cluster numbers (storage locations) for each chunk of the file. These clusters are then no longer 'allocated' and hence can be re-used for storing chunks from other newer files. However, the actual file content within the clusters initially remains untouched. (In the analogy of the airline passenger list, emptying the recycle bin is analogous to removing the entire family from the passenger list without removing them physically from their seats on the plane. The seats are still physically occupied, but the booking system shows the seats as empty and available for re-booking.) The digital forensic investigator can search the 'unallocated' clusters for chunks of a previously extant file and attempt to recover it. (In the analogy, this is like walking through the plane to see if the seats marked as unoccupied on the booking system really are vacant. The entire family might still be found in the seats, and could then be rebooked into the same seats or allocated to other free seats.) If a computer has not been used much since the file was deleted, the prognosis for full data recovery is generally good.

The third stage of file deletion arises when files are partially (or fully) overwritten as the computer continues to be used. The clusters containing the chunks of the 'deleted' file are at risk of being used for other files, and the remaining data may be partially or fully overwritten. (Returning to the analogy, this is akin to a new passenger being allocated to a seat listed as vacant but still occupied by a family member; the family member would have to vacate the seat. So any attempt to find the entire family in their seats would now at best produce an 'incomplete' family). Hence, the more the computer is used after a file is deleted, the worse the prognosis for data recovery – new files are created and allocated to clusters, thereby overwriting old data.

In addition if a file does not fill up a whole number of clusters there will be a residual amount of 'slack space' in the final cluster which will not have been fully overwritten. The slack space might contain remnants of a previously deleted file (Carrier, 2005) which can be recovered by using 'file carving' software which attempts to find certain characteristics patterns that can be used to distinguish different types of files. When it encounters a particular pattern in several fragments it will then attempt to rebuild the file (Pal and Memon, 2009).

Web browsers such as Internet Explorer, Chrome and Firefox can provide a number of traces of internet activity. Having identified one or more incriminating files, the digital forensic analyst can examine the internet history records on the computer to identify a timeline of browsing behaviour. The files containing the records will vary with browser, for Internet Explorer it would be an index.dat file and the 'TypedURLs' area of the registry. (The latter also contains records of sites that have been 'copied and pasted' into the browser's address bar). In addition, temporary internet files (such as graphics from a page visited by a user) are kept by the Windows OS. However, most browsers also include a privacy mode that attempts to hide a user's activity, although these have only varying degrees of success. For example Firefox private browsing does not obscure Macromedia Flash Player history, so even if a user had been browsing in private mode there may still be a record of certain Flash video related sites (Aggarwal et al., 2010, p. 6), and obviously this may be useful for an investigator. As well as website addresses visited, any keywords submitted to search engines such as Google, or data entered into online forms can also be recovered. Records of access to both local and remote files (for example, files located on a network drive or USB device) can also be recovered from internet history records.

Internet history is one of the most useful records of user activity as it can demonstrate both the likely intent (through searching) and probable action (through browsing or downloading) of the user. Each of these records is stored with the date and time against the user logged in at the time of the action. The small size of these records makes them quite resilient to being overwritten by other data. Indeed, the recovery of deleted internet history records can produce detailed user activity records going back a number of years.

Countering the 'Pop-up Defence'

A digital forensic analysis will normally be required when a suspect puts forward a 'pop-up defence'. This is the claim that the presence of incriminating material on a computer is the result of malware rather than the suspect's own actions. For example, in the UK an individual recently came to the attention of law enforcement after downloaded images of child sexual abuse imagery were found on his computer. Following a dawn raid and the seizure of the computer, a total of 2,400 illegal images were recovered and produced as evidence. The quantity of material far exceeded that required for indictments and so a representative sample was selected and the remainder of the material collated into what is termed a 'roll-up' charge. Following the initial prosecution report, a defence expert was engaged and his statement introduced doubt about the provenance of the material recovered, and suggested the material had come to be on the computer as a result of pop-ups during a normal browsing session.

The prosecution therefore needed to establish the behaviour of the suspect around the time the incriminating files were created. On examination the computer was found to be running the Windows XP operating system. The Protected Storage area of the registry was examined and 'autocomplete' data collected from web-based forms indicated that search terms associated with images of child sexual abuse had been used. Login details were also recovered for a number of password secured websites:

Item:	http://xxx.xx.xx/:StringData
Username:	<username>@talk21.com
Password:	3757121
Item:	http://yyy.yy.yyy/:StringData
Username:	<username>@talk21.com
Password:	3757121
Item:	http://www.website.com/login/login.asp:StringData
Username:	<username>@talk21.com
Password:	3757121

The 'TypedURLs' area of the registry included the website <http://xxx.xx.xx> (one of the addresses found in the protected storage area of the registry with a username and password). This indicated that access to that particular website was restricted and required the entry of a username and password or PIN number.

The internet cache was also recovered – this is an area created by a web browser (such as Internet Explorer) on the hard disk which in effect becomes a temporary storage area in which webpages (including embedded images) are stored as they are viewed. By examining the date and time the registry had been updated and then correlating it with the internet cache, it was possible to argue that the address had been manually entered moments before the page was rendered on the computer's screen. To support this further the webpage was extracted from the cache and reconstructed to show the court what would have been visible on the screen. The defence team had claimed the page was a 'pop-up', but it was in fact rendered following access through a login page.

To proceed beyond this screen, the user had to enter login credentials and press the 'LOGIN' button. Examination of the code 'underneath' this button showed that clicking the button would take the user to the URL

<http://xxxxxx-xxx.com/cgi-local/index.cgi?;165158558;1031249585>.

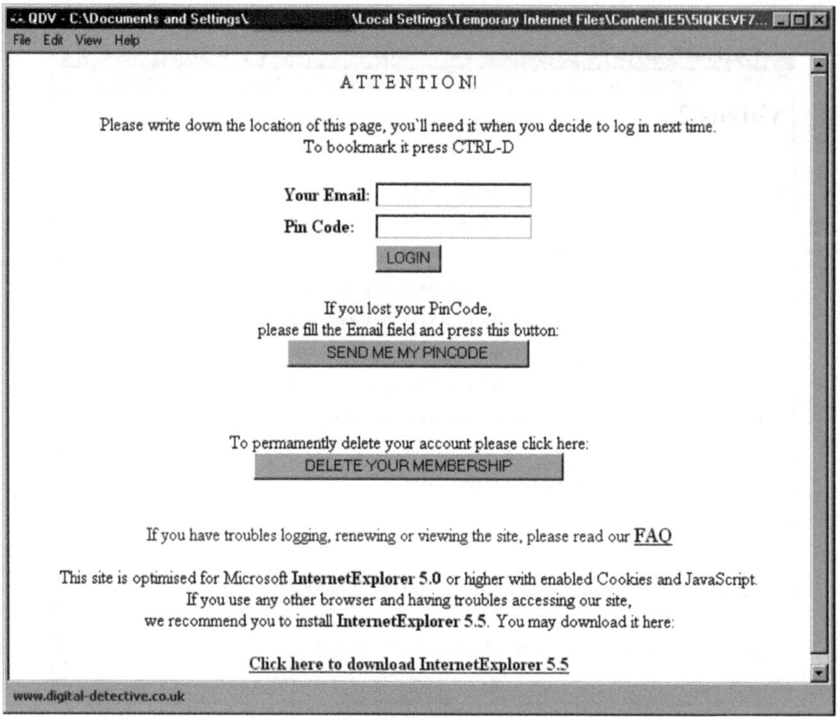

Figure 8.10 The Login Screen (image reproduced with the permission of Digital Detective)

The internet history entry immediately following the visit to the login page showed that the user was indeed taken to that URL, and the most likely explanation for this is that the user clicked the Login button. The date and time of this event (that is, when the user logged in) correlated with the date and time the form-data was recorded in the registry. There were now two independent records of when the user logged into the web-site; the manual entry of data on the login form and the subsequent accessing of the URL.

It was then possible (again using the internet cache) to reconstruct the first page the user had accessed after the login process. It contained a number of links with names associated with different sexual activities. The internet history showed that the user clicked on one of these within two seconds and was taken to a new page that contained further links to a number of video files.

The internet history also contained the following entry:

Visited: 17/09/2002 12:06:25 Tue

URL: http://xxxxx-xxx.com/cgi-local/videos2/video.cgi?raygolddance.mpeg

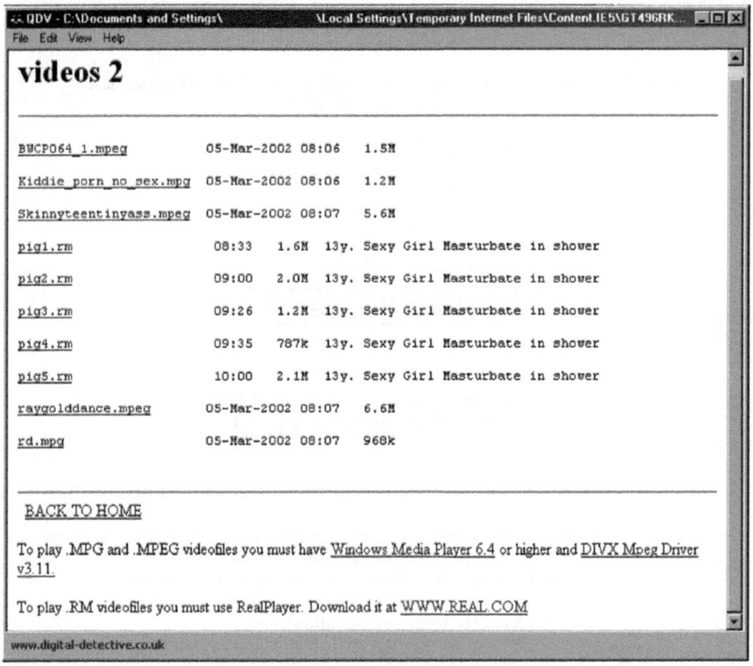

Figure 8.11   The Page with Links to Video Files (image reproduced with the permission of Digital Detective)

This showed that the user had then clicked on the raygolddance.mpg. Further examination of the internet history (in the temporary internet files location in the registry) revealed numerous episodes of browsing sessions over an extended period and that the user had visited web-sites that appeared to contain images of child abuse.

The combination of manually typed URLs, the entering of credentials and the clicking on a sequence of links to eventually view a movie file on the screen together amount to activities that do not support the hypothesis of automated pop-up downloads. Furthermore, it was pointed out in the final report from the analyst involved that there were 1,281 currently live indecent images and 1,199 located in unallocated areas, and that as the approximate size of the average picture was around 35Kb this amounted to approximately 84Mb of data in total. The computer was connected to the internet via an ISDN connection which could run at maximum speed of 64Kb per second, and could therefore download no more than about 8Kb per second. To download all of the indecent images identified on the computer from the internet would have taken over three hours. The prosecution argued that this length of time is again not indicative of pop-ups, which by their nature are bursts of short-term unsolicited activity which are subsequently dismissed by a user. In light of the analysis presented in the prosecution's response to the defence statement, the defence team withdrew their contention that the material that formed the indictment could have been produced as a result of pop-up activity. The defendant was found guilty and sentenced to a custodial term.

Analysis of USB-connected Devices

As part of a digital forensic analysis an investigator might need to test the hypothesis that a file located on a USB-connected device originated from a specific computer (or vice-versa). One of the ways of doing this would be to examine the records kept by the Windows OS relating to the USB devices that have been plugged into the computer. When a USB device is plugged in for the first time a record is made of the date and time of the event, together with two codes representing the vendor and the product name of the device. Often the device serial number is recorded as well. By examining the original device in a forensically sound manner using specialist software (such as that produced by Nirsoft (2001)), this same information can be extracted from device itself, see Figure 8.12 (below).

Windows will also record the drive letter assigned to the USB device in the registry. This will allow the digital forensic investigator to create a timeline showing the insertion of a USB-connected device and user activity relating to files located on it.

Email Forensics

As part of the analysis process a digital forensic investigator will often look for indications of communication between the suspect and other individuals (for

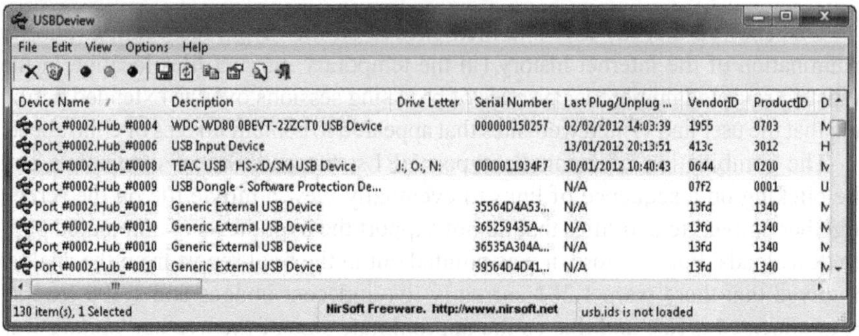

Figure 8.12   Examination of a USB Device (image reproduced with permission of NirSoft)

example other suspects, or victims). One such source of communication evidence is email. An email examination can also produce evidence to support or refute a hypothesis of when, and from whom, a file was obtained, or demonstrate that it was distributed to a third party.

Broadly speaking, email evidence exists on a computer in two forms: multiple email messages stored within a single file (also known as a 'container' file, as used by Microsoft Outlook), or in multiple files (often the case for web-based email such as Yahoo or Hotmail). Emails in container files are typically stored in a way that is similar to how files are stored on a disk, so references are used internally to identify where each individual email is stored. The forensic analyst is thus able to search not only for deleted email container files, but individually deleted emails within such files.

Email messages themselves can contain a wealth of information about their provenance. An examination of an email's underlying code (the 'header') can provide clues to both the source and route taken by the message in its delivery (see Figure 8.13).

Generally speaking, the path an email has taken can be determined by examining the list of servers identified in the email header. The most reliable of this information is located at the top, where the recipient's own email server is identified. (The further down the entry, the greater the risk that the email header has been fabricated).

One of the lines in Figure 8.13 is indicated by an arrow and shows the recorded source Internet Protocol (IP) address for the email. The IP address functions much like a telephone number, with each address being allocated to an Internet Service Provider (ISP). Publicly available databases such as CentralOps (Hexillion, 1997) can be interrogated to identify an organisation assigned to a particular IP address, and other online tools such as ip-adress.com (2004) can provide an approximate geographical location of the email source, as shown in Figure 8.14. In this example the ISP is located in Japan.

```
Received: from Svr2.global.company.com (192.168.87.37) by
 Svr1.global.company.com (192.168.87.110) with Microsoft SMTP Server
 id 14.1.289.1; Thu, 2 Feb 2012 03:39:03 +0000
Received: from service90.mimecast.com ([195.130.217.14]) by
 Svr2.global.company.com with Microsoft SMTPSVC(6.0.3790.4675);
     Thu, 2 Feb 2012 03:39:02 +0000
Received: from web100501.mail.kks.yahoo.co.jp (web100501.mail.kks.yahoo.co.jp
 [183.79.28.131]) by service90.mimecast.com; Thu, 02 Feb 2012 03:39:01 +0000
Received: (qmail 39625 invoked by uid 60001); 2 Feb 2012 03:38:59 -0000

<snip>

Received: from [219.108.113.213] by web100501.mail.kks.yahoo.co.jp via HTTP;
 Thu, 02 Feb 2012 12:38:59 JST
X-Mailer: YahooMailClassic/6.0.19_43 YahooMailWebService/0.7.289.12_42
Date: Thu, 2 Feb 2012 12:38:59 +0900
From: "Keith. T" <********@yahoo.co.jp>
Subject: RE: Busy as a bee
To: Ian Kennedy <ian.kennedy@company.com>
```

Figure 8.13   Example of an Email Header

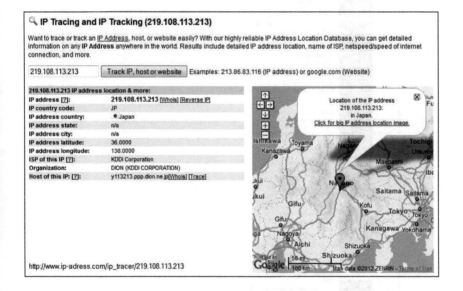

Figure 8.14   Tracking an IP address (reproduced with the permission of IP-address.com; Google and the Google logo are registered trademarks of Google Inc., used with permission)

In the UK, powers granted by the Regulation of Investigatory Powers Act 2000, permit law enforcement bodies to approach ISPs and require them to provide details of the individual business or organisation using the IP address on the date and time in question.

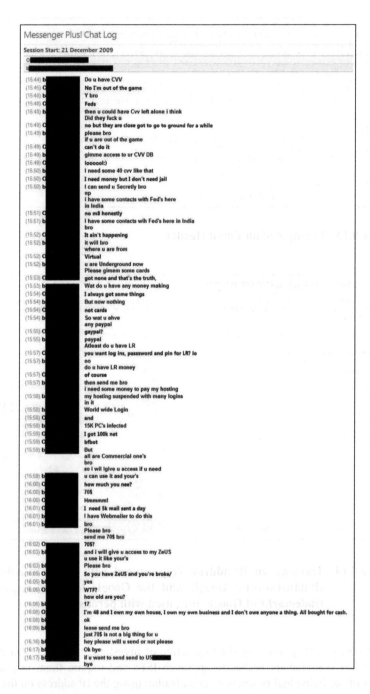

Figure 8.15   Incriminating Online Chat (used with permission from Microsoft)

Social Network Forensics

Instant messaging (IM) software such as Windows Live Messenger or the IM facility in Facebook can leave a number of forensically useful artefacts on PCs (Van Dongen, 2007), and also on mobile phones (Husain and Sridhar, 2010) and smartphones. Instant messaging allows users to conduct one-to-one conversations whereas chat allows for many-to-many conversations. Images, sound recordings, video and chat logs may all be recoverable. Many of the IM and chat programs available record the contents of each conversation between individuals by default, for example, Yahoo! Messenger for PC records conversations, unless the user has selected the option 'Do not keep a record of my conversations', (Yahoo, 2013). Typically, these records are stamped with a time and date and can support the hypothesis that one individual knew another, or even provide a confession of a crime, as in Figure 8.15.

Mobile Phone Forensics

The situation for digital forensics for mobile phones is very different from that of the PC. This is mainly due to the fast-paced changes in the mobile phone market: recent statistics suggest that in the first quarter of 2011, only three years after the first commercial Android handset was released, over 36 million Android handsets were sold (Gartner, 2011) and by September 2012 Google claimed that 500 million Android OS handsets had been activated (Barra, 2012). Mobile phones tend to have a shorter life than PCs and also have a wider variety of OSs and architectures, and it is therefore difficult for manufacturers of forensic tools to keep pace with the fast changing technology.

Another difficulty is that mobile phones cannot be imaged in the same way as PC hard drives (see above) because the data retrieval process for phones requires a two way communication with the device. This does not provide an exact copy of all data and can potentially alter data on the device, in apparent contravention of the UK's recommended practice (ACPO's first principle – see Chapter 7). The National Institute of Standards and Technology (NIST) in the US have produced guidelines on 'Cell Phone Forensics' (Special Publication 800–101) but these do not prescribe how law enforcement should actually analyse mobile devices (Jansen and Ayers, 2007, p. 1). Furthermore, due to the variety of handsets on the market, the currently available forensic software is not capable of analysing all devices, so investigators may have no choice other than to manually examine a device, and photograph or video their findings (ACPO, 2012).

A decision will need to be made concerning the level of analysis required for a suspect's mobile phone. The examination could range from the relatively simple check of phone number against billing information to support identification, to the much more complex, technically demanding and expensive removal and examination of on-board memory modules (in the UK, reference is made to Levels 1 to 4).

The degree of analysis conducted is likely to depend on the seriousness of the alleged offence.

Within a mobile phone there are a number of 'layers' that are forensically important. These are (Owen and Thomas, 2011, p. 136):

- the 'hardware layer' consisting of a processor chip (for example in the Samsung Galaxy S, the ARM Cortex-A8 CPU);
- the RAM;
- the ROM;
- antennae (such as GPS, wifi, Bluetooth) and other hardware for input and output of data;
- the Original Equipment Manufacturer ('OEM') layer, the proprietary software of the manufacturer for booting and configuration files; and
- the 'application layer' which includes internet browsers, word processing applications.

Just as with computers, phones can contain videos, images and documents, and of course they can also be used to browse the internet. Phones also have address books and call histories (Curran et al., 2010), and many have GPS capabilities which can be used to determine where they have been used. Removable SD cards are often used for data storage on phones, but the situation is complicated for investigators because the technical specifications of SD cards vary. Some can be thought of in much the same way as PC hard drives but others are more like solid-state drives and changes may occur when merely powered-on (see Chapter 10 on SSDs). Information is likely to be much harder to retrieve than on PCs due to the variety of OSs used on mobile devices, and so sometimes it might be necessary to examine mobile data at the level of hexadecimal code.

The mobile phone network for the UK follows the GSM/UMTS standard which requires phones to have a SIM card. One important piece of information stored on the SIM card is the International Mobile Subscriber Identity (IMSI) which identifies the person or corporation that has an account with the NSP (Willassen, 2003). This allows for portability of SIM between handsets (Jansen and Ayers, 2007) and handsets between SIMs, which can be useful from a forensic perspective since a number of phones can be linked to the same person or group of people, thus potentially providing evidence of associations between individuals.

When examining a phone, a decision will have to be made on what to examine first, since removal of the SIM card normally requires removing the battery. This can lead to the alteration of data on the device, and also a password or PIN number might be required for access when it is switched back on. When examining a phone, connection to a phone by cable is by far the most preferable method as it is more secure (ACPO, 2007), but wifi, Bluetooth, or infrared could also be used.

Location data is also available from mobile phones, and this may be used to determine suspects' movements and to help determine event timelines. For GPS-enabled phones, the location accuracy depends in part on how well the phone 'sees' the satellites sending signals to the phone (the phone uses these to determine its location). An alternative location method is Cell Site Analysis, which uses records about which cell phone mast the phone was connected to at a particular time (Denby et al., 2008). Such data was used in the investigation of the 1998 car bomb attack in Omagh in Northern Ireland in the UK, which resulted in 31 deaths. A series of phones were linked to the incident using cell site data (Cormack, 2010).

Emerging technologies provide other ways to track phone locations, for example phones can act as carriers and readers in Radio Frequency Identification (RFID) systems. (RFID systems allow contactless communication between devices that carry data and readers; the Oyster card system on London's public transport systems work this way). Location Based Services can use RFID technology, for example particular adverts can be sent to a phone when it is in the vicinity of a shop selling the relevant product (Denby et al., 2008), thus leaving a record of the phone's location at a particular time. Near-field communications (NFC) are very close range RFID communications for which the devices must be generally be no more than 20cm apart. It is expected that NFC technology will become widespread in mobile phones and may lead to significant increases in the use of phones as payment devices (Finkenzeller and Müller, 2010). In the future, the data relating to such 'touch payments' could be used by investigators to retrospectively track the location of a particular phone.

Many aspects of the investigation of mobile phones can be automated using commercial tools such as Paraben's device seizure, Radiotactics' XRY, Oxygen's Forensics Suite, AccessData's Mobile Phone Examiner Plus (MPE+) and Guidance Software's EnCase Neutrino/Smartphone Examiner. Some of these tools are exclusively software whereas others such as XRY include hardware, for cloning SIM cards for example.

Data may be extracted from mobile phones either logically (making a copy of a logical structure) or physically (making an identical copy of a storage area), or both. Due to the large number of phones released each year, commercial tools are inevitably limited in the make and model of mobile phones that they are able to logically or physically analyse. The ability to conduct a physical extraction in particular is often limited, but there are alternative methods available for this type of process. JTAG (Joint Action Test Group) is a direct interface to a phone's memory structure, bypassing its OS and is the most commonly used form of physical extraction. Another alternative physical extraction is via a 'chip off' procedure, which as its name suggests, involves removing chips from phones and reading them directly (Casey and Turnbull, 2011).

Chapter 9
Network Forensics

Paul Stephens

Introduction

Network forensics has been defined variously as 'the art of collecting, protecting, analyzing, and presenting network traffic to support remediation or prosecution' (Bejtlich, 2005). A rather more detailed definition was agreed by the DFRWS as '[t]he use of scientifically proven techniques to collect, fuse, identify, examine, correlate, analyze, and document digital evidence from multiple, actively processing and transmitting digital sources for the purpose of uncovering facts related to the planned intent, or measured success of unauthorized activities meant to disrupt, corrupt, and or compromise system components as well as providing information to assist in response to or recovery from these activities' (DFRWS, 2001, p. 27). Although long and detailed, the DFRWS definition does have relatively wide currency.

Network forensics might at first sight appear a specialist and arcane topic to include under the heading of 'Policing Digital Crime', but even a cursory audit of the number, ubiquity and functionality of network-connected devices in use suggests otherwise. Networks are commonly encountered in the course of a digital investigation that forms part of a wider criminal investigation, and the forensic examination and analysis of networks is increasingly important. For example, key information and potentially incriminating evidence might only be available from captured or recovered 'session data' of email traffic between two suspects. However, the volatile and transitory nature of many forms of electronic communication through these channels means that network forensics presents a number of additional challenges to digital forensic investigators, when compared with more established forms of evidence recovery such as hard disk forensics. The challenge might be further compounded by the use of data distortion techniques. For example, suspects making calls might well have employed encrypted VoIP services (such as 'Skype', which routinely employs 256 bit encryption; Skype, 2013).

In terms of the prevention of digital crime, many large organisations are aware of the dangers of an 'always on' internet connection (for example, the threats from viruses, worms, and deliberate attackers), and often employ suitably qualified systems and network administrators to manage these systems. But anyone using ADSL services at home has also unwittingly become a systems and network administrator. Domestic computers are therefore particularly vulnerable to a myriad of computer-related threats, including their use for the perpetration of crimes such as concerted DDoS attacks. Users are often unaware of the dangers, the problem is compounded by ISPs, software suppliers, and hardware vendors all frequently supplying services, applications and equipment with little or no security enabled as standard (see the discussion on the 'Market for Lemons' in Chapter 1).

Whilst the collection, protection, analysis and presentation of data is very much in keeping with the rest of digital forensics as a discipline, the 'art' of network forensics perhaps refers to the unique difficulties associated with network-based evidence. These difficulties include problems in terms of the interpretation of the captured data, and the number of sources and the total volume of network traffic data that an investigator might need to examine. Interpretation can also be difficult and time-consuming because data has been compressed and may also have been encrypted. Subtleties in the use of covert channels (a form of hidden network communication intended to avoid detection by the system administrators) could also be a factor, for example, steganography could be used, as could very slight changes in some of the fields of a packet header.

It is worth noting that Bejtlich uses the word 'support' in relation to 'remediation or prosecution' in the quotation cited above. The network data on its own may not be enough to isolate a problem or secure a prosecution, however it may assist in both endeavours (see also Potential Problems with Network Forensics Data below). It is also of note that he uses the word 'remediation' perhaps indicating that for some examiners (for example, systems administrators), the evidence collected would be sufficient simply to confirm their suspicions so that they can remedy the situation.

Sources of Evidence

The networks to be examined may be wired or wireless (for example, Bluetooth), and the equipment can include modems, switches, hubs, routers and network cards, all of which might potentially contain data that is forensically useful. There are many sources of network traffic data (Casey, 2004b and Nikkel, 2005) including:

- Log files generated by server applications such as HTTP, FTP, and SMTP;
- Intrusion Detection System (IDS) logs;
- Firewall and proxy/cache server logs;
- Network traffic capture using a tool such as a packet sniffer; and
- Host-based forensic analysis of systems, containing traces of network-based evidence including network traffic, routing and ARP tables.

The number of sources as well as the amount of data generated by each means that realistically not all data can necessarily be examined.

Careful thought has to be given to how to handle any seizure of networks equipment. If lights are illuminated on switches, hubs and routers this may indicate data traffic on the network, and a decision will have to be made whether to stop running the processes. In the case of corporate networks, any consequential impact on a business needs to be considered when disrupting data traffic. Law enforcement advice in the UK is that prior to seizure the network's apparent physical layout should be visually recorded in a diagram so it can be recreated if required. The location of wifi networks may not be immediately obvious, so the use of a wireless detector to locate them is often advised (for example, by ACPO, 2012, p. 25).

Investigations involving networks can also be complicated by the fact that peripheral devices such as printers may be shared amongst users, making identification of 'who did what' more difficult. In addition networks may be remotely accessed, so a suspect may never have had physical access to the network machines and may even reside in a different country from the network location (ACPO, 2007). Such is the case when a series of machines are networked using the internet as part of a botnet, a network of machines under the control of a third party, usually unbeknown to the owners of the machines (Rajab, Zarfoss, Monrose and Terzis, 2006). Data may be stored remotely on a server that is part of a network, or using 'the cloud' where data is stored by an online service (Hayes, 2008).

Networking Fundamentals

Although the particular understanding of networking required for an investigation will vary there are a number of fundamental concepts that underpin networking which are common. (Further information may be found in a variety of sources but a particularly clear and comprehensive account of networking fundamentals is Tanenbaum, 2003). Note that the concepts described below are not mutually exclusive (there is some overlap) nor is the list exhaustive.

- *Protocols*: these are agreed ways in which computer communication takes place. Particularly important are those that make up the TCP/IP model of network communication. These include: IP, ARP, ICMP, TCP, UDP, DNS, SMTP, HTTP, and FTP. For example, HTTP is the Hypertext Transfer Protocol, employed when accessing websites and following links. Note also that many of these protocols interlink; so for example HTTP employs TCP (the Transmission Control Protocol) during web sessions to make the request for a page on another website. The forensic aspects of each protocol are reasonably well-understood and documented– for example, HTTP requests are in plain text which makes capture of information and evidence in this case in principle relatively straightforward.
- *Layered Protocol Models*: particularly the Seven Layer ISO/OSI Reference Model. The ISO/OSI model is essentially a set of rules for communication through networks which, in principle, means that different devices are still able to communicate with each other despite their differences. The 'layers' represent the stages of communication and represent what is needed to successfully transmit and receive communication (Level 1 is the physical

level, Level 2 is the data link, Level 3 is network, Level 4 is transport, Level 5 is session, Level 6 is presentation and Level 7 is application).

- *The Transmission Control Protocol/Internet Protocol (TCP/IP) Model*: TCP/IP is the protocol stack upon which the internet is based, this means it is used by most of the world for network communication. The TCP/IP model has four layers: the link (or host-to-network) layer, used for the local network; the internet layer itself (the 'IP' part) which connects local networks together through the internet; the transport layer (the 'TCP' part) which facilitates communication between these networks and finally the application layer (for example, HTTP which specifies the web browser communication with a web server – see above).

- *The IEEE 802 LAN Standards*: with the TCP/IP model, the means by which host-to-network communication takes place is flexible, and as a consequence almost any networking technologies can utilise TCP/IP protocols. The implications for the network forensic investigator is that an understanding of a wide variety of TCP/IP-utilising means of networking such as Ethernet (IEEE 802.3) and wifi (IEEE 802.11) is necessary.

- *Network Devices*: understanding the functioning of devices in a network such as hubs, switches and routers is often necessary as the specific configuration of some forensic network tools will need to be determined. For example, a switch does not broadcast traffic to all computers plugged into it, whereas a hub does.

- *Operating Systems* (such as Microsoft Windows 7): log files used for network forensic analysis will in many cases be specific to the operating system being used. For example, the Windows operating system 'Security log' is often of interest to network forensic investigators as it might (but not always) contain information concerning log-ons, authentication, file access and similar.

- *Application Servers and Services*: a network forensic investigator often needs to know exactly how certain applications work, for example email, web hosting, and database systems. This knowledge should include the port numbers each application uses. For example, an email client employing the Simple Mail Transfer Protocol (SMTP) will employ port number 25 to transfer from client to server and client to client (Banday, 2011, p. 233).

- *Connectivity Utilities*: these are often 'command line' methods to view and test network connections. Examples include ifconfig (UNIX or Linux)/(ipconfig (Windows), ping, traceroute (UNIX or Linux)/(tracert (Windows), netstat, arp, and nslookup. For example, running ipconfig/ all on the command line in the Windows operating system will elicit potentially important information including the current hostname, physical and logical networks, and the IP address and MAC address for each network interface.

Types of Network Forensics Data and Practical Network Forensics

Many of the tools and techniques associated with network forensics are extremely powerful and could also be used by an offender to illegally gain access to sensitive information. In fact 'hackers' and 'investigators' often employ similar techniques and the same software tools. (In terms of the latter there has been some concern expressed concerning the degree of forensic validity and reliability testing conducted on the software – see Chapter 10). Many countries have data protection safeguards and 'good practice' guidelines for the use of network forensics (for example ACPO, 2012, Appendix A and IOCE/G8, 2002). In many countries an investigator carrying out network forensics activities might need to ensure that the network owner has given permission to perform an analysis, and the legal limitations and implications of carrying out such an analysis should be clarified in advance. Many companies have an 'acceptable use policy' that contains a clause stating that users should have no expectation of privacy on the company network, and companies reinforce the message periodically using methods such as pop-ups. By signing such agreements users often give express permission (in the 'small print') to the network owner to carry out network forensic investigation and analysis.

Although network forensics is sometimes associated simply with the examination of log files and the use of packet sniffers to collect data, it has been suggested that there are actually four categories of network-based evidence (Jones, Betjlich and Rose, 2006) and that an understanding of these and how they inter-relate forms the theoretical basis for network forensic analysis. The four types of evidence Jones, Betjlich and Rose (2006) define are:

- *Session Data*: a summary of the network conversations that have taken place during a particular communication session. It is often gathered routinely, and at the simplest level the information collected would include an explanation message, the protocol used, a date and time-stamp, the source IP address, the destination IP address, source port number, and destination port number.
- *Alert Data*: a subset of session data which only records events that are defined in some way as significant.
- *Full Content Data*: a record of all packets transmitted on a network, including headers and application data.
- *Statistical Data*: provides a useful overview of patterns of activity on a network, and can be derived from any of the above sources, or separately.

Jones, Betjlich and Rose (2006) also distinguish between proactive and reactive monitoring. Proactive monitoring refers to information collected before a malicious event occurs, for example a routine examination of session data, alert data, or statistical data. Reactive monitoring is set up in response to a malicious incident. If proactive monitoring led an administrator to suspect that an incident had occurred he/she may then reactively deploy full content data monitoring.

Session Data

Session data is usually captured in log files. Proxy/cache logs and Apache logs (for example, access logs in the file /var/log/apache2/access.log) are examples of session data. Although not all the detail of network activity can be ascertained from the logged data, it provides an overview record of what network conversations have taken place. The disadvantage of session data is that very large amounts of data can be generated (if it is collected in an automated fashion, which is the norm), most of which is likely to be irrelevant to an enquiry. However, the relevance sometimes only becomes known after the event (unless specific session data is being monitored for).

'Squid' (2013) is a popular HTTP proxy/cache server application that runs under Linux and UNIX systems. Squid allows the administrator to restrict the websites that can be visited (based upon IP address and/or URL) and also which ports can be used. In a standard installation of Squid the logs can be found in the /var/log/squid directory. The default or native format of the 'access.log' for example contains several fields as shown in the table (Squid Cache, 2007).

Table 9.1   Access Log Fields

Field	Description
time	The number of seconds that have elapsed since the 'UNIX Epoch' (beginning 1st January 1970). It is a common way of recording time under UNIX and Linux systems and conversion utilities are widely available.
duration	The time taken in milliseconds for the proxy/cache to process the client request.
client_address	The IP address of the client machine making a request.
result_codes	This is actually two entries separated by a slash (that is, of the form */*). The first entry is a Squid result code stating the type of request made, how it was satisfied or if it failed. The second is a HTTP status code as detailed in RFC 2616 for HTTP 1.1 (this RFC can be found on the internet). If for example the result code was TCP_HIT/200 it would mean that a copy of the requested object (for example a webpage) was in the cache (so it would not need to pass on the request to the web server) and after the slash the '200' means that the request was successful (OK).
bytes	The amount of data delivered to the client, measured in bytes.
Request method	The request method as defined in RFC 2616 for HTTP 1.1, for example a GET or READ request.
URL	The address of the server the client is attempting to access.
RFC931	By default this protocol is not turned on by a server as it detrimentally affects the performance of the proxy/cache. When it is not enabled a dash (-) is often inserted in the log, giving no information about the client making the HTTP request. If RFC931 is used it will detail the ident lookups of the requesting client.

Field	Description
hierarchy_code	This concerns how Squid deals with the request. For a TCP_HIT the hierarchy_code would be NONE. For a TCP_MISS (i.e. the object is not in the cache) the result may be DIRECT, meaning that cache would need to go 'direct' to the server to satisfy the request. The hierarchy code will also consist of the IP address or hostname of the web server accessed.
type	The object's type of content, as seen in the HTTP reply header.

One way of searching and analysing this under Linux is to use the 'grep' command to search for the suspect's IP address. A worked example is shown in the case study below.

Alert Data

An intrusion detection system (IDS) can be configured to recognise specific patterns of malicious network activity, and to inform an administrator if such activity is detected. However configuring an IDS correctly can be difficult, but is essential in order to avoid generating false positives (that is, the system incorrectly flags an 'innocent' event as an intrusion).

Further information about the use of IDSs in particular and network forensics in general is available on the Honeynet Project website (The Honeynet Project, 2013). The project was set up to attempt to learn the tools, strategies, and motivations of system crackers, and to disseminate the findings. Project members gather information by setting up 'honeynets', a network infrastructure around a server that is intended to attract hackers (the honeypot, see Chapter 6). System crackers are then tracked from the initial break-in to their subsequent unauthorised activities on the honeynet. All packets to and from the honeynet are monitored, captured and analysed. Restrictions are placed on the outgoing packets to limit the harm that a honeynet could possibly inflict if used as part of an attack (The Honeynet Project, 2004). The IDS used by The Honeynet Project is Snort, which can be used for both preventing and detecting network break-ins (Snort, 2013)

Full Content Data

This method provides a network forensic investigator with the best chance of correctly interpreting the significance of each packet within an investigation. Unencrypted communications can also be observed. The disadvantage of this method is that much data storage space is required due to the large volume of information generated, and hence there may be problems in the sheer physical collection of such data. Therefore, full content data analysis is generally only used reactively when responding to an incident or suspected incident, or if network monitoring is taking place for the purposes of troubleshooting. If needed, full content data can be collected using a packet sniffer.

One of the most popular full content data capture and analysis tools is the open source software Wireshark (available at http://www.wireshark.org/). In many jurisdictions the use of Wireshark will require the network owner's permission. There may be additional problems in relation to the ISP's policy if the intention is also to run the sniffer on a network.

Statistical Data

When full content data capture is performed for any length of time a vast amount of information is generated. Wireshark can display statistical data concerning the captured packets, and this can provide an overview of the network activities including those carried out by a particular user. For example, an organisation seeking to identify users who are participating in illegal file-sharing may look at the network usage statistics. The users of machines that are shown to have high data traffic volumes could then be added to a list of suspects. Similarly, statistical analysis of the protocols used on the network could flag up a form of communication that should not be occurring.

Potential Problems with Network Forensics Data

It is rare for network forensics to provide a single source of information or evidence to confirm or refute an investigative hypothesis (see Chapter 6). Instead, much of the data collected using network forensic methods is viewed as supplementary or supporting information or evidence. The main reason for this is the potential for obfuscation and interference by a suspect. This potential includes:

- Anonymous browsing capabilities: some suspects employ an additional 'anonymous proxy' server between the user and the servers accessed for information. The user's requests are carried out by the proxy server and passed back, so the user's activity is disguised as it appears to be coming from the proxy server. This can make it difficult to trace the suspect.
- Anonymous email services: similar to anonymous browsing; they allow the user to send emails that are difficult to trace because few, if any, records are kept by the service provider.
- Email address spoofing: altering the email header which contains the sender's information. This means that not only can the email appear to be from someone it is not, but also that the real sender is no longer identifiable (see Chapter 8).
- IP address spoofing: similar to email address spoofing; the source field of the IP packet header is changed in order to conceal the real sender's identity or to attempt to implicate another sender.
- Tunnelling: transmitting one protocol encapsulated within another so that data traffic may appear 'normal'. For example, a network using a HTTP

proxy server may allow HTTP traffic but may wish to disallow other protocols. Illegal traffic could be encapsulated within HTTP traffic to circumvent this security measure.
- DNS cache poisoning: the DNS entries of legitimate machines are replaced with the addresses of servers owned by the attacker. Users affected by the 'poisoning' are then redirected to the attacker's servers.
- 'Man-in-the-middle' attacks: an attacker intercepts messages between sender and receiver. Any unencrypted messages can be read and/or changed before the attacker then forwards them to the receiver.

In addition to these weaknesses, further problems may arise when dealing with an incident; information on the systems from which network-based evidence is collected could be compromised and the data changed or deleted. Caution must also be exercised with any tools used for data collection, because some must be run with administrative privileges (with fewer restrictions) and they may introduce vulnerabilities which could be exploited by an attacker. Further complications may arise due to the nature of the internet: there are many administrators of a plethora of networks, all of which are subject to the policies and jurisdictions of the network managers.

Case Study

As an illustration of practical network forensics consider the case of an employee of a major corporation (we'll call her JKM) who was suspected of supplying confidential commercial files and documents to a competitor via her company's network. Her employer also suspected that she was considering launching some sort of attack against the company's servers. JKM had been using a laptop to connect to the company network, which she took home at the end of each day. This lack of accessibility made a forensic analysis of the laptop for evidence of industrial espionage difficult.

The company proxy server logs were analysed for session data using Squid. The grep command (under Linux) was used to search for her IP address (192.168.1.2) as follows:

```
grep 192.168.1.2 access.log
```

This returned all the lines containing the IP address 192.168.1.2, including the line is shown below:

```
1195068000.965  1234  192.168.1.2  TCP_MISS/200  27548  GET  http://
www.2600.com/index.html - DIRECT/www.2600.com text/html
```

The line can be interpreted as follows:

- The time stamp (1195068000.965) can be converted to a real time by using the Perl script located at Squid Cache (2007) or through a website such as http://www.unixtimestamp.com/index.php. The conversion reveals the time to be 14th November 2007 at 2:20pm.
- It took 1234 milliseconds for the proxy/cache to process the request.
- The request came from IP address 192.168.1.2.
- The requested object was not in the cache (TCP_MISS) but the request was OK (allowed).
- 27548 bytes were downloaded.
- There was a HTTP GET request for http://www.2600.com/index.html (the home page of The Hacker Quarterly online magazine).
- RFC 931 was not in use (-).
- The cache retrieved the webpage (DIRECT) from www.2600.com.
- The object was a text/html document, i.e. a webpage.

It is clear that the she was probably spending a considerable amount of time transferring files, messaging others, and visiting 'hacking' websites. Full content data monitoring was set up using Wireshark (version 0.99.6a and supporting documentation). The WinPCap library was also installed when prompted and the default installation instructions were accepted. The operating system used was Windows XP.

The digital forensic analyst involved in the case tested further investigative hypotheses by:

- Launching the application by clicking on Start->All Programs->Wireshark->Wireshark.
- Clicking on Capture->Interfaces bringing up a window displaying all the network interface cards.
- Selecting the relevant Ethernet connection.

Full content data capture had been set up correctly and Figure 9.1 shows the results of taking the following actions on JKM's machine:

- Clicking on Start->Run and typing 'cmd' in the Open: text box.
- Typing ping www.bbc.co.uk in the command window
- Clicking on Capture->Stop in the Wireshark application.

A 'ping' request at the command prompt is made a total of four times, and four replies should be received (unless there is a network problem). The outcome at this stage of the analysis is a full content data capture which can now be analysed using Wireshark.

One hypothesis tested by the network forensic investigators was that JKM was transferring files to a rival organisation by using FTP. (It was indeed unusual that a proxy/cache server and direct FTP access were possible on the same network).

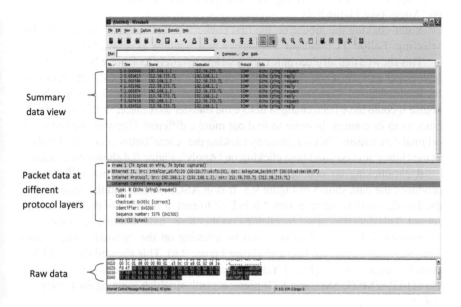

Figure 9.1 Wireshark (image reproduced under the GNU General Public License)

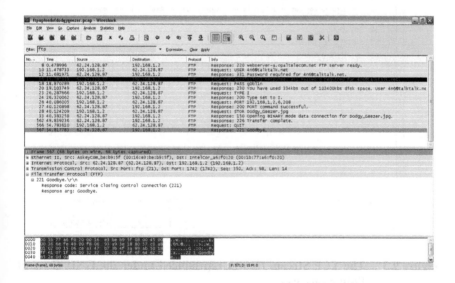

Figure 9.2 Applying a Filter for FTP (image reproduced under the GNU General Public License)

They applied a filter by entering 'ftp' in the text box labelled 'Filter' and clicking on 'Apply'(see Figure 9.2).

Right-clicking the mouse on the first packets in the 'summary data view' and selecting 'Follow TCP Stream' produced a new window as shown in Figure 9.3.

This showed that an electronic conversation definitely took place between JKM's laptop and an FTP server. The details were saved using 'Save As'. The details of the file transferred were also revealed. The file name is 'Dodgy_Geezer.jpg' but of course it could have been changed before the transfer took place, so this provides no clues as to its content. In order to find out more a different filter was applied to the original data stream. This was done by clicking the 'Clear' button, entering 'ftp-data' in the 'Filter' text box and then clicking on 'Apply'. Figure 9.4 shows the results.

Right-clicking on one of these packets and selecting 'Follow TCP Stream' produced the data shown in Figure 9.5. It is in ASCII format and the beginning of the file (the header) indicates that it is in Exif format, a variation of the JPEG image format. This data was saved by clicking on the 'Raw' radio button and 'Save As'.

Statistical data was then accessed by clicking on the 'Statistics' menu item and 'Statistics->Protocol Hierarchy' (see Figure 9.6). This showed that JKM had probably been using FTP and Yahoo Messenger during office hours, and using the HTTP, YMSG, SSL, and FTP protocols, all of which were against company policy.

Figure 9.3   The TCP Stream (image reproduced under the GNU General Public License)

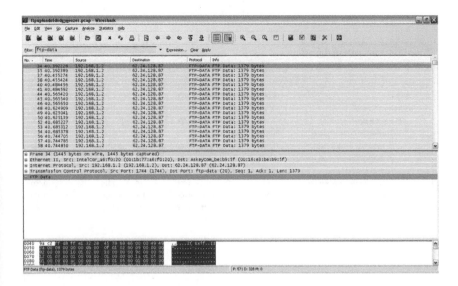

Figure 9.4   Filtering for FTP Data (image reproduced under the GNU General Public License)

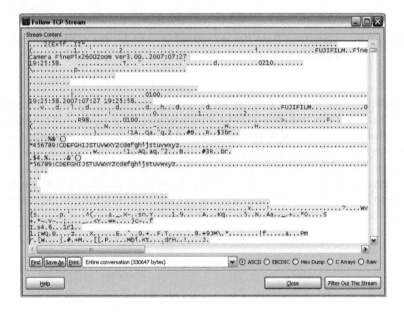

Figure 9.5   The Output Produced by Selecting 'Follow TCP Stream' (image reproduced under the GNU General Public License)

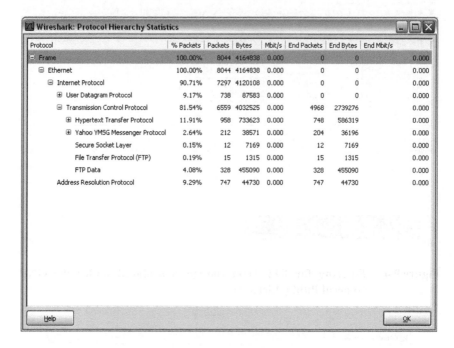

Figure 9.6   **Statistical Data (image reproduced under the GNU General Public License)**

To conclude, the network forensic investigators were able to identify messages, documents and files that should not have been leaving the company. On the balance of probabilities, it seemed likely that JKM had been passing trade secrets to a rival company and perhaps planning an attack against some of the company computer systems. However, there was no evidence that she had mounted an attack against the servers, but some of the sites she was visiting suggest that she might have done so in the future. Confronted with the evidence she resigned and the company sought legal advice concerning the breach in security.

Chapter 10

Opportunities and Challenges for the Future

Robin Bryant, Ed Day and Ian Kennedy

Introduction

In this chapter we look at some of the opportunities and challenges for the policing of digital crime in the future. This includes developments in digital criminal investigation, (digital forensics and anti-forensics) and some of the problems with the use of expert witnesses in court. The challenges and opportunities often reside in the same phenomenon, for example cloud computing offers the opportunity for distributed approaches for dealing with large amounts of data from mobile phones (see below) but also provides challenges in terms of the recovery of evidence.

Developments in Digital Forensic Investigation

Garfinkel (2010, p. 64) argues that we are now reaching the end of the 'Golden Age of Digital Forensics' as we encounter volumes and types of data that defy analysis with existing tools. It is certainly true that the processing of digital data using automated tools such as FTK or EnCase is a lengthy process. It can take hours or sometimes days to pre-process the various pieces of digital evidence for a single case, and this must be done before analysts even consider what aspects might require further examination (Cantrell et al., 2012). The explosion in the sheer quantity of digital data and the vastly increased storage capacity of devices has placed increased pressure on digital investigators. However there are various ways the workload of digital forensics labs can be mitigated: outsourcing, triage, workload management and automation (Jones and Valli, 2008).

The rise in the amount of information to be processed in a digital investigation requires a concomitant increase in processing power, which can potentially be achieved either via faster or multiple computers, or a combination of the two. The use of multiple machines working on different aspects of a task at the same time is known as 'parallel processing', and this is often performed by using distributed resources that are situated and maintained remotely (ie distributed computing, using a 'grid').

There has long been a call for distributing forensic digital processing (Richard and Roussev, 2004), but so called 'first generation' forensic tools such as EnCase and Forensic ToolKit were limited in terms of both automation of tasks and their ability to exploit parallel or distributed processing (Ayers, 2009). A 'second generation' of organisations and individuals began using such tools with increased computing power. For example AccessData in partnership with Dell claim to provide enhanced processing speeds through the use of a 'data centre' with 'high performance servers' to run FTK processing (Dell, 2009). Multiple core machines such as a Beowulf cluster (50–100 cores), and a supercomputer (4096 cores) have been used to reduce processing times (Ayers, 2009), but the disadvantage of such approaches is the need for expensive hardware.

Grid computing however provides an alternative means of providing the necessary increase in processing power. It reduces the need for new hardware by utilising existing resources such as spare desktop capacity, and provides a far more powerful (parallel) computing resource than would normally be available to an individual investigator. In essence this type of computing links a number of resources together in a grid, and enables a user to run a program using vast but distributed resources that are remotely situated and maintained. Grids allow a number of nodes to process the data in parallel with potentially substantial time benefits (Voss et al., 2009). For example the FBI uses an internal grid computing network, the 'Grid Computing Initiative' which utilises unused capacity from their users' PCs (FBI, 2010). One of the contributors to this book is currently involved in a research project to determine the viability of grid computing for mobile phone forensic investigation utilising the National e-Infrastructure Service (formerly the National Grid Service). The National e-Infrastructure Service (NES) is a computing grid which has already been successfully used for a number of research applications where massive computing power is needed, for example to model criminal behaviour of individuals within a city (Malleson et al., 2009).

Increasing the number of processors or machines to complete an investigative task reduces the time spent on each task but can be expensive, and is best used in conjunction with triaging. Digital investigation triaging is a heuristic (experience-based) method which identifies a hierarchy of importance of digital tasks. Some work has been done on formalising this process, for example Rogers et al., (2006), but they say very little about triaging other than reiterating it requires prioritisation of tasks. Nor does the model identify how best to triage between cases, an important task for efficient caseload management for digital forensic labs. Instead focus is given to triaging within a case, for example on deciding whether the analysis of chat logs is worth the time and monetary expense for that case. ADF Solutions have recently developed software that claims to triage between cases (ADF, 2010).

Many aspects of the digital forensic investigation of PCs can also be automated using commercial tools such as X-ways' WinHex, Guidance Software's Encase, and AccessData's FTK. There are also free and open source tools which perform a similar function, although more of these are available for Linux than for Windows. Ideally such tools should be forensically sound – the Computer Forensic Tool Testing (CFTT) project at the United States National Institute of Standards and Technology (NIST) carries out tests on forensic tools using a standardised methodology. The UK lags far behind in tool evaluation (Sommer, 2010) and it remains to be seen how the anticipated granting of regulatory powers for the Forensic Science Regulator will affect this situation, if at all (Adetunji, 2011).

Solid-state Drives (SSDs)

Currently most PCs use a hard disk drive (HDD) for storage of data, and in forensic terms this type of drive is reasonably well-understood and documented. Increasingly though, PCs are being fitted with solid-state drives (SSDs) instead of, or in addition to HDDs. The SSDs have a number of advantages over HDDs: they are smaller, quicker (with decreased 'latency'), quieter, more energy efficient and more robust (able to withstand sudden shocks). They are however more expensive, but as with much digital technology the price is steadily falling. From the outset netbooks were often fitted with SSDs and by default most tablets are now fitted with SSDs; for example the new Microsoft Surface Pro tablet contains a 64GB or 128GB SSD according to customer choice.

However, the increasing use of SSDs has significant implications for digital forensic investigation. Digital information is represented as binary digits as an aid to human understanding and manipulation, but the real data has to be stored in some physical manner. For example RAM consists of memory cells filled with capacitive charge, optical media such as CDs and DVDs contain lands and pits on a reflective surface, and magnetic hard drive storage involves small magnets oriented north or south (Bell and Boddington, 2010). The conceptual basis of the magnetic storage system used in HDDs has changed little since the 1950s (Hughes, 2002) and a drive's controller chip acts predictably: any processes it carries out do not generally interfere with the forensic investigation. The investigation and analysis of HDDs follows a well-established set of procedures that enable law enforcement to, amongst other things, extract data that a user had deleted. This is reasonably straightforward because HDDs merely mark deleted files as deleted, but the file content remains on the drive until the space is needed for new data (see the section on the forensic analysis of PCs in Chapter 8 for more detail).

Modern SSDs store data using Flash NAND memory chips which retain data on power-off (in contrast to RAM which requires an electric current to retain data). At the physical level the NAND within the SSDs consists of transistors (technically, 'floating gate MOSFETs', see OCZ, 2013) that are in one of two electronic conditions even when power is removed. These two conditions represent the binary states of 0 or 1 in our simplified description. At the logical level SSDs can be thought of as being divided into blocks, a typical block being about 512KB. Each block is divided into pages of about 4KB in size, and so it follows that each block contains approximately 128 pages. As data is written to the drive, it occupies a page. While each page can be read and written to, it is only possible to delete an entire block. Also, pages cannot be overwritten; they must be empty before they can be written to.

An SSD (unlike a USB pen drive, which also uses Flash NAND and is not considered here) has a controller chip that performs more complex processes than an HDD controller (Chen et al., 2009). The SSD controller runs an application known as the Flash Translation Layer (FTL) which acts as an intermediary between the operating system (OS) and the actual data storage within the blocks. To write data, an OS sends a request to the FTL via a standard hard drive interface (such as SATA) and the FTL translates this logical request and maps it to actual data on the SSD NAND chips (Bell and Boddington, 2010). The number of such writes to SSDs chips is limited, with chips failing after as few as 10,000 writes (Olson and Langlois, 2008). With modern SSDs, in order to avoid failure, a process known as wear-levelling is performed by the FTL (older SSDs behave somewhat differently). This involves directing writes to storage areas that have been written to less often (rather than to where the OS requests), thus levelling out the number of writes per storage area. The FTL 'tells' the OS that it has logically written to the correct place even though it may have physically written to a very different area from that stated by the original logical address (Bell and Boddington, 2010). If an OS deletes a file then tries to write new data to the logical location of the deleted file the SSD cannot overwrite the deleted file since it must erase data before re-writing. Therefore the FTL also performs a process known as 'Garbage Collection' which moves used data pages to other data blocks in preparation for future writes to that block. Garbage Collection occurs independently of the operating system – it is a feature of the SSD's internal firmware, and occurs even when the SSD is merely powered-on (but not otherwise busy reading or writing data).

An ATA command 'TRIM' was introduced (first available in Windows 7), that allows OSs to tell the SSD that the file is deleted thus reducing the amount of data moving required by the SSD (King and Vidas, 2011). Unfortunately (for the digital forensic investigator) when Garbage Collection occurs on a TRIM-enabled SSD, the file becomes effectively irrecoverable (unlike with HDDs where deleted files are usually recoverable). This process of permanent deletion is sometimes known as 'SSD self-corrosion' (Bell and Boddington, 2010) or 'SSD self-contamination'. This has significant forensic implications because it means that as soon as the SSD is powered-on it is possible for permanent data deletion to occur within minutes, and it is certain that the original data will be altered before an exact image can be made (even if a write-blocker is used; Sheward, 2012). This would be a serious breach of most current digital forensic guidelines (for example, ACPO, 2012). Indeed Bednar and Katos (2012, p. 6), are clear that the information and advice contained in the earlier 2010 ACPO guidelines 'cannot be used for [the] handling of SSD devices'. However, the updated 2012 ACPO guidelines do not appear to deal explicitly with SSDs (although NAND memory chips are discussed in the NPIA mobile phone Standard Operating Procedures). The only known way to avoid SSD self-contamination is by removing the controller, detaching the memory chips from the SSD and by using specialist hardware to access and read the data content (Gubanov and Afonin, 2012) – a time-consuming process and not guaranteed to succeed.

Further, as well as the garbage collection, wear-levelling and TRIM problems, the way an FTL behaves is also not necessarily consistent between devices, and its algorithms are protected proprietary data. Thus investigators are faced with FTLs that could work in a number of different ways (Bell and Boddington, 2010) which also makes the analysis of SSDs much more difficult for forensic investigators. However the outlook is not entirely bleak since magnetic drives are likely to still be encountered for many years and there are also hybrid drives: part SSD and part magnetic drive which may yet provide other forensic opportunities.

Developments in Cloud Computing

In 2012 the university sector employer of four contributors to this book (in Canterbury in south East England) decided to replace their previous email, calendar and contacts software with the new Microsoft Office 365. Instead of the webmail and other services being physically provided by the university they are now provided through the 'Microsoft Online Portal', a data server based somewhere in the European Union, probably several hundred miles from Canterbury. Much of the services and data are now accessed from 'the Cloud'. Many other organisations, particularly small and medium sized businesses, are also migrating to cloud computing due to the obvious economic benefits and flexibility it provides, compared with traditional in-house IT infrastructure and services. Individuals too are increasingly using cloud computing, in many cases with no great knowledge of doing so (or the need to know). For example a user of an iPad with the iOS6 OS has the option of turning on 'iCloud'; 'Gmail' is a popular cloud-based form of email; Google Apps is a convenient way of cloud-sharing documents with others; many users of android-based smartphones employ 'Dropbox' for online storage; and Microsoft offer free online cloud storage with their 'SkyDrive' service. These services have developed in part because of the greater availability and speed of broadband services and the advent of Web 2.0.

Traditionally a user's own machine (for example, the PC on their desk) would store data and run software applications, and for the work-place a machine or server centrally located within the organisation could alternatively be used. But now the data and services can be located elsewhere and accessed through the internet, and through a variety of devices (PC, tablet, smartphone). The metaphor is a 'Cloud' floating somewhere above the user, somewhat ephemeral and delocalised, and not within the control of those on the 'ground'.

Vaquero et al. and others have proposed a more formal definition of a cloud computing service (a CCS) as: "[...] a large pool of easily usable and accessible virtualized resources (such as hardware, development platforms and/or services)'. An even more detailed definition is offered by Grance and Mell (2009): 'Cloud computing is a model for enabling convenient, on-demand network access to a shared pool of configurable computing resources (for example, networks, servers, storage, applications, and services) that can be rapidly provisioned and released with minimal management effort or service provider interaction'. There is a general distinction between a 'public' cloud computing (the internet used for data transfer) and 'private' cloud computing (where an organisation's intranet is employed). Sometimes however the two are linked, with private clouds off-loading some tasks and data to a public cloud. Within the field of the policing of digital crime, more attention is currently directed at public cloud computing services as these provide a greater challenge to law enforcement.

Svantesson and Clarke, (2010) outline five characteristics of a CCS:

- the CCS is delivered over a telecommunications network;
- users of the CCS rely on it for access to and/or processing of data;
- the data is under the legal control of the user of the CCS;
- the CCS is 'virtualised', so the user is unaware of which server is running or which host is delivering the service, or where the host is located; and
- the CCS is delivered through a relatively flexible contractual arrangement in terms of the volume of data the CCS stores for a client.

A CCS can operate in three main ways, and supply different types of services as shown in Table 10.1, although it should be noted that these can be combined with a single provider (Taylor et al., 2010, p. 304).

Table 10.1   The Three Main types of Cloud Computing Service

CCS	Description	Example
Platform as a Service (PaaS) Infrastructure as a Service (IaaS)	CCS provides the operating system, applications, data storage etc. for the end user through the internet	Oracle Cloud
Software as a Service (SaaS)	Software applications are run on CCS provider's system, accessed by the end user through the internet	Google Apps

Security of data is an issue for all providers of cloud computing services, and by implication, for their clients. As noted elsewhere in this book, personal data is a valuable commodity and is likely to be a subject of interest for many people intent on its criminal exploitation. The attempted malicious hacking of cloud services is almost certainly a regular occurrence. Some CCSs are also hosted in countries where privacy laws are inadequate, and security is perhaps less of a priority. There is also some indication that the Cloud is already being utilised by those with criminal intentions, for example allegations include the use of cloud computing services to 'run command and control services for botnets, to launch spam campaigns and to host phishing websites' (Wolpe, 2010 citing Rik Ferguson, Trend Micro). For investigators, indications that a CSS has been used can often be found on a digital device, for example, Dropbox leaves traces in the Windows operating system (McClain, 2011).

There are a number of forensic opportunities for the investigator in cases where it seems likely that potential evidence is located in the Cloud. For example a CCS could be automatically recording storage usage, number of logins, data displayed and accessed, and perhaps most importantly the IP addresses of users together with dates and times of access, with some of this information being retained for significant periods (Taylor et al., 2010, p. 305). However, it is probably correct to argue in terms of the forensic capture and analysis of digital data, that the current investigator mind-set is still 'off line', and the guidelines provided in many good practice manuals for example seem to implicitly assume that the investigator has control of the storage medium. Part of the problem is that evidence 'is more ethereal and dynamic in the cloud environment with non-or semi-permanent data' (Taylor et al., 2010, p. 304). Some of the information which is normally written to the operating system (for example date stamps) will instead be written to the cloud with the attendant difficulties in recovery. The legal basis for the seizure of equipment is also somewhat more uncertain (Mason and George, 2011). Data is also moved around in the Cloud from server to server and this might pose difficulties in terms of a digital investigator tracking the data down, and there will then be the added problem of gaining the legal authority to require the Cloud supplier to provide the data. Finally, there are likely to be increased difficulties with the audit trail the Cloud is likely to provide (continuity logs in particular) when compared with, say, hard drive forensics.

However, cloud computing provides a number of opportunities for the policing of digital crime. For example, a distributed cluster of PCs on the cloud can provide the power to break a password used for encryption. Cloud computing also provides new forensic opportunities because even if the data is securely erased at one location there might still be a copy at another. The Cloud also provides the facility to enable an organisation to back up and utilise data whilst digital evidence is being collected in situ.

Policing the Deep Web

Most users interface with the internet through search engines such as Google. To 'find something' on the web a person will simply type a description into the conveniently provided Google search box which will generally produce an impressive number of 'hits'. The user will then explore the so-called 'visible' web, often jumping from one website to the next. Occasionally a bookmark will be used to access a website or the website address will be typed in for direct navigation to the site. Many people will also be familiar with other visible parts of the internet, for example portals to SNSs such as Facebook or Hyves, or through apps such as Apple 'Maps'. However, beneath this readily accessible surface there is a less visible region of the internet that is more difficult to access; the 'deep web' (sometimes known as the 'hidden web' or 'invisible web'). Most users will be aware that access to some parts of the internet is controlled in some way, through gatekeeping such as the use of usernames and passwords, and that they may have to manually enter the web address of the site to access resources. These include web-based email services to special interest forums, commercial services (such as the 'Sky Go' portal for subscribers to view subscription satellite broadcasts online), and databases of academic journals available to students and others.

The deep web is undoubtedly very much larger (in terms of volume of data) than the visible web. In 2001 Michael Bergman (widely acknowledged as the originator of the term deep web and citing a 'Bright Planet' survey (Bergman, 2001)) estimated that deep web contained some 7,500 terabytes of information and 550 billion individual documents, compared to 19 terabytes of information and one billion documents in the visible web. Most of the deep web consists of entirely legitimate content and is not connected with criminal activity. It is also utilised by people, such as political dissidents within repressive regimes, who need to keep their identities secret for reasons of personal safety: indeed this was one of the original intentions when the 'Freenet' part of deep web was first developed.

However, the deep web is inevitably also used for illegal activities and these criminally-oriented 'sub nets' are sometimes collectively known as the 'dark web' or the 'dark net' (note however that there is much variation in the meanings of 'deep web', 'dark web', 'dark net' and similar terms). Examples of dark web activities include invite-only and password-protected chatrooms and forums used by cyber-criminals for sharing information or trading. Some attempt will generally have been made to conceal the existence of the forums, for example by using obscure naming systems, and casual users of the internet will not generally access the criminally oriented parts of deep web or indeed even be aware of its existence. Deeper still are the parts of the deep web which can only be accessed using specialist software such as 'I2P' or 'Tor' (the latter also is available as a plugin for some internet web browsers). The open source software available to access the deep web varies, but most of it can supposedly conceal the identity (IP address) of a user, for example by using random pathways to communicate between parts of the network, and encryption. (The anonymity provided by Tor is also sometimes employed as a tool by investigators to conceal their surveillance of suspects.)

Furthermore, a suspect using the dark website 'The Armoury' (which purports to specialise in the supply of firearms and other weapons) might not only employ the in-built anonymity provided by Tor and similar software, but also conduct business through 'stealth listings' of weapons which are not visible unless the specific URL is known. The transaction is also conducted using a number of 'tumbler boxes' which further complicate attempts to trace and demonstrate payment.

As with the visible surface web, internet services such as forums, data warehouses and wikis are all available within the dark web. These hidden parts are not simply stored as single items on a particular server but instead are distributed through networks. Lurid claims are made for the supposed availability of nefarious services and items on the dark web including hyperbole surrounding child abuse imagery, the supply of illegal drugs and firearms and even offers to conduct murder (for example see the popular British newspaper the 'Daily Mirror' (2012)). Claims are also sometimes made for the terrorist use of the deep web. However, the very nature of deep web (for example the need for particular software and the anonymity) might make it less attractive to those seeking to profit from crime. For example, organised criminal groups attempting to make money from the supply of child sexual abuse imagery need to market their services, and this is much more easily conducted on the surface web. Similarly, radical groups attempting to recruit new members from disaffected communities are likely to wish to display their message in locations which will be seen by potential recruits.

However, although claims of serious criminal activity within the deep web are usually unsubstantiated there is nonetheless clear evidence for the availability of a number of illegal products and services, and there are certainly also forums for sharing information on how to perpetrate illegal activities. For example, the dark web 'Silk Road' website claims to offer illegal drugs by mail order. In 2012 it was offering for sale prescription anti-depressants and opiates, steroids and illegal street drugs including marijuana, ecstasy, heroin and cocaine, together with 'date rape' drugs such as GHB. There are a number of indications that the Silk Road illegal offer is 'for real' and not an elaborate scam, for example, a man from Melbourne was arrested in 2012 for importing narcotics he had allegedly sourced from the Silk Road (AFP, 2012). The Silk Road uses a form of 'anonymised' currency called 'bitcoins' (often referred to as 'BTCs'). Potential purchasers first exchange traditional forms of money (for example, using a debit card and an online trading site such as Mt. Gox) for bitcoins, and these are then used for transactions and trading. In mid-2012 it was estimated that approximately 1.9 million US dollars was being generated through the Silk Road site (Christin, 2012, p. 3). The site is currently the subject of attention from the LEAs around the world, including the US Drug Enforcement Agency.

The investigation of both the deep web and the dark web can inevitably pose problems for investigators given its closed and particularly in the case of the dark web, often bogus nature. In terms of the 'legitimate' parts of deep web, a number of search tools are being developed including some from Google. Although these will not necessarily allow access to password-controlled resources they will at least reveal the existence of some of these resources.

Proactive investigations of the dark web will often employ software such as Tor (see above), and could include investigators posing as a customer for an illegal service or establishing a connection with individuals or organisations involved in the sharing of illegal imagery. Reactive investigations in the dark web (for example, attempting to collect intelligence against an identified suspect) are perhaps more problematic, but use of the dark web does not guarantee anonymity for a suspect, largely because of the naivety of most users of Tor and other similar software. An indication that Tor had been used to access dark web would be an SSL request to the user's ISP to become the first Tor node in the communication pathway, together with the use of encryption. However, if users employ Tor through a web browser they might still have cookies enabled, and may also be running javascript, both of which will assist a digital forensic investigator in testing hypotheses in terms of a suspect accessing illegal material.

Anti-forensics

The term 'anti-forensics' is used to describe a range of methods, techniques and actions that are intended to thwart the efficacy of a forensic examination of a digital artefact. At the outset, it should be noted that 'anti-forensic' methods are often also employed by individuals for what we would regard as entirely legitimate and non-criminal reasons – for example, for reasons of privacy, to protect themselves against the actions of oppressive regimes or simply on grounds of principle and ideology. The use of anti-forensic tools by an individual should not necessarily be seen as a 'smoking gun' that indicates guilt. That said, organised crime groups in particular are likely to be fully cognisant of the advantages of adopting an 'anti-forensic' mind-set.

We can identify five main categories of anti-forensics activities and these are described in Table 10.2. Note that the categories are not mutually exclusive.

Table 10.2   Five Categories of Anti-forensic Activities

Category	Explanation	Example
Source elimination	Use of methods to attempt to stop any evidence accruing, particular at source	Using an 'incognito' window with the Firefox browser. Using Trojan commands
Destruction	Attempting to completely erase data.	Using software that employs algorithms to repeatedly overwrite data. Physically destroying the medium that held the data.
Obfuscation	Covering tracks, changing file attributes to confuse time of origination etc.	Use of 'log cleaners' Spoofing IP addresses The 'Zeus Botnet Crime-ware toolkit'
Hiding	Altering data in such a way that it is not visible or not 'readable'	Steganography. Encrypting files. Hiding data in Windows 'slack space'
Counterfeiting	Attempting to present one form of data as another innocuous form	Changing a file extension on an image file (for example, .gif) to another extension that is less 'suspicious' (for example, .xls)

(Derived in part from Harris (2006) and Rogers (2005) but authors' interpretation and description).

Cryptography, the science of encryption, is an important part of anti-forensics, and presents particular challenges to the investigation of digital crime. It involves changing data into a form which is unreadable (encrypted) and has been used for thousands of years, often as a means of retaining the confidentiality of information, particularly important in times of war. A well-known example was the Enigma code used by the German military in World War 2 and its decryption at Bletchley Part in the UK by a group of workers that included Alan Turing. Encryption can be used for text and data, not just for data representing text, and also includes data conveyed over a communication network such as the internet. All data, including images, videos and audio files (if not already in in numerical form) can be converted into a digital format.

Modern forms of encryption use a mathematical set of instructions (an algorithm) and a 'key', or set of keys. The encrypted data can be converted back to its original intelligible form, using the algorithm and a key, but not usually the same key as was originally used to perform the encryption. The lengthy and complex processing work of encryption is performed by software, much of which is easily available via the internet. Examples include, PGP ('Pretty Good Privacy') and its derivatives (such as GNU Privacy Guard), and other software such as TrueCrypt and AxCrypt. A number of popular applications, such as the Microsoft Office suite also provide encryption as an option for the user. Encryption can be used for a complete hard drive, for individual files, or for network traffic. (Many readers will be familiar with the existence of the latter when using secure online payment methods).

The algorithms used for encryption are derived from theorems that originated in number theory (a branch of pure mathematics), and particularly 'trap door' mathematics which provides algorithms that in practice will only work in one direction. This makes modern forms of encryption very powerful, and almost impossible to 'crack' if correctly implemented.

A commonly used form of encryption uses public and private keys, and in this context a key is a number or several numbers. A 'public key' is potentially accessible to anyone and a 'private key' is kept secret by an individual. A public key is shared with others who may then use it to encrypt messages. The encrypted messages can be decrypted by the recipients, each using his or her private key. To illustrate both the process, and just how difficult encryption can be to crack we will take a simple example (adapted from Bryant and Bryant, 2008, pp. 100–101) in which Brian wants to encrypt the message 1234 and send it to Anneka using the RSA method of encryption (in practice the encryption is done automatically using software).

Anneka first chooses two prime numbers such as 26,863 and 102,001 (a prime number is any number that is not divisible by any whole number other than one and itself). Next she multiplies these two prime numbers together: $26{,}863 \times 102{,}001 = 2{,}740{,}052{,}863$. She then reduces each of the chosen prime numbers by exactly one, and multiplies the answers: $26{,}862 \times 102{,}000 = 2{,}739{,}924{,}000$. Next she needs to find two other numbers that must have a particular mathematical connection with the second result (that is, with 2,739,924,000). These two numbers (a) and (b) have to be chosen so that:

- number (a) shares no common divisor (other than one) with the number 2,739,924,000;
- number (b) shares no common divisor (other than one) with 2,739,924,000; but also when multiplied by the number (a) and then divided by 2,739,924,000 leaves a remainder of exactly one.

Using the mathematical process 'Euclid's Extended Algorithm', Anneka finds two numbers that satisfy the criteria, namely (a) = 103, and (b) = 1,143,851,767.

(To check this, calculate $103 \times 1,143,851,767 = 117,816,732,001$. Then check that 2,739,924,000 divides into this (43 times) leaving a remainder of exactly 1).

The numbers 103 and 2,740,052,863 are Anneka's public key. (It would in fact be more appropriate to describe this as Anneka's public lock, but the term 'public key' is the one normally used). To help the explanation we will designate 103 as the first part of her public key and 2,740,052,863 as the second part of her public key. The number 1,143,851,767 ((b) from above) is Anneka's private key, and she keeps this to herself. She sends both parts of her public key to Brian.

Brian now sets about encrypting his plaintext message 1234, to be sent to Anneka. First he raises 1234 to the power of the first part of Anneka's public key, 103 (that is 1234^{103}; a very large number), and then divides this result by the second part of her public key, (2,740,052,863) and notes the remainder. The remainder is the encrypted message. In this case the remainder is 1,063,268,443 and hence the encrypted version of 1234 that Brian sends to Anneka is 1,063,268,443. Note that Brian has not used any information that has been kept secret – he has only used Anneka's public key.

Anneka now takes Brian's encrypted message and raises it to the power of her private key, (1,143,851,767), and then divides by the second part of her public key (2,740,052,863). Without the private key this part of the decryption process is impossible to achieve by 'trial and error'. The remainder in this case is exactly 1234; Anneka has successfully decrypted Brian's message.

This form of encryption is certainly difficult to decipher, but there are other advantages; by not using a secret key in the transmission process the danger of compromising the security of the message is practically eliminated. Public key systems can also be used to communicate securely with groups of people. All of this has obvious advantages to those who wish to share data securely, and inevitably this will include those with criminal intent, such as individuals sharing child abuse imagery. Over the past 20 years or so there have been frequent examples of offenders (including terrorist suspects), employing encryption as an anti-forensics method. For example, in 1995 members of the Aum Shinri Kyo sect released Sarin gas on the Tokyo underground, killing 12 people and injuring thousands more. Members of the cult had used RSA encryption (see above) on computer files in an attempt to hide their plans to deploy weapons of mass destruction.

The existence of an encrypted artefact will be reasonably clear to the investigator: for example, an encrypted word file will appear as a 'nonsense' string of letters and symbols when viewed with forensic software, and will not contain intelligible text (although the file might contain readable information concerning the software used for encryption). Encryption poses significant problems for digital criminal investigations (Reyes et al., 2007), as without the password a robustly encrypted digital artefact is near-impossible to 'crack'. For this reason it is best to capture information using live forensics when possible, perhaps using covert means (for example, surveillance), using surreptitious installation of key-logging software through a back door method, physical key-loggers, electromagnetic capture of emanations from a suspect's PC and similar methods (but see the discussion in Chapter 4 on the legal considerations in the UK surrounding covert methods). We provide an overview in Chapters 3 and 6 of some methods open to the investigator (within the law) to secure passwords.

Expert Evidence

The expert's opinion, findings and associated methodologies in a range of specialist fields are now subject to an increasing level of scrutiny. We have perhaps moved on from Garfinkle's (2010), 'Golden Age' of digital forensics (the period from 1999 to 2007) with the implicit trust in the digital investigator as expert. This change has been mirrored elsewhere in the world, with Beckett and Slay observing (2011, p. 214) that 'National bodies in the United States and elsewhere are beginning to call into question the validity of science and forensics in general, with a call for reform across all disciplines'. The absence of scientific principles in several forensic disciplines is well documented (Beckett and Slay, 2007; Sean Peisert et al., 2008; Saks and Faigman, 2008; Haack, 2009; Sommer, 2010). Following the bad press that exposed the weaknesses of expert evidence within the CJS (BBC, 2003 and BBC, 2005), a review of science as applied to expert evidence is now underway. This is in part due to recent problems with expert evidence, for example high profile miscarriages of justice with flawed expert evidence (Law Commission, 2011). The Solicitors Journal (2011) cites the Law Commissioner, Professor David Ormerod as saying that judges are 'in the unsatisfactory position of having no real test to gauge the unreliability of expert evidence'. In the case of *R v Clark* [1999], Professor Sir Roy Meadow made claims regarding infant cot death which had 'no statistical basis' (Royal Statistical Society, 2001). As a paediatrician (not a statistician), Meadow was testifying outside of his area of expertise, and this occurred in other cases too (*R v Cannings* [2002] and *R v Patel* [2003]). All these convictions were quashed on appeal, and the Law Commission subsequently reviewed the admissibility of expert evidence for use in criminal trials (Law Commission, 2011). Their report calls for a move to incorporate a test of the level of reliability of the opinion of an expert witness to ensure that the evidence is based on sound scientific principles, techniques and assumptions.

Requiring greater levels of scientific rigour as the basis for expert evidence derived from a forensic science presents a number of challenges, not least of which is that the term 'forensic science' is itself a misnomer. It is claimed that forensic science lacks the scientific principles that underpin more traditional scientific disciplines (Kennedy, 2003). With little formal research and no research agenda, there is a correlation between 'dubious forensic science and wrongful convictions' (Cooley, 2004). The absence of a body of knowledge, established through accepted scientific methodologies has led to criticism of practitioners, and suggestions that they are rhetorical in their application of substance or methodology (Saks and Faigman, 2008). Saks and Faigman go on to state that scientific principles such as rigorous empirical testing, inductive methodologies and reporting of error rates are all absent from many of the 'non-science forensic science' disciplines.

Without this scientific pedigree, many of the specialties within forensic science face the risk of being labelled as 'junk science' in court (Huber, 1993). Epstein (2009) cites fingerprints, handwriting and firearms as three examples of such science, and goes on to suggest that evidence from such sources should be excluded from trials. Other examples of problematic forensic science include voice identification, footprints, ear-prints, bite marks, tool marks, blood spatter and hair comparison (Edmond, Biber, Kemp and Porter, 2009). Broadly speaking, all of these specialties concern themselves with applying individualisation to link an artefact to a suspect. Disciplines such as computer forensics and malware forensics likewise utilise the automated record-keeping nature of computer software and operating systems to apply provenance to identified artefacts.

It is not uncommon to discover malware in the course of any forensic computer investigation, and suspects frequently offer the 'Trojan Defence', arguing that the contentious actions were performed as a result of some form of malware (or cyber-criminal) having gained control of his or her computer (see Chapter 8). Both civil and criminal forensic practitioners of course have a duty to consider such a defence (in the UK this would be under the Civil Procedure Rules (Ministry of Justice, 2010) and the Criminal Procedure Rules (Ministry of Justice, 2011)). Forensic practitioners are reliant on their tools, skills and knowledge of malware to detect, identify and study the behaviour of any identified malware, and they need to form an opinion on the impact any identified malware has had. But the lack of a scientific footing for malware forensics has a greater impact for the discipline than it does for computer forensics. The availability of both undergraduate and post-graduate qualifications in computer forensics provides an opportunity for practitioners to engage with their discipline on an academic and scientific footing, but although included as modules on some courses, there are no such equivalent academic qualifications specifically dedicated to malware forensics. Malware is designed to obfuscate its true intentions and hinder attempts to analyse it, and there is therefore already a level of uncertainty associated with any conclusions drawn from malware analysis, and this can be used in a case to raise 'reasonable doubt' about the true nature and intentions of a particular piece of malware. The complexity of the subject matter and the specialist skills required to study it (e.g.

reverse engineering and assembly language) may also make the specialty less accessible to practitioners.

Lawyers seeking to undermine evidence produced from malware analysis currently have a rich choice of methods of attack for introducing reasonable doubt. Even one of the most fundamental requirements of digital evidence, the ability to verify and hence corroborate the findings of the expert, is open to challenge. An established tenet of science is that hypotheses are supported by reproducible experiments (Beckett, 2010) and that hypotheses are tested through falsification, or refutability (Popper, 1968). Although there are some examples of the use of falsifiability in forensic hypothesis testing (see Willassen, 2008b, in the case of the investigation of digital time-stamps) these are few and far between.

Practitioners intending to present digital evidence must expect to be required to defend their findings, and disclose enough detail to enable an opposing expert to verify and possibly provide an alternative explanation for an artefact. 'Dual-tool validation' is often promoted as a tenet of a scientific approach to forensic computing, and hence good practice (for example, SWGDE, 2004) and is explained in Chapter 8 – in essence it means using one forensic software tool to check the results achieved by another. But there are problems with this, for example one forensic provider states 'Dual-tool verification can confirm result integrity during analysis' (Forensic Control, 2011), a bold claim, but open to challenge if a third tool or manual inspection of the raw data identify a discrepancy. Another provider makes the less radical claim that the forensic software products EnCase and FTK 'allow for a dual-tool approach for the verification of findings' (Cy4or, 2009). However, as in the previous example, no scientific studies or supporting evidence are cited. A third example is a freelance forensic investigator who states on his website (in relation to tool validation), that 'I don't validate my tools – I validate my results. Generally I do this with dual tool verification' (Drinkwater, 2009). This statement is contradictory, as a second tool is used to check the results of another.

Dual-tool 'verification' thus falls short of the standard scientific criterion for of verification: that of the need of falsification as the test of hypotheses. Put simply, both software tools could arrive at the same wrong conclusion either because both are using the same erroneous method or by coincidence. Arriving at the same result is not a scientific 'proof' is that the outcome is true. Although it is accepted that there are no documented examples of two tools making the same error (Beckett and Slay, 2007), this nonetheless could arise, for example, by the use of the same underlying Windows API call, and in such circumstances both tools are making the same erroneous assumption (Sommer, 2010). Errors from an API can arise due to vulnerabilities in the design (similar to those utilised by malware) or simply because a given API function was not written with a forensic application in mind. The scientific approach is not to repeatedly look for confirmation of the hypothesis but instead to formulate ways in which it can be falsified and test for this.

Although dual-tool verification cannot scientifically 'confirm' a result, it can provide corroboration, if only at the level of probability rather than certainty. However, the main benefit in applying a dual-tool approach arises where there is a discrepancy in results (Turner, 2008), thereby highlighting the need for closer analysis. An example of this was during the trial of Casey Anthony who was charged with the murder of Caylee Marie Anthony in Orlando, Florida. During this trial a discrepancy was identified between two internet history tools used to produce expert testimony. As a result of this discovery, the developer of one of the tools corroborated the tool's output by reverting to the underlying raw data and interpreting the data manually (Wilson, 2011). Ideally, an independent party unaware of the expected outcome should have undertaken this step.

The acceptance of a tool or methodology sanctioned by others is common practice in both legal and scientific circles. In judicial processes, legal precedent can be cited from prior cases where particular techniques have been admitted into proceedings, but scientific work advances by citing and carefully extending a previously established body of knowledge through hypothesis testing. The difference arises in how these precedents are determined and hence accepted. Kritzer (2009) argues that scientific and legal inquiries differ in how they persuade and hence accept propositions. He explains that the scientific tenet of general acceptance and peer review is advanced through repeated attempts to falsify a hypothesis, and that truth in a scientific context is complex and elusive, and can only be approached by a process of eliminating falsehoods. This is very different from the concept of truth as applied within the legal context, which is revealed through the adversarial process. In accepting a given truth, the legal enquirer values certainty, whilst the scientist values doubt and scepticism, argues Marsico (2004). He goes on to state that if justice is blind, then it will 'blindly follow evidence presented as truth'. The role of judges, he continues, should be limited to evaluating the admissibility of evidence, rather than to evaluate the credibility of scientific evidence.

The Daubert test (or Daubert standard) in the US developed in 1993 from the Supreme Court decision in the case of *Daubert v Merrell Dew Pharmaceuticals*, provides a framework to assist the judiciary in evaluating scientific evidence and the admissibility of this evidence from expert witnesses under Federal Rule of Evidence 702. As explained in Chapter 4, one of the four considerations of the Daubert test is the acceptability (to the relevant scientific community) of the theory or technique used to derive the evidence. However, within the field of digital forensics there is no established 'scientific community' to draw upon (Marsico, 2004). Instead justification for the scientific basis of a particular digital forensic method or software application is often based upon one of two forms of fallacious argument (*ad populum* and *consensus gentium*), that a conclusion is true simply on the basis it is believed by a large number of people; that is by 'common consent'. We can see clear *consensus gentium* arguments in a number of examples in relation to the validity of particular software and hardware for informing expert scientific testimony. For example, Guidance Software (2011) state that they have evaluated their EnCase software product against the Daubert test. In addressing the general acceptance criteria of this test, they argue that with in excess of 30,000 licensed users their product is generally accepted. However, Carrier (2002) points out that a forensic tool will probably be chosen on the basis of interface and support, and that the size of the user community is not a valid measure of procedural acceptance.

Van Buskirk and Liu (2006) have observed that statements such as those by Guidance Software lead to a tendency within the judicial system to presume that forensic software is reliable. They identify EnCase reliability issues, but Limongelli (2008) of Guidance Software defends its reliability, citing *Williford v State* [Texas, 2004] in which the court concluded that EnCase software is reliable. However this conclusion was based on the anecdotal testimony of a single police officer. Limongelli however goes on to cite *Sanders v State* [Texas, 2006] in which it was concluded that once the scientific reliability of a specific methodology is determined, 'other courts may take judicial notice' of the result. No consideration is given to the possible effects new versions of the software, or to bugs and/or errors that might arise in particular environments.

Sommer (2010) identifies how (in the UK) through the application of Part 33.6 of the Criminal Procedure Rules, at a pre-trial hearing just two individuals (the opposing experts in a case) can accept the validity of digital forensic evidence derived using a novel approach as 'sufficient' for the purposes of the case under consideration (but without implying a more general acceptance of the technique). Beach (2010) suggests that the scientific approach of falsification of hypotheses is not an issue for practitioners operating within the legal arena, as the concept of 'truth' differs between the science and legal profession – the law's objective is to resolve conflicts rather than to increase knowledge. Within the bounds of a single case, truth is deemed 'static' and not open to re-evaluation. Denning (2005) argues this acceptance of untested theories is a wider problem within the computer science community as a whole.

In the UK, partly in response to a number of miscarriages of justice, the Forensic Regulator was formed in 2008 with a remit to 'establish and monitor compliance with quality standards for the provision of forensic science services to the police and wider criminal justice system' (Forensic Science Regulator 2009) as described in Chapter 6. The Regulator's 'Codes of Practice and Conduct' (Home Office, 2011b) are aligned to BS EN ISO/IEC 17025:2005 (ISO 2005) and some police forces are now beginning to award contracts for outsourced work partly on the condition that the provider is ISO 17025 accredited.

One of the drawbacks of the standard for forensic service providers is that it is a quality based standard. It therefore clearly addresses what a provider should do, but not how it should be done. So although a provider must demonstrate it has a validation procedure for a forensic process, a description of the validation method itself is not required.

Given the appointment of a Forensic Regulator and emerging regulatory standards, it can be argued that the issues identified currently undermine the trust that can be placed in findings tendered in criminal proceedings. The production of electronic evidence therefore requires the use of reliable tools and competent operators, both currently areas of active research.

References

AccessData, 2009. *The Importance of Memory Search and Analysis*. [online] Available at: <http://accessdata.com/downloads/media/The_Importance_of_Memory_Search_and_Analysis.pdf> [Accessed 23 March 2013].

AccessData, 2010. *AccessData Product Support Downloads*. Available at: <http://accessdata.com/support/adownloads#FTKImager> [Accessed 23 March 2013].

AccessData, 2011. *e-Discovery, Computer Forensics & Cyber Security Software*. [online] Available at: <http://accessdata.com/> [Accessed 23 March 2013].

ACPO, 2009. *ACPO e-Crime Strategy*. [online] Available at: <http://www.met.police.uk/pceu/documents/ACPOecrimestrategy.pdf> [Accessed 8 July 2011].

ACPO, 2012. *ACPO Good Practice Guide for Digital Evidence*. (March 2012) [online] Available at: <http://library.npia.police.uk/docs/acpo/digital-evidence-2012.pdf> [Accessed 23 March 2013].

ACPO/Centrex, 2005. *Practice Advice on Core Investigative Doctrine*. Camborne: National Centre for Policing Excellence.

Adetunji, J., 2011. *Forensic Science Regulator Could Gain Statutory Powers*. [online] Available at: <http://www.guardian.co.uk/public-leaders-network/2011/apr/28/forensic-science-regulator-statutory-powers?INTCMP=SRCH> [Accessed 29 May 2011].

AFP, 2012. *Media Release: AFP and Customs warn users of Silk Road*. [online] Available at: <http://www.afp.gov.au/media-centre/news/afp/2012/july/afp-and-Customs-warn-users-of-silk-road.aspx> [Accessed 23 March 2013].

Afuah, A. and Tucci, C., 2003. *Internet Business Models and Strategies*. New York: McGraw-Hill.

Aggarwal, G., Bursztein, E., Jackson, C. and Boneh, D., 2010. *An Analysis of Private Browsing Modes in Modern Browsers*. In Proceedings of the 19th USENIX conference on Security USENIX Association.

Akdeniz, Y., 1996. *Section 3 of the Computer Misuse Act 1990: An Antidote for Computer Viruses!* [online] Available at: <http://webjcli.ncl.ac.uk/1996/issue3/akdeniz3.html> [Accessed 23 March 2013].

Akerlof, G., 1970. The market for "Lemons": Quality uncertainty and the market mechanism, *The Quarterly Journal of Economics*, [online] Available at: <http://www.eco.uc3m.es/docencia/microii-phd/G%20Akerlof.pdf> [Accessed 23 March 2013].

Aldrich, R., 2010. Cyber Security Operations Centre begins full range of activity, *Department of Politics and International Studies, University of Warwick*. [online] Available at: <http://www2.warwick.ac.uk/fac/soc/pais/people/aldrich/vigilant/lectures/gchq/csoc/> [Accessed 23 March 2013].

All Party Parliamentary Internet Group, 2004. *Revision of the Computer Misuse Act, Report of an Inquiry by the all Party Internet Group.* [online] Available at: <http://www.apcomms.org.uk/apig/archive/activities-2004/computer-misuse-inquiry/CMAReportFinalVersion1.pdf> [Accessed 23 March 2013].

Anderson, R., Barton, C., Böhme, R., Clayton, R., van Eeten, M.J.G., Levi, M., Moore, T., and Savage, S., 2012. *Measuring the Cost of Cybercrime.* [online] Available at: <http://weis2012.econinfosec.org/papers/Anderson_WEIS2012.pdf> [Accessed 6 August 2012].

Angulo, J and Wästlund, E., 2011. *Exploring Touch-screen Biometrics for User Identification on Smart Phones.* [online] Available at: <http://www.kau.se/sites/default/files/Dokument/subpage/2011/11/exploring_touch_screen_biometrics_for_user_identif_16753.pdf> [Accessed 23 March 2013].

Apple, 2011. *Apple (United Kingdom) – iCloud.* [online] Available at: <http://www.apple.com/uk/icloud/ [Accessed 3 February 2012].

Apple, 2012. *iOS Security May 2012.* [online] Available at: <http://images.apple.com/ipad/business/docs/iOS_Security_May12.pdf> [Accessed 23 March 2013].

Etoundi, A., Mboupda, R. and Moyo, A., 2012. Multi-perspective cybercrime investigation process modeling, *International Journal of Applied Information Systems*, 2(2), June 2012 pp. 14–20.

Axelrod, R., 1984. *The Evolution of Cooperation.* New York: Basic Books Inc.

Ayers, D., 2009. A second generation computer forensic analysis system, *Digital Investigation*, 6, pp. 34–42.

Baggili, I. and Rogers, M., 2009. Self-reported cyber crime: An analysis on the effects of anonymity and pre-employment integrity, *International Journal of Cyber Criminology*, 3(2), pp. 550–65.

Bainbridge, D., 1989. Hacking—The unauthorised access of computer systems: The legal implications, *The Modern Law Review*, 52(2), pp. 236–45.

Bainbridge, D., ed. 2008. *Introduction to Information Technology Law.* Harlow: Pearson.

Baker, J., 2012. *EU Regulators Drop Legal Case after UK Implements ePrivacy Legislation.* [online] Available at: <http://www.computerworld.com/s/article/9223730/EU_regulators_drop_legal_case_after_UK_implements_ePrivacy_legislation> [Accessed 23 March 2013].

Ball, J. and Travis, A., 2012. *Home Secretary Upholds Decision to Extradite Richard O'Dwyer.* [online] Available at: <http://www.guardian.co.uk/uk/2012/jul/09/theresa-may-richard-odwyer-extradition> [Accessed 23 March 2013].

Banday, M., 2011. Techniques and tools for forensic investigation of email, *International Journal of Network Security & its Applications*, [online] Available at: <http://airccse.org/journal/nsa/1111nsa17.pdf> [Accessed 23 March 2013].

Barendt, E. 2011. Religious hatred laws: Protecting groups or belief? *Res Publica*, 17(1), pp. 41–53.

Barnard-Wills, D., 2012. E-safety education: Young people, surveillance and responsibility, *Criminology & Criminal Justice*, 12(3), pp. 239–255.

Barra, H., 2012. 500 Million, [online] Available at: <https://plus.google.com/110023707389740934545/posts/R5YdRRyeTHM#110023707389740934545/posts/R5YdRRyeTHM> [Accessed 8 March 2013].

Barrett, M., Steingruebl, A. and Smith, B., 2012. *Combating Cybercrime: Principles, Policies, and Programs*, PayPal, [online] Available at: <https://www.paypal-media.com/assets/pdf/fact_sheet/PayPal_CombatingCybercrime_WP_0411_v4.pdf> [Accessed 24 March 2013].

Barron, A., 2011. Graduated response 'a l'Anglaise': Online copyright infringement and the Digital Economy Act 2010, *Journal of Media Law*, 3(2), pp. 305–47.

Baryamureeba, V. and Tushabe, F., 2006. The enhanced digital investigation process model, *Asian Journal of Information Technology*, 5, pp.790–794.

Battula, B.P., Prasad, S. and Sudha, T., 2009, Techniques in computer forensics: A recovery perspective, *International Journal of Security*, 3(2), p. 27.

BBC, 2000. *Nailbomber set out to 'terrorise'*. [online] Available at: <http://news.bbc.co.uk/1/hi/uk/782876.stm> [Accessed: 22 March 2013].

BBC, 2003. *Patel case raises questions*. [online] Available at: <http://news.bbc.co.uk/1/hi/england/2982302.stm> [Accessed 12 March 2011].

BBC, 2005. *Sir Roy Meadow struck off by GMC*. [online] Available at: <http://news.bbc.co.uk/1/hi/health/4685511.stm> [Accessed 12 March 2011].

BBC, 2008a. *60,000 devices are left in cabs*. [online] Available at: <http://news.bbc.co.uk/2/hi/technology/7620569.stm> [Accessed 24 March 2013].

BBC, 2008b. *Five Students Win Terror Appeal*. [online] Available at: <http://news.bbc.co.uk/1/hi/7242724.stm>.[Accessed 24 March 2013].

BBC, 2009. *Previous cases of missing data*. [online] Available at: <http://news.bbc.co.uk/1/hi/uk/8409405.stm> [Accessed 24 March 2013].

BBC, 2010. *$2m file-sharing fine slashed to $54,000*. [online] Available at: <http://news.bbc.co.uk/1/hi/technology/8478305.stm> [Accessed 24 March 2013].

BBC, 2012a. *April Jones: Matthew Woods jailed for Facebook posts*. [online] Available at<http://www.bbc.co.uk/news/uk-england-lancashire-19869710> [Accessed 10 October 2012].

BBC, 2012b. *BMW: Open to car theft*. [online] Available at: <http://www.bbc.co.uk/programmes/b006mg74/features/bmw-car-theft-technology> [Accessed 24 March 2013].

BBC, 2012c. *Hacker Gary McKinnon will not face UK charges*. [online] Available at: <http://www.bbc.co.uk/news/uk-20730627> [Accessed 24 March 2013].

BBC, 2012d. *Rothko damage 'could take up to 18 months to repair'*. [online] Available at: <http://www.bbc.co.uk/news/entertainment-arts-20424251> [Accessed 24 March 2013].

BBC, 2012e. *York Facebook Hacking Student Glenn Mangham Jailed*. [online] Available at: <http://www.bbc.co.uk/news/uk-england-york-north-yorkshire-17079853> [Accessed 24 March 2013].

BBC, 2012f. *Greater Manchester Police fined over stolen data stick*. [online] Available at: <http://www.bbc.co.uk/news/uk-england-manchester-19960966> [Accessed 24 March 2013].

BBC, 2013. *Frozen Android phones give up data secrets.* [online] Available at: <http://www.bbc.co.uk/news/technology-21697704> [Accessed 24 March 2013].

Beaman, A.L., Klentz, B., Diener, E. and Svanum, S., 1979. Self-awarenesss and transgression in children: Two field studies, *Journal of Personality and Social Psychology*, 37(10), pp. 1835–46.

Beck, U., 1992. *Risk Society: Towards a New Modernity.* London: Sage Publications.

Beckett, J., 2010. *Forensic Computing: A Deterministic Model for Validation and Verification through an Ontological Examination of Forensic Functions and Processes.* [PhD, University of South Australia] (Personal communication from author, September 2011).

Beckett, J. and Slay, J., 2007. Digital forensics: Validation and verification in a dynamic work environment. *Proceedings of the 40th Hawaii International Conference on System Sciences* [online] Available at: <http://www.computer.org/csdl/proceedings/hicss/2007/2755/00/27550266a.pdf> [Accessed 24 March 2013].

Bednar, P. and Katos, V., 2012. *SSD: New Challenges for Digital Forensics.* [online] Available at: <http://www.cersi.it/itais2011/pdf/30.pdf> [Accessed 24 March 2013].

Bejtlich, R., 2005. *Network Forensics? Please.* [online] Available at: <http://taosecurity.blogspot.com/2005/11/network-forensics-please.html> [Accessed 24 March 2013].

Bell, D., 1974. *The Coming of Post-Industrial Society: A Venture in Social Forecasting.* London: Heinemann Educational Books.

Bell, D., 1979. The Social Framework of the Information Society. In: M.L. Dertoozos and J. Moses, eds. 1980. *The Computer Age: A 20 Year View.* Cambridge, MA: MIT Press, pp. 500–549.

Bell, S., 2001. *A beginner's guide to uncertainty in measurement.* [online] Available at: <http://publications.npl.co.uk/dbtw-wpd/exec/dbtwpub.dll?&Q B0=AND&QF0=ID&QI0=2284&TN=NPLPUBS&RF=WFullRecordDetails &DL=0&RL=0&NP=4&AC=QBE_QUERY> [Accessed 24 March 2013].

Bell, G.B. and Boddington, R., 2010, Solid state drives: The beginning of the end for current practice in digital forensic recovery? *Journal of Digital Forensics, Security and Law*, 5(3) pp. 1–20.

Bergman, M., 2001. White Paper: The Deep Web: Surfacing Hidden Value, *Journal of Electronic Publishing*, [online] Available at: <http://dx.doi.org/10.3998/3336451.0007.104> [Accessed 24 March 2013].

Betz, C., 2005. *DFRWS 2005 Forensics Challenge: Memparser Analysis Tool.* [online] Available at: <http://www.dfrws.org/2005/challenge/memparser.shtml> [Accessed 24 March 2013].

Beverly, R., Garfinkel, S. and Cardwell, G., 2011. Forensic carving of network packets and associated data structures, *Digital Investigation*, 8(0), pp. S78–S89.

Bickley, J.A., and Beech, R., 2002. An empirical investigation of the Ward & Hudson self-regulation model of the sexual offence process with child abusers, *Journal of Interpersonal Violence*, 17, pp. 371–93.

Blackburn, R., 1993. *The Psychology of Criminal Conduct.* Chichester: John Wiley and Sons.

Bonneau, J. and Preibusch, S., 2010. *The password thicket: technical and market failures in human authentication on the web.* [online] Available at: <http://weis2010.econinfosec.org/papers/session3/weis2010_bonneau.pdf> [Accessed 24 March 2013].

Bonneau, J., 2011. *Measuring Password Re-use Empirically.* [online] Available at: <http://www.lightbluetouchpaper.org/2011/02/09/measuring-password-re-use-empirically/> [Accessed 24 March 2013].

BOP Consulting, 2010. *Changing Attitudes and Behaviour in the 'non-Internet' Digital World and their Implications for Intellectual Property.* London: SABIP.

Bowcott, O., 2012. *Twitter Joke Trial: Paul Chambers Wins High Court Appeal Against Conviction.* [online] Available at: <http://www.guardian.co.uk/law/2012/jul/27/twitter-joke-trial-high-court> [Accessed 24 March 2013].

Brasier, L., 2011. *Felony Charges Put on Hold for Man Who Read Wife's e-Mail.* [online] Available at: <http://www.freep.com/article/20110621/NEWS03/106210343/Felony-charges-put-hold-man-who-read-wife-s-e-mail> [Accessed 24 March 2013].

Brasier, L.L., 2012. *Final charge dropped in Rochester Hills e-mail hacking case.* [online] Available at: <http://www.freep.com/article/20120720/NEWS03/207200450/Final-charge-dropped-in-Rochester-Hills-e-mail-hacking-case> [Accessed 24 March 2013].

Brenner, S., 2004. *Cybercrime Metrics: Old Wine, New Bottles?* [online] Available at: <http://www.vjolt.net/vol9/issue4/v9i4_a13-Brenner.pdf Brenner, S. (2010) Cybercrime: criminal threats from Cyberspace>* [Accessed 24 March 2013].

Brenner, S. and Clarke, L., 2006. Distributed Security: Preventing Cybercrime, *John Marshall Journal of Computer and Information Law,* [online] Available at: <http://www.jcil.org/journal/articles/434.html> [Accessed 24 March 2013].

Brewster, T., 2013. *European Cybercrime Centre impresses on cautious opening.* [online] Available at: <http://www.techweekeurope.co.uk/news/european-cybercrime-centre-opening-2-104013> [Accessed 24 March 2013].

Britz, M.T., 2004. *Computer Forensics and Cyber Crime: An Introduction.* Upper Saddle River, NJ: Prentice Hall Press.

Bryant, R. and Bryant, S. eds. 2008. *Investigating Digital Crime.* Chichester: John Wiley & Sons.

Bryant, R. and Bryant, S. eds. 2013. *Blackstone's Handbook for Policing Students 2013.* Oxford: Oxford University Press.

Bryant, R., Cockcroft, T. and Dileone, N., 2012. *Cybercrime Investigation – developing and disseminating an accredited international training programme for the future,* (ISEC Project JLS/2008/ISEC/FP/C4-077) [online] Available at: <http://ec.europa.eu/dgs/home-affairs/financing/fundings/projects/stories/cybercrime_en.htm> [Accessed 24 March 2013].

Buerger, M. and Mazerolle, L., 1998. Third party policing: A theoretical analysis of an emerging trend, *Justice Quarterly,* 15(2), pp. 301–28.

Burke, A., Sowerbutts, S., Blundell, S., and Sherry, M., 2001. Child pornography and the internet: Policing and the treatment issues, *Psychiatry, Psychology & Law*, 9, pp. 79–84.

Burke, R., 2005. *An Introduction to Criminological Theory*. Cullompton: Willan Publishing.

Busch, A., 2012. The Regulation of Privacy. In: D. Levi-Faur, ed. *Handbook on the Politics of Regulation*. [online] Available at: <http://levifaur.wiki.huji.ac.il/images/Handbookr.pdf> [Accessed 24 March 2013]. Ch 16.

Business Insider, 2011. *Notorious Hacker Group LulzSec Just Announced That It's Finished*. [online] Available at: <http://www.businessinsider.com/lulzsec-finished-2011-6> [Accessed 24 March 2013].

Cabinet Office, 2010. *A Strong Britain in an Age of Uncertainty: The National Security Strategy*. [online] Available at: <http://www.direct.gov.uk/prod_consum_dg/groups/dg_digitalassets/@dg/@en/documents/digitalasset/dg_191639.pdf> [Accessed 24 March 2013].

Cabinet Office, 2011. *Cyber Security*. [online] Available at: <http://www.cabinetoffice.gov.uk/content/cyber-security [viewed July 7th 2011].

Cabinet Office, 2012. *The UK Cyber Security Strategy*. [online] Available at: <http://www.cabinetoffice.gov.uk/sites/default/files/resources/Cyber_Security_Strategy_one_year_on_achievements.pdf> [Accessed 24 March 2013].

Caida, 2003. *The Spread of the Sapphire/Slammer Worm*. [online] Available at: <http://www.caida.org/publications/papers/2003/sapphire/sapphire.html>.

Carrier, B., 2003. Defining digital forensic examination and analysis tools using abstraction layers, *International Journal of Digital Evidence*, 1(4).

Carrier, B., 2005. *File System Forensic Analysis*. Upper Saddle River, NJ: Addison-Wesley Professional.

Carrier, B. and Spafford, H., 2006. *Getting physical with digital forensic process*. [online] Available at: <http://citeseerx.ist.psu.edu/viewdoc/download?doi=10.1.1.76.pdf>

Carstensen, J., 2011. *European Cybercrime 10 Years on – Why It's Not Working*. [online] Available at: <http://www.infosecisland.com/blogview/13139-European-Cybercrime-10-Years-On-Why-Its-Not-Working.html>.

Carter, D.L., Prentky, R.A., Knight, R.A., Vanderveer, P., and Boucher, R.J., 1987. Use of pornography in the criminal and developmental histories of sexual offenders. *Journal of Interpersonal Violence*, 2, pp. 196–211.

Casey, E., 2004a. *Digital Evidence and Computer Crime*. Waltham, MA: Elsevier Academic Press.

Casey, E., 2004b. Network traffic as a source of evidence: Tool strengths, weaknesses, and future needs. *Digital Investigation*, 1(1), pp. 28–43.

Casey, E., 2011. *Digital Evidence and Computer Crime Forensic Science, Computers and the Internet*. Salt Lake City: Academic Press.

Casey, E. and Turnbull, B., (2011) 'Digital evidence on mobile devices'. In: E. Casey, ed. *Digital Evidence and Computer Crime*, London: Academic Press.

Cash, W., 2011. *Draft Directive on attacks against information systems will require the UK to amend existing criminal law.* [online] Available at: <http://www. europeanfoundation.org/my_weblog/2011/03/draft-directive-on-attacks-against-information-systems-will-require-the-uk-to-amend-existing-criminal-law.html> [Accessed 8 March 2013].

Castells, M., 1996. *The Rise of the Network Society.* Blackwell: Oxford

Castells, M. (1998) *The Information Age: Economy, Society and Culture, The Information Age, Vol. III (End of Millennium).* Blackwell: Oxford.

Castells, M., 2000. Materials for an explanatory theory of the network society, *British Journal of Sociology,* 1(1), pp. 5–24.

Castells, M. and Cardoso, G. eds., 2005. *The Network Society from Knowledge to Policy.* Washington DC: Center for Transatlantic Relations.

CCDCOE, 2013. *Cooperative Cyber Defence Centre of Excellence Mission.* [online} Available at: <http://www.ccdcoe.org/images/147.pdf>

CEOP, 2012a. *About the CEOP Centre.* [online] Available at: <http://ceop.police. uk/About-Us/> [Accessed 24 March 2013].

CEOP, 2012b. *A Picture of Abuse A thematic assessment of the risk of contact child sexual abuse posed by those who possess indecent images of children.* [online] Available at: <http://ceop.police.uk/Documents/ceopdocs/CEOP%20 IIOCTA%20Executive%20Summary.pdf>

CEOP, 2013. *Welcome to CEOP's thinkuknow website.* [online] Available at: <http://www.thinkuknow.co.uk/>

CGI, 2011. *The Commonwealth Cybercrime Initiative.* [online] Available at: <http:// www.commonwealthigf.org/cybercrime/the-commonwealth-cybercrime-initiative/he Commonwealth Cybercrime Initiative>

Chen, F., Koufaty, D.A., and Zhang, X. 2009. Understanding intrinsic characteristics and system implications of flash memory based solid state drives. In: ACM *Proceedings of the eleventh international joint conference on Measurement and modeling of computer systems,* Seattle, USA, 15–19 June 2009. (pp. 181–192).

Cheng, E.K. and Yoon, A.H., 2005. Does Frye or Daubert matter? A study of scientific admissibility standards. *Virginia Law Review,* [online] Available at: <http://papers.ssrn.com/sol3/papers.cfm?abstract_id=609581pp.   471-513> [Accessed 24 March 2013].

Cheng, J., 2010. *Appeals Court: Pirate Bay Admins Still Guilty, Now with Higher Fines.* [online] Available at: <http://www.wired.com/threatlevel/2010/11/ appeals-court-pirate-bay-admins-still-guilty-now-with-higher-fines/.

Christin, N., 2012. *Traveling the Silk Road: A measurement analysis of a large anonymous online marketplace* [online] Available at: <http://arxiv.org/ pdf>/1207.7139v1.pdf>

Ciampa, M., (forthcoming, 2014) *Security Awareness: Applying Practical Security in Your World.* Cengage: USA.

CIFAS, 2012. *Welcome to CIFAS.* [online] Available at: <http://www.cifas.org.uk>

Clarke, N. and Furnell, S., 2007. Authenticating mobile phone users using keystroke analysis. *International Journal of Information Security*, 6(1), pp. 1–14.

Clarke, R., 1997. *Situational Crime Prevention Successful Case Studies*. New York: Harrow and Heston Publishers.

Clarke, R., 1999. Hot products: Understanding, anticipating and reducing demand for stolen goods *Police Research Series Paper 112*, Home Office: UK.

Clarke, R. and Felson, M. eds., 1993. *Routine Activity and Rational Choice. Advances in Criminological Theory*, Vol. 5. New Brunswick, NJ: Transaction Books.

Clough, J., 2010. *Principles of Cybercrime*. Cambridge: Cambridge University Press.

Clough, J., 2012. The Council of Europe Convention on Cybercrime: Defining 'crime' in a digital world, *Criminal Law Forum*, 23(4), pp. 363–91

CNET, 2010. *Rustock botnet responsible for 39 percent of all spam*. [online] Available at: <http://news.cnet.com/8301-1009_3-20014690-83.html>

Commission of the European Communities, 2007. *Communication from the Commission to the European Parliament, the Council and the Committee of the Regions Towards a general policy on the fight against cybercrime*. [online] Available at: <http://eur-lex.europa.eu/LexUriServ/LexUriServ.do?uri=COM: 2007:0267:FIN:EN:PDF>

Constitutional Council, 2009. *Decision n° 2009-580*. [online] Available at: <http://www.conseil-constitutionnel.fr/conseil-constitutionnel/root/bank/ download/2009-580DC-2009_580dc.pdf>.

Cormack, P.S., 2010. *The Omagh bombing: some remaining questions, fourth report of session 2009-10, report, together with formal minutes, oral and written evidence*. [online] Available at: <http://www.parliament.the-stationery-office.co.uk/pa/cm200910/cmselect/cmniaf/374/374.pdf>   [Accessed   24 March 2013].

Cornish, W. Llewelyn, D. and Aplin, T. 2010. *Intellectual Property: Patents, Copyright, Trade Marks and Allied Rights*, 7th edn. London: Sweet & Maxwell.

Corsaro, V., 2012. From Betamax to YouTube: How Sony Corporation of America v. Universal City Studios, Inc. could still be a standard for new technology. *Federal Communications Law Journal*, 64(2), pp. 449–75.

Council of Europe, 2001. *Convention on Cybercrime*. [online] Available at: <http:// conventions.coe.int/Treaty/EN/Treaties/Html/185.htm>   [Last   accessed: 6 October 2010].

Council of Europe, 2006. *Additional Protocol to the Convention on Cybercrime, concerning the criminalisation of acts of a racist and xenophobic nature committed through computer systems (ETS No. 189)* [online] Available at: <http://conventions.coe.int/Treaty/EN/Reports/Html/189.htm>

Council of Europe, 2011. *Specialised cybercrime units – Good practice study*. [online] Available at: <http://www.coe.int/t/dghl/cooperation/economiccrime/

cybercrime/Documents/Reports-Presentations/Octopus2011/2467_HTCU_ study_V30_9Nov11.pdf> [Accessed 24 March 2013].

Council of Europe. 2012. *Council of Europe: 800 Million Europeans.* [online] Available at: <http://www.coe.int/AboutCoe/media/interface/ publications/800_millions_en.pdf>.

Council of Europe Treaty Office, 2012. *Action against economic crime.* [online] Available at: <http://www.coe.int/t/DGHL/cooperation/economiccrime/ cybercrime/default_en.asp>

CPS, 2011. *Section 3A CMA – Making, Supplying Or Obtaining Articles.* [online] Available at: <http://www.cps.gov.uk/legal/a_to_c/computer_misuse_act_ 1990/#an10>.

CPS, 2012. *CPS statement on conviction of two men over incitement on Facebook* [online] Available at: <http://www.cps.gov.uk/news/press_statements/cps_ statement_on_conviction_of_two_men_over_incitement_on_facebook/index. html>

CPS, unknown. *Guidance on Prosecuting Cases of Racist and Religious Crime.* [online] Available at: <http://www.cps.gov.uk/publications/prosecution/ rrpbcrpol.html>.

Curran, K., Robinson, A., Peacocke, S. and Cassidy, S. 2010, Mobile phone forensic analysis. *International Journal of Digital Crime and Forensics*, 2(3), pp. 15–27.

Daily Mirror, 2012. *Deep web: Drugs, guns, assassins, jet planes all for sale on vast anonymous network*, [online] Available at: <http://www.mirror.co.uk/ news/uk-news/deep-web-drugs-guns-assassins-1337131>

Daily Telegraph, 2010. *Anti-Piracy Agency's Logo Broke Copyright.* [online] Available at: <http://www.telegraph.co.uk/news/worldnews/europe/france/ 6974249/Anti-piracy-agencys-logo-broke-copyright.html>.

Dasgupta, D. and S. Saha, 2010. Password Security through Negative Filtering. In: EST, *2010 International Conference on Emerging Security Technologies*, Canterbury, UK, 6–7 Sep 2010.

DataGenetics (2012) *PIN Analysis.* [online] Available at: <http://www. datagenetics.com/blog/september32012/index.html>

Davies, C., 2012. *Former Boris Johnson Aide Cleared of Possession of 'Extreme Pornography'* [online] Available at: <http://www.guardian.co.uk/uk/2012/ aug/08/boris-johnson-aide-extreme-pornography-cleared?newsfeed=true>.

Davies, C., 2011. *Car crime fall attributed to technological drive.* [online] Available at: <http://www.guardian.co.uk/uk/2011/jun/16/car-crime-fall- technological-drive?INTCMP=SRCH> [Accessed 24 March 2103].

Davis, M., Kennedy, R., Pyles, K., Strickler, A. and Shenoi, S., 2006. Detecting data concealment programs using passive file system analysis, *Advances in Digital Forensics*, II, pp. 171–83.

Deibert, R. and Rohozinski, R., 2010. Risking security: Policies and paradoxes of cyberspace security, *International Political Sociology*, 4, pp. 15–32.

Dell, 2009. *Dell Transforms how Police Analyse Digital Evidence with Digital Forensics Solution.* [online] Available at: <http://content.dell.com/uk/en/corp/d/press-releases/2009-07-07-digital-forensic-uk.aspx> [viewed July 18th 2011].

Denby, B., Oussar, Y. and Ahriz, I., 2008, Geolocalisation in cellular telephone networks. In: F. Fogelman-Soulie, D. Perrotta, J. Piskorski and R. Steinberger, eds. *Mining Massive Data Sets for Security: Advances in Data Mining, Search, Social Networks and Text Mining, and Their Applications to Security*, Amsterdam: IOS Press, pp. 357–65.

Desfossez, J., Dieppedale, J. and Girard, G., 2009. Stealth malware analysis from kernel space with Kolumbo, *Journal in Computer Virology*, 7(1), pp. 83–93.

Detica, 2011. *The Cost of Cyber Crime A Detica Report in Partnership with the Office of Cyber security and Information Assurance in the Cabinet Office.* [online] Available at: <http://www.baesystemsdetica.com/uploads/press_releases/THE_COST_OF_CYBER_CRIME_SUMMARY_FINAL_14_February_2011.pdf>

Detica with the John Grieve Centre for Policing and Security, 2012. *Organised Crime in the Digital age: the real picture.* [online] Available at: <http://www.baesystemsdetica.com/uploads/resources/ORGANISED_CRIME_IN_THE_DIGITAL_AGE_EXECUTIVE_SUMMARY_FINAL_MARCH_2012.pdf>

DFRWS, 2001. *DTR – T001-01 Final DFRWS Technical Report A Road Map for Digital Forensic Research.* [online] Available at: <http://www.dfrws.org/2001/dfrws-rm-final.pdf>

DFRWS, 2005. DFRWS 2005 Forensics Challenge. [online] Available at: <http://www.dfrws.org/2005/challenge/> [Accessed 3 February 2012].

Digital Detective, 2011. *Digital Detective – Digital Forensic Data Recovery Software.* [online] Available at: <http://www.digital-detective.co.uk/> [Accessed 12 November 2011].

Directive, E.U.C. 2005. Council Framework Decision 2005/222/JHA of 24 February 2005 on Attacks Against Information Systems, *Official Journal of the European Union*, 69, pp. 67–71.

Dowell, B. 2012. *Twitter Users to be Arrested over Naming of Ched Evans Rape Victim.* [online] Available at: <http://www.guardian.co.uk/technology/2012/apr/24/twitter-users-arrested-ched-evans-rape>.

Dropbox, 2012. *Dropbox Privacy Policy.* [online] Available at: <https://www.dropbox.com/privacy>

Dropbox, 2007. *Dropbox – Files – Simplify your life.* [online] Available at: <https://www.dropbox.com> [Accessed 3 February 2012].

Dupont, B., 2004. Security in the Age of Networks, *Policing & Society*, 14(1), pp. 76–91.

Blank, G. and Dutton, W., 2012. The emergence of next generation internet users. In: J. Hartley, J. Burgess and A. Bruns, eds. 2013. *The Blackwell Companion to New Media Dynamics*. London: Wiley-Blackwell.

Dwyer, D., 2003. Duties of expert witnesses of fact and opinion: R v. Clark (Sally), *International Journal of Evidence & Proof*, 7, p. 264.

Easton, C., 2012. ICANN's core principles and the expansion of generic top-level domain names, *International Journal of Law and IT*, 20(4), pp. 273–290.

Edwards, L., Rauhofer, J. and Yar, M., 2010. Recent developments in UK cybercrime law. In: Y. Jewkes and M. Yar eds. 2010, *Handbook of Internet Crime*, Cullompton, UK: Willan, pp. 413–36.

e-fense, 2013. *Don't let your company data walk out the door!* [online] Available at: <http://www.e-fense.com/products.php> [Accessed 24 March 2013].

El-Guindy, M., n.d. *Steganography & Cybercriminals* [online] Information Systems Security Association. Available at: <http://www.netsafe.me/pres/Stego.pdf> [Accessed 25 March 2013].

Elliott, I. and Beech, A., 2009. Understanding online child pornography use: Applying sexual offense theory to internet offenders, *Aggression and Violent Behavior*, 14, pp. 180–93.

Endrass, J., Urbaniok, F., Hammermeister, L.C., Benz, C., Christian, E., Elbert, T., Laubacher, A. and Rossegger, A., 2009 PsycINFOBMC, *Psychiatry*. 9, Art. ID 43.

Engineering the Future, 2012. *E-crime Home Affairs Select Committee call for evidence*, [online] Available at: <http://www.theiet.org/policy/submissions/sub942.pdf>[Accessed 25 March 2013].

ENISA, 2011. *Activities*. [online] Available at: <http://www.enisa.europa.eu/about-enisa/activities> [Accessed 7 July 2011].

EPSRC, 2012. *Consortia for Exploratory Research in Security (CEReS)*, [online] Available at: <http://www.epsrc.ac.uk/SiteCollectionDocuments/Calls/2012/CEReSCall.pdf> [Accesed 18 May 2012].

Epstein, R., 2009. *Attacking the Government's "Junk Science"*, Seminar, Charlston, South Carolina, USA, [online] Available at: <http://www.fd.org/pdf>_lib/WinningStrategies2009/Attacking_the_Gov_Junk_Science.pdf> [Accessed 11 December 2011).

Epstein, Z., 2011. *'Anonymous' hackers to FBI: There is nothing you can do to stop us*, [online] Available at: <http://www.bgr.com/2011/07/21/anonymous-hackers-to-fbi-there-is-nothing-you-can-do-to-stop-us/>[Accessed 25 March 2013].

EU Commission, 2010. *Proposal for a Directive on Attacks Against Information Systems, Repealing Framework Decision 2005/222/JHA*. [online] Available at: <http://europa.eu/rapid/pressReleasesAction.do?reference=MEMO/10/463>. [Accessed 25 March 2013].

European Commission. 2010. *Directive of the European Parliament and of the Council on Attacks Against Information Systems and Repealing Council Framework Decision 2005/222/JHA*. [online] Available at: <http://ec.europa.eu/dgs/home-affairs/policies/crime/1_en_act_part1_v101.pdf> ed>. [Accessed 25 March 2013].

European Commission, 2013. *European Cybercrime Centre (EC3) opens on 11 January.* [online] Available at: <http://europa.eu/rapid/press-release_IP-13-13_en.htm>[Accessed 25 March 2013].

European Union, 2008. *EU Relations with the Council of Europe.* [online] Available at: <http://eeas.europa.eu/organisations/coe/index_en.htm>.[Accessed 25 March 2013].

Europol, 2012a. *About Europol.* [online] Available at: <https://www.europol. europa.eu/content/page/about-europol-17> [Accessed 17 August 2012].

Europol, 2012b. *The European Cybercrime Centre Bulletin of the EC3.* Den Haag: Europol.

Europol, 2013. *New European Cybercrime Centre (EC3) opens at Europol.* [online] Available at: <https://www.europol.europa.eu/node/1899> [Accessed 25 March 2013].

Fafinski, A., Dutton, W. and Margetts, H., 2010. *Mapping and Measuring Cybercrime,* Oxford Internet Institute Forum Discussion Paper No. 18 [online] Available at: <http://www.law.leeds.ac.uk/assets/files/staff/FD18.pdf> [Accessed 25 March 2013].

Fafinski, S., 2008. Computer misuse: The implications of the Police and Justice Act 2006, *Journal of Criminal Law,* 72, pp. 53.

Fafinski, S., 2009. *Computer Misuse: Response, Regulation and the Law.* London: Willan Publishing.

FastMail, 2012. *SSL vs TLS vs STARTTLS.* [online] Available at: <https://www. fastmail.fm/help/technology_ssl_vs_tls_starttls.html> [Accessed 25 March 2013].

FBI, 2010. *On the Grid: Computers Crunch Numbers in their Sleep.* [online] Available at: <http://www.fbi.gov/news/stories/2010/january/grid_012210/on-the-grid-computers-crunch-numbers-in-their-sleep>.

FBI, 2013. *Computer Intrusions.* [online] Available at: <http://www.fbi.gov/ about-us/investigate/cyber/computer-intrusions> [Accessed 25 March 2013].

Felson, M. and Clarke, R., 1998. Opportunity makes the thief: Practical theory for crime prevention. In: B. Webb, ed. *Police Research Series Paper 98.* London: The Policing and Reducing Crime Unit.

FFA, 2012. *Card-not-present Fraud.* [online] Available at: <http://www. financialfraudaction.org.uk/Financial-cnp-fraud.asp> [Accessed 25 March 2013].

Finch, E., 2003. What a tangled web we weave: Identity theft and the Internet. In: Y. Jewkes, ed. *Dot.cons: Crime, deviance, and identity on the Internet.* Collompton, UK: Willan. pp. 86–104.

Finkenzeller, K. and Müller, D., 2010. *RFID Handbook: Fundamentals and Applications in Contactless Smart Cards, Radio Frequency Identification and Near-Field Communication,* 3rd edn. Chichester: Wiley.

Finklea, K. and Theohary, C., 2013. *Cybercrime: Conceptual Issues for Congress and U.S. Law Enforcement.* [online] Available at: <http://www.fas.org/sgp/crs/ misc/R42547.pdf> [Accessed 25 March 2013].

Fitchard, K., 2012. *National Database Aims to Catch Smartphone Thieves.* [online] Available at: <http://gigaom.com/mobile/national-database-aims-to-catch-smartphone-thieves/>.[Accessed 25 March 2013].

Foresight Future Identities, 2013. *Future Identities Changing identities in the UK the next 10 years Final Project Report.* London: The Government Office for Science.

Forward Discovery, 2011. *Forward Discovery.* [online] Available at: <http://forwarddiscovery.com/> [Accessed 9 November 2011].

Franky, 2002. *The Cannibal Cafe Forum.* [online] Available at: <http://web.archive.org/web/20021204051051/<http://www.necrobabes.org/perroloco/forum/messages/1218.html>.[Accesed 4 July 2012].

Fullwood, C., Melrose, K., Morris, N., and Floyd, S., 2012. Sex, blogs and baring your soul: Factors influencing UK blogging strategies, *Journal of the American Society for Information Science and Technology*, 64(2), pp. 345–55.

Garfinkel, S., 2010. Digital forensics research: the next 10 years, *Digital Investigation*, 7, pp. 64–73.

Garland, D., 1996. The limits of the sovereign state: Strategies of crime control in contemporary society, *British Journal of Criminology*, 36(4), pp. 445–71.

Garland, J. and Chakraborti, N., 2012. Divided by a common concept? Assessing the implications of different conceptualizations of hate crime in the European Union, *European Journal of Criminology*, 9(1), pp. 38–51.

Garner, G., 2005. *DFRWS 2005 Forensics Challenge.* [online] Available at: <http://www.dfrws.org/2005/challenge/kntlist.shtml. [Accessed 24 March 2013].

Gartner. 2011, *Gartner Says 428 Million Mobile Communication Devices Sold Worldwide in First Quarter 2011, a 19 Percent Increase Year-on-Year.* [online] Available at: <http://www.gartner.com/it/page.jsp?id=1689814> [Accessed 29 May 2011].

Gillespie, A.A., 2010. Racially offensive web postings, *Journal of Criminal Law*, 74, p. 242.

Goff, E., 2008. Adding the temporal and spatial aspects of routine activities: A further test of routine activity theory, *Security Journal*, 21(1/2), pp. 95–116.

Golan, T., 2004. *Laws of Men and Laws of Nature: The History of Scientific Expert Testimony in England and America.* Cambridge, MA: Harvard University Press.

Goldstein, R. and Volkow, N., 2002. Drug addiction and its underlying neurobiological basis: Neuroimaging evidence for the involvement of the frontal cortex, *American Journal of Psychiatry*, 159(10), pp. 1642–52.

Goodchild, S., 2011. *Hospital Patients' Details Lost Or Stolen 1,000 Times in Three Years.* [online] Available at: <http://www.thisislondon.co.uk/standard/article-23963531-hospital-patients-details-lost-or-stolen-1000-times-in-three-years.do> [Accessed 7 July 2011].

Goode, S., 2011. *Paedophiles in Society Reflecting on Sexuality, Abuse and Hope,* Basingstoke: Palgrave Macmillan.

Google, 2011. *An Update on Android Market Security*, [online] Available at: <http://googlemobile.blogspot.co.uk/2011/03/update-on-android-market-security.html> [Accessed 25 March 2013].

Google, 2012. *Chrome & Apps @ Google I/O: Your web, everywhere.* [online] Available at: <http://googleblog.blogspot.co.uk/2012/06/chrome-apps-google-io-your-web.html> [Accessed 25 March 2013].

Grabosky, P., 2001. Virtual criminality: Old wine in new bottles? *Social & Legal Studies*, 10(2), pp. 243–9.

Grabosky, P., 2007. *Electronic Crime.* New Jersey: Pearson Education Inc.

Grabosky, P. and Smith, R., 2001. Telecommunications fraud in the digital age: The convergence of technologies. In: D. Wall, ed. 2001. *Crime and the Internet.* London: Routledge, pp. 29–43.

Grobler, M., 2012. The need for digital evidence standardization, *International Journal of Digital Crime and Forensics*, 4(2), pp. 1–12.

Gromov, G.R., 2002. *The roads and crossroads of internet history.* [online] Available at: <http://vclass.mgt.psu.ac.th/~parinya/MISMBA2004/pdf>/x-bad-Netvalley-Internet-History-2.pdf> [Accessed 8 March 2013].

Guardian Newspaper, 2013. *Fall in UK crime rate baffles experts.* [online] Available at: <http://www.guardian.co.uk/uk/2013/jan/24/fall-uk-crime-rate-baffles-experts> [Accessed 25 March 2013].

Gubanov, Y. and Afonin, O., 2012. *Why SSD Drives Destroy Court Evidence, and What Can Be Done About It.* [online] Available at: <http://forensic.belkasoft.com/download/info/SSD%20Forensics%202012.pdf> [Accessed 25 March 2013].

Guinchard, A., 2011. Between hype and understatement: Reassessing cyber risks as a security strategy, *Journal of Strategic Security*, IV(2), pp. 75–96.

Haberfeld, M., Clarke, C. and Sheehan, D., eds., 2012. *Police Organisation and Training: Innovations in Research and Practice*, New York: Springer.

Hafner, K. and Lyon, M., 1996, *When Wizards Stay Up Late: The Origins of the Internet.* London: Simon & Shuster.

Halliday, J., 2012. *The Pirate Bay to Defy International Crackdown on Filesharing Websites.* [online] Available at: <http://www.guardian.co.uk/technology/2012/feb/21/pirate-bay-defy-crackdown-filesharing?INTCMP=SRCH> [Accessed 25 March 2013].

Hansard, 2012. *House of Commons Written Answers 16 May 2012.* [online] Available at: <http://www.publications.parliament.uk/pa/cm201213/cmhansrd/cm120516/text/120516w0002.htm#12051655002281> [Accessed 25 March 2013].

Hardin, 1968. *The Tragedy of the Commons.* [online] Available at: <http://homes.chass.utoronto.ca/~mturner/ec313/readings/Hardin_Science_1968.pdf> [Accessed 25 March 2013].

Hardy, K., 2011. WWWMDs: Cyber-Attacks against Infrastructure in Domestic Anti-Terror Laws, *Computer Law & Security Review*, 27(2), pp. 152–61.

Hargreaves, C.J., 2009. *Assessing the Reliability of Digital Evidence from Live Investigations Involving Encryption.* Ph.D. Cranfield University.

Harris, D. and Drexel, G., 1971. *Basic Elements of Intelligence*, Washington: US Government Printing Office.

Harris, R., 2006, Arriving at an anti-forensics consensus: Examining how to define and control the anti-forensics problem, *Digital Investigation*, 3, pp. 4–49.

Hayes, B., 2008, Cloud computing, *Communications of the ACM*, 51(7), pp. 9–11.

Heaton, R., 2000. The prospects for intelligence-led policing: Some historical and quantitative considerations, *Policing and Society*, 9(4), pp. 337–56.

Hexillion, 1997. *Free online network tools - traceroute, nslookup, dig, whois lookup, ping – IPv6. Central Ops.* [online] Available at: <http://centralops.net/co/>. [Accessed 3 February 2012].

Higgins, G., 2007. Digital piracy, self-control theory, and rational choice: An examination of the role of value, *International Journal of Cyber Criminology*, 1(1).

Holt, T. and Kilger, M., 2012 Examining willingness to attack critical infrastructure online and offline, *Crime & Delinquency*, 58(5), pp. 798–822.

Home Office, 1989. *Criminal and Custodial Careers of those Born in 1953, 1958 and 1963*, London: Home Office.

Home Office, 2010. *Forensic Science Regulator.* [online] Available at: <http://www.homeoffice.gov.uk/police/forensic-science-regulator/ > [Accessed 10 July 2010].

Home Office, 2011a. *The National Crime Agency A plan for the creation of a national crime-fighting capability.* London: Stationery Office.

Home Office, 2011b. *Draft Codes of Practice and Conduct | Home Office. Forensic Science Regulator - Draft Codes of Practice and Conduct.* [online] Available at: <http://www.homeoffice.gov.uk/publications/police/forensic-science-regulator1/codes-conduct-practice> [Accessed 8 April 2011].

Honeynet, 2013. *The Honeynet Project.* [online] Available at: <http://www.honeynet.org/> [Accessed 25 March 2013].

Howard, P.N., Duffy, A., Freelon, D., Hussain, M., Mari, W. and Mazaid, M., 2011. *Opening Closed Regimes: What Was the Role of Social Media During the Arab Spring?* [online] Available at: <http://pitpi.org/index.php/2011/09/11/opening-closed-regimes-what-was-the-role-of-social-media-during-the-arab-spring/> [Accessed 22 May 2012]

Hudson, B., 2003. *Justice in the Risk Society.* London: Sage.

Hunton, P. 2009. The growing phenomenon of crime and the Internet: A cybercrime execution and analysis model, *Computer Law & Security Review*, 25(6), pp. 528–35.

Hunton, P., 2012. Data attack of the cybercriminal: Investigating the digital currency of cybercrime, *Computer Law & Security Review*, 28(2), pp. 201–7.

Husain, M.I. and Sridhar, R., 2010. *iForensics: Forensic Analysis of Instant Messaging on Smart Phones.* [online] Available at: <http://books.google.co.uk/books?id=fb5F6LGz9_sC&pg=PA9&dq=Forensics:+Forensic+Analy

sis+of+Instant+Messaging+on+Smartphones+husain&hl=en&sa=X&ei=LR ZPUde0K9Oa1AWkvoCgCg&sqi=2&ved=0CDoQ6AEwAA> [Accessed 24 March 2013].

Innes, M. and Sheptychi, J., 2004. From detection to disruption: Intelligence and the changing logic of police control in the United Kingdom, *International Criminal Justice Review*, 14, pp. 1–24.

Interpol, 2012. *Overview.* [online] Available at: <http://www.interpol.int/About-INTERPOL/Overview> [Accessed 17 August 2012].

Interpol, 2013. *Cybercrime.* [online] Available at: <https://secure.interpol.int/Public/ICPO/FactSheets/FHT02.pdf> [Accessed 25 March 2013].

IOCE/G8, 2002. *Guidelines for Best Practice in the Forensic Examination of Digital Technology.* [online] Available at: <http://www.ioce.org/fileadmin/user_upload/2002/ioce_bp_exam_digit_tech.html>#Principles> [Accessed 25 March 2013].

IP-Adress.com, 2004. *IP Address | IP Address Tracer | IP-Adress.com.* [online] Available at: <http://www.ip-adress.com/ip_tracer/> [Accessed 3 February 2012].

ISO, 2005. ISO/IEC 17025:2005 – General requirements for the competence of testing and calibration laboratories, *International Standards Organisation*, [online] Available at: <http://www.iso.org/iso/catalogue_detail.htm?csnumber=39883> [Accessed 11 March 2011].

ISO, 2012a. *Guilty or not? New ISO/IEC standard for credible digital evidence.* [online] Available at: <http://www.iso.org/iso/home/news_index/news_archive/news.htm?refid=Ref1677>

ISO, 2012b. *Information technology — Security techniques — Guidelines for identification, collection, acquisition, and preservation of digital evidence* ISO/IEC

IWF, 2012. *IWF International Trends 2011.* [online] Available at: <http://www.iwf.org.uk/resources/trends> [Accessed 25 March 2013].

IWF, 2013a. *Current Members.* [online] Available at: <http://www.iwf.org.uk/members/current-members> [Accessed 25 March 2013].

IWF, 2013b. *European Union and UK Safer Internet Programme Partners.* [online] Available at: <http://www.iwf.org.uk/partnerships/eu-consortium> [Accessed 25 March 2013].

Jaishankar, K., 2008. Space Transition Theory of Cyber Crimes. In: F. Schmallager, and M. Pittaro, eds. *Crimes of the Internet.* Upper Saddle River, NJ: Prentice Hall. pp. 283–301.

Jansen, W. and Ayers, R., 2007. *Guidelines on Cell Phone Forensics Recommendations of the National Institute of Standards and Technology.* [online] Available at: <http://csrc.nist.gov/publications/nistpubs/800-101/SP800-101.pdf> [Accessed 25 March 2013].

Jewkes, Y. and Andrews, C., 2007. Killed by the internet: cyber homicides, cyber suicides and cyber sex crimes, In: Y. Jewkes, ed. *Crime online.* Cullompton, UK: Willan Publishing. pp. 1–11.

Jian, G., 2010. *Strengthening international cooperation and joining hands in fighting against transnational cybercrime Ministry of Public Security, People's Republic of China.* [online] Available at: <http://www.china.org.cn/business/2010internetforum/2010-11/09/content_21306503.htm> [Accessed 25 March 2013].

Jones, A., Valli, C., and Dabibi, G., 2009. *The 2009 Analysis of Information Remaining on USB Storage Devices Offered for Sale on the Second Hand Market.* [online] Available at: <http://igneous.scis.ecu.edu.au/proceedings/2009/forensics/Jones_Valli_Dabibi.pdf> [Accessed 24 March 2013].

Jones, K.J., Bejtlich, R., and Rose, C.W., 2006. *Real Digital Forensics: Computer Security and Incident Response.* Upper Saddle River, NJ: Addison-Wesley.

Jones, A. and Valli C., 2008. *Building a Digital Forensic Laboratory: Establishing and Managing a Successful Facility,* Oxford: Butterworth Heinemann.

Karatgozianni, A., 2010. Blame it on the Russians: Tracking the portrayal of Russian hackers during cyber conflict incidents, *Digital Icons: Studies in Russian, Eurasian and Central European New Media,* 4, pp. 127–50.

Kaye, L., 2012. *Why we are Breaking the Pirate Bay Ban.* [online] Available at: <http://www.guardian.co.uk/commentisfree/2012/jul/11/pirate-bay-ban> [Accessed 25 March 2013].

Keierleber, J.A. and Bohan, T.L., 2005. Ten years after Daubert, the status of the States, *Journal of Forensic Sciences,* 50(5), pp. 1154–63.

Kerr, O.S., 2003. Cybercrime's scope: Interpreting access and authorization in computer misuse statutes. *NYUL Rev.,* 78, pp. 1596–668.

Kigerl, A., 2012. Routine activity theory and the determinants of high cybercrime countries *Social Science Computer Review,* 30(4), pp. 470–86.

King, C. and Vidas, T., 2011. Empirical analysis of solid state disk data retention when used with contemporary operating systems. *Digital Investigation,* 8, S111–S117.

Kleinman, Z., 2013. *Has chip and pin had its day?* [online] Available at: <http://www.bbc.co.uk/news/technology-21085738> [Accessed 25 March 2013].

Kleinwächter, 2013. *Internet Governance Outlook 2013: "Cold Internet War" or "Peaceful Internet Coexistence"?* [online] Available at: <http://www.circleid.com/posts/20130103_internet_governance_outlook_2013/> [Accessed 8 March 2013].

Knetzger, M. and Muraski, J., 2008. *Investigating High-Tech Crime.* Upper Saddle River, NJ: Pearson.

Kolata, G., 2001. *Veiled Messages of Terror May Lurk in Cyberspace,* [online] Available at: <http://www.nytimes.com/2001/10/30/science/veiled-messages-of-terror-may-lurk-in-cyberspace.html>?pagewanted=all> [Accessed 25 March 2013].

Kornblum, J., 2007. Using every part of the buffalo in Windows memory analysis, *Digital Investigation,* 4(1), pp. 24–9.

Krohn, M., Lizotte, G. and Jeffrey, A., 2009. *Handbook on Crime and Deviance.* Springer: London.

Kshetri, N., 2005. Pattern of global cyber war and crime: A conceptual framework, *Journal of International Management*, 11, pp. 541–62.

Laidlaw, E., 2012. The responsibilities of free speech regulators: An analysis of the Internet Watch Foundation, *International Journal of Law and IT*, 20(4), pp. 312–45.

Lakhani, A., 2003. *Deception techniques using Honeypots.* MSc Thesis, Royal Holloway, University of London.

Lapidot-Lefler, N. and Barak, A., 2012. Effects of anonymity, invisibility, and lack of eye-contact on toxic online disinhibition, *Computers in Human Behavior*, 28, pp. 434–43.

Las Vegas Sun, 2012. *More than $2.8 million seized in Las Vegas as part of gambling probe.* [online] Available at: <http://www.lasvegassun.com/news/2012/oct/25/25-arrested-alleged-nationwide-illegal-sports-bett/>

Laskar, S. and Hermachandran, K., 2012. High capacity data hiding using LSB steganography and encryption, *International Journal of Database Management*, 4(6), pp. 57–68.

Law Commission, 1989. *Criminal Law: Computer Misuse* (Law Com. No. 186), Cm 819, HMSO, 1989. National Audit Office

Lee, A.F., Li, N.-C., Lamade, R., Schuler, A., and Prentky, R.A., 2012, April 16). Predicting hands-on child sexual offenses among possessors of internet child pornography, *Psychology, Public Policy, and Law*. Advance online publication. doi: 10.1037/a0027517

Lewis, S. and Lewis, D., 2011. Digitalizing crime prevention theories: How technology affects victim and offender behavior, *International Journal of Criminology and Sociological Theory*, 4(2), pp. 756–69.

Libicki, M., 2009. *Cyberdeterrence and Cyberwar.* [online] Available at: <http://www.rand.org/content/dam/rand/pubs/monographs/2009/RAND_MG877.pdf> [Accessed 25 March 2013].

Livingstone, S. and Haddon, L., 2009. *EU Kids online: Final report.* LSE, London: EU Kids online.

Logicube, 2011. *Logicube.com, hard drive duplication, copying hard drives & computer forensics*, [online] Available at: <http://www.logicubeforensics.com/> [Accessed 9 November 2011].

Lovet, G., 2009. Fighting cybercrime: technical, juridical, and ethical challenges, *Virus Bulletin 2009*. [online] Available at: <http://www.fortiguard.com/sites/default/files/VB2009_Fighting_Cybercrime_-_Technical%2CJuridical_and_Ethical_Challenges.pdf> [Accessed 25 March 2013].

McCarthy, J., 2010. Internet sexual activity: A comparison between contact and non-contact child pornography offenders, *Journal of Sexual Aggression*, 16(2), pp. 181–95.

McClain, F., 2011. *Dropbox Forensics.* [online] Available at: <http://www.forensicfocus.com/dropbox-forensics>

MacEwan, N.F., 2008. The Computer Misuse Act 1990: Lessons from its past and predictions for its future, *Criminal Law Review*, 12, pp. 955–67.

McGuire, M., 2007. *Hypercrime: The New Geometry of Harm.* Abingdon, Oxford: Routledge-Cavendish.

Mac Sithigh, D., 2009. Law in the last mile: Sharing internet access through wifi, *Communication Law & Policy*, 231, p. 274.

Maguire, M., Morgan, R. and Reiner, R., eds. 2002. *The Oxford Handbook of Criminology*, 3rd edn. Oxford: Oxford University Press.

Maimon, D., Kamerdze, A., Cukier, M. and Sobesto, B., 2013. Daily trends and origin of computer-focused crimes against a large university computer network An Application of the Routine-Activities and Lifestyle Perspective, *British Journal of Criminology*, 53, pp. 319–43

Malleson, N., Evans, A. and Jenkins, T., 2009. An agent-based model of burglary, *Environment and Planning B: Planning and Design*, 36(6), pp. 1103–23.

Mangham, G., 2012. *The Facebook Hack - what really Happened.* [online] Available at: <http://gmangham.blogspot.co.uk/2012/04/facebook-hack-what-really-happened.html> [Accessed 25 March 2013].

Marion, N., 2010. The Council of Europe's Cyber Crime Treaty: An exercise in symbolic legislation, *International Journal of Cyber Criminology*, 4(1&2).

Marsden, C.T., 2011. *Internet Co-Regulation: European Law, Regulatory Governance and Legitimacy in Cyberspace.* Cambridge: Cambridge University Press.

Marshall, A., 2008. *Digital Forensic.* Chichester: Wiley.

Marshall, L., O'Brien, M., Marshall, W., Booth, B., and Davis, A., 2012. Obsessive-compulsive disorder, social phobia, and loneliness in incarcerated internet child pornography offenders, *Sexual Addiction & Compulsivity: The Journal of Treatment & Prevention*, 19(1–2), pp. 41–52.

Mason, S. and George, E., 2011. Digital evidence and 'cloud' computing, *Computer Law & Security review*, 27, pp. 524–28.

Mattice, L., 2012. Measuring the Wild West Risks of Cyber Crime, *Security Magazine*, [online] Available at: <http://www.securitymagazine.com/articles/83545-measuring-the-wild-west-risks-of-cyber-crime>

Metropolitan Police Authority, 2009. *Appendix 1 Examples of MPS e-Crime Cases Example 5* [online] Available at: <http://www.mpa.gov.uk/downloads/committees/mpa/070125-10-appendix01.pdf> [Accessed 25 March 2009].

Microsoft, 2013a. *Microsoft Digital Crimes Unit.* [online] Available at: <http://www.microsoft.com/government/ww/safety-defense/initiatives/pages/digital-crimes-unit.aspx> [Accessed 25 March 2012]

Microsoft, 2013b. *Microsoft's digital crimes and Internet piracy unit combine forces, hello Cybercrime Center.* [online] Available at: <http://www.winbeta.org/news/microsofts-digital-crimes-and-internet-piracy-unit-combine-forces-hello-cybercrime-center> [Accessed 25 March 2012]

Microsoft, 2013c. *Law Enforcements Requests Report.* [online] Available at: <http://download.microsoft.com/download/F/3/8/F38AF681-EB3A-4645-A9C4-D4F31B8BA8F2/MSFT_Reporting_Data.pdf> [Accessed 25 March 2012]

Microsoft, 2013d. *2012 Law Enforcement Requests Report*. [online] Available at: <http://www.microsoft.com/about/corporatecitizenship/en-us/reporting/transparency/#FAQs1> [Accessed 25 March 2012]

Miller, M., 2004. *Metasploit's Meterpreter*. [online] Available at: <www.exploit-db.com/download_pdf/15948/>. [Accessed 25 March 2012]

Mitchell, S., 2010. *Spy tool highlights Android app store security issues*. [online] Available at: <http://www.pcpro.co.uk/news/security/360370/spy-tool-highlights-android-app-store-security-issues> [Accessed 25 March 2012]

Mitchell, S., 2012. *Anger Over Mass Web Surveillance Plans*. [online] Available at <http://www.pcpro.co.uk/news/security/372985/anger-over-mass-web-surveillance-plans>. [Accessed 25 March 2012]

Molloy, I. and Li, N., 2011. Attack on the GridCode one-time password, *Proceedings of the 6th ACM Symposium on Information, Computer and Communications Security*, 2011.

Moody, G., 2012. *Digital Economy Act: Respond Or Repeal?* [online] Available at: <http://blogs.computerworlduk.com/open-enterprise/2012/07/digital-economy-act-initial-obligations-code-consultation/index.htm>. [Accessed 25 March 2012]

Moore, R., 2011. *Cybercrime: Investigating High-Technology Computer Crime*. Cincinnati: Anderson Publishing.

Morgan, T.D., 2008. Recovering deleted data from the Windows registry, *Digital Investigation*, 5, pp. S33–S41.

Mueller, M.L., 2010. *Networks and States: The Global Politics of Internet Governance*. Cambridge, MA: MIT Press.

Murdoch, S. and Anderson, R., 2010. Verified by Visa and Mastercard Securecode: Or, how not to design authentication. *Financial Cryptography and Data Security*, 2010, pp. 336–42.

Natarajan, R., 2011. *Password Vs Passphrase: Here's 5 Reasons to Use Passphrase*. [online] Available at: <http://www.passworddragon.com/password-vs-passphrase>

National Institute of Justice, 2004. *Forensic Examination of Digital Evidence: A Guide for Law Enforcement*. [online] Available at: <http://www.nij.gov/pubs-sum/199408.htm> [Accessed 3 February 2012].

NATO, 2011. *NATO Cooperative Cyber Defence Centre of Excellence*. [online] Available at: <https://www.ccdcoe.org/> [Accessed 25 March 2012]

NATO, 2013. *Focus areas*. [online] Available at: <https://www.ccdcoe.org/37.html> [Accessed 25 March 2012]

netmarketshare.com, 2011. *OS market share news*. [online] Available at: <http://www.netmarketshare.com/os-market-share.aspx?qprid=9 > [Accessed 29 May 2011].

Newburn, T., 2007. *Criminology*. Cullompton, UK: Willan Publishing.

Newman, G. and Clarke, R., 2003. *Superhighway Robbery: Preventing E-commerce Crime*. Portland, OR: Willan Publishing.

Nikkel, B.J. (2005) Generalizing sources of live network evidence. *Digital Investigation*, 2(3), pp. 193–200.

Nirsoft, 2001. NirSoft - freeware utilities: password recovery, system utilities, desktop utilities. Available at: <http://www.nirsoft.net/ [Accessed 3 February 2012].

NIST, 1994. *Security Standards for Cryptographic modules.* [online] Available at: <http://csrc.nist.gov/publications/fips/fips1401.htm > [Accessed 25 March 2012]

Niveau, G., 2010. Brief Communication Cyber-pedocriminality: Characteristics of a sample of internet child pornography offenders, *Child Abuse & Neglect*, 34, pp. 570–75.

Nola, R. and Sankey, H., 2000. *A Selective Survey of Theories of Scientific Method. After Popper, Kuhn and Feyerabend*, Dordrecht; Kluwer. pp. 1–65.

Ó Ciardhuáin, S., 2004. An extended model of cybercrime investigations, *International Journal of Digital Evidence*, 3(1), pp. 1–22.

OCZ, 2013. *SSDs – A look inside.* [online] Available at: <http://www.ocztechnologyforum.com/staff/praz/download/ssd/ssd_1.pdf>

Office for National Statistics, 2012. *Statistical bulletin: Internet Access – Households and Individuals, 2012.* [online] Available at: <http://www.ons.gov.uk/ons/rel/rdit2/internet-access---households-and-individuals/2012/stb-internet-access--households-and-individuals--2012.html>

Office of the Attorney General of Texas, 2012. *Criminal Investigations.* [online] Available at: <https://www.oag.state.tx.us/criminal/investigation.shtml>

O'Floinn, M. and Ormerod, D. 2011. Social networking sites, RIPA and criminal investigations, *Criminal Law Review*, 10, pp. 766–89.

Olson, A.R. and Langlois, D.J., 2008. *Solid state drives data reliability and lifetime.* (Imation White Paper) [online] Available at: <cs.umbc.edu/~squire/images/ssd1.pdf> [Accessed 25 March 2013].

Osborn, J., Elliott, I.A., Middleton, D. and Beech, A.R., 2010. The use of actuarial risk assessment measures with UK internet child pornography offenders, *Journal of Aggression, Conflict and Peace Research.* 2(3), pp. 16–24.

OST, S., 2009. *Child Pornography and Sexual Grooming: Legal and Societal Responses.* Cambridge: Cambridge University Press.

Ou, G., 2005. *Why the computing world chose PKI.* [online] Available at: <http://www.zdnet.com/blog/ou/why-the-computing-world-chose-pki/89> [Accessed 25 March 2013].

Owen, P. and Thomas, P., 2011. An analysis of digital forensic examinations: Mobile devices versus hard disk drives utilising ACPO & NIST guidelines, *Digital Investigation*, 8(2), pp. 135–40.

Pal, A. and Memon, N., 2009. The evolution of file carving: The benefits and problems of forensics recovery, *IEEE Signal Processing Magazine*, 26(2), pp. 59–71.

Palmer, G., ed., 2001. *A Road Map for Digital Forensic Research: Report from the First Digital Forensic Workshop, 7–8 August 2001*. [online] Available at: <http://www.dfrws.org/dfrws-rm-final.pdf> [Accessed 30 June 2004]

Park, B., Park, J. and Lee, S., 2009, Data concealment and detection in Microsoft Office 2007 files, *Digital Investigation*, 5(3–4), pp. 104–14.

Parliamentary Office of Science and Technology, 2006. *postnote, October 2006, Number 271, Computer Crime*. [online] Available at: <http://www.parliament. uk/documents/post/postpn271.pdf> [Accessed 6 August 2012].

Patton, J. and Stanford, M., 2012. Psychology of Impulsivity. In: J. Grant and M. Potenza, eds. *The Oxford Handbook of Impulse Control Disorders*. Oxford: Oxford University Press.

Reich, P.C., Weinstein, S., Wild, C. and Cabanlong, A.S., 2010. Cyber warfare: A review of theories, law, policies, actual incidents – and the dilemma of anonymity, *European Journal of Law and Technology*, 1(2).

PceU, 2009. *Computer Crime Team*. [online] Available at: <http://www.met. police.uk/pceu/computer_crime_team.html> [Accessed 25 March 2009].

PCeU, 2012. *PCeU – Police Central e-crime Unit*. [online] Available at: <http:// www.met.police.uk/pceu/index.htm> [Accessed 17 August 2012].

PCeU, n.d.. *PCeU – Police Central e-Crime Unit*. [online] Available at: <http:// www.met.police.uk/pceu/remit_and_exclusions.html> [Accessed 7 July 2011].

Pfleeger, C.P. and Pfleeger, S.L., 2007. *Security in Computing*, 4th edn. Upper Saddle River, NJ: Prentice Hall.

Pratt, T., Holtfreter, K. and. Reisig, M., 2010. Routine online activity and internet fraud targeting: Extending the generality of Routine Activity Theory, *Journal of Research in Crime and Delinquency*, 47(3), pp. 267–96.

Prichard, J., Watters, P. and Spiranovic, C. (2011) Internet subcultures and pathways to the use of child pornography, *Computer Law and Security Review*, 27(6), pp. 585–600

Quayle, E., 2012. Pedophilia, child porn, and cyberpredators, In C. Bryant, ed. *The Routledge Handbook of Deviant Behaviour*, pp. 390–96.

Quayle, E. and Jones, T., 2011. Sexualized images of children on the Internet, *Sexual Abuse: Journal of Research and Treatment*, 23(1), pp. 7–21.

Reid, R., 2012. *The $8 billion iPod*. [online] Available at: <http://www.youtube. com/watch?v=GZadCj8O1-0> [Accessed 6 August 2012].

Reijnen, L., Bulten, E. and Nijman, H., 2009. Demographic and personality characteristics of internet child pornography downloader's in comparison to other offenders, *Journal of Child Sexual Abuse: Research, Treatment, & Program Innovations for Victims, Survivors, & Offenders*, 18(6), pp. 611–22.

Reith, M., Carr, C. and Gunsch, G., 2002. An Examination of Digital Forensic Models, *International Journal of Digital Evidence*, [online] Available at: http://www.ijde.org/docs/02_fall_art2.html [Accessed 30 June 2004].

Reyes, A., O'Shea, K., Steele, J., Hansen, J.R., Jean B.R. and Ralph, T., 2007. *Cyber Crime Investigations: Bridging the Gaps between Security Professionals, Law Enforcement, and Prosecutors*. Rockland, MA: Syngress.

Reyns, B., Henson, B. and Fisher, B., 2011. Being pursued online: Applying cyberlifestyle-routine activities theory to cyberstalking victimisation, *Criminal Justice and Behaviour*, 38, pp. 1149–69.

Richard III, G.G. and Roussev, V., 2004. Breaking the performance wall: The case for distributed digital forensics, *Proceedings of the 2004 digital forensics research workshop*, Baltimore, Maryland, 11–13 August 2004.

Rogers, M., Goldman, J., Mislan, R., Wedge, T. and Debrota, S., 2006. computer forensic field triage process model, *Journal of Digital Forensics, Security and Law*, 1(2), pp. 19–38.

Rogers, M., 2005. *Anti-Forensics*, [online] Available at: <http://www.cyberforensics. purdue.edu/documents/AntiForensics_LockheedMartin09152005.pdf> [Accessed 25 March 2013].

Ruff, N., 2008. Windows memory forensics, *Journal in Computer Virology*, 4(2), pp. 83–100.

Rushe, D., 2012. *The online Copyright War: The Day the Internet Hit Back at Big Media*. [online] Available at: <http://www.guardian.co.uk/technology/2012/ apr/18/online-copyright-war-internet-hit-back?INTCMP=SRCH>.

Said, E., 1979. *Orientalism*. New York: Knopf Doubleday Publishing Group.

Sammes, T. and Jenkinson, B., 2007. *Forensic Computing: A Practitioner's Guide*, 2nd edn. New York: Springer-Verlag Inc.

Sandywell, B., 2010. On the globalisation of crime: The Internet and new criminality. In: Y. Jewkes and M. Yar, eds. *Handbook of Internet Crime*. Cullompton, UK: Willan Publishing, pp. 38–66.

Savoldi, A. and Gubian, P., 2008. Towards the virtual memory space reconstruction for Windows live forensic purposes. In: SADFE, *Third International Workshop on Systematic Approaches to Digital Forensic Engineering, 2008*. Berkeley, California, USA, 22 May 2008, pp. 15–22.

Schneier, B., 1996. *Applied Cryptography*, 2nd edn. Chichester: John Wiley & Sons.

Schneier, B., 2000. *Secrets and Lies: Digital Security in a Networked World*. Chichester: John Wiley & Sons.

Schneier, B., 2005. *Schneier on Security*. [online] Available at: <http://www. schneier.com/blog/archives/2005/06/write_down_your.html> [Accessed 9 November 2012].

Schneier, B., 2008. *Passwords Are Not Broken, but How We Choose them Sure Is*. [online] Available at: <http://www.schneier.com/essay-246.html> [Accessed 9 November 2012].

Schneier, B. (2010) *Changing Passwords*. [online] Available at: <http://www. schneier.com/blog/archives/2010/11/changing_passwo.html> [Accessed 25 March 2013].

Segel, L., 2008. *Criminology: The Core*, 4th edn. Stamford, CT: Wadsworth Cengage Learning.

SETI, 2012. *SETILive*. [online] Available at: <http://setilive.org/>.[Accessed 25 March 2013].

Sharif, M., Lanzi, A and Giffin, J., 2009. Automatic Reverse Engineering of Malware Emulators. In: *Proceedings of the IEEE Symposium on Security and Privacy*, Hong Kong, Hong Kong, 22–24 March 2011.

Sheldon, B., 2006. Printing in forensic analysis of Windows systems. In: E. Casey, ed., *Handbook of Computer Crime Investigation: Forensic Tools and Technology*, Elsevier, London, pp. 161–4.

Sheward, M., 2012. *Rock Solid: Will Digital Forensics Crack SSD's?* [online] Available at: <http://resources.infosecinstitute.com/ssd-forensics/> [Accessed 25 March 2013].

Siegfried, K.C., Lovely, R.L. and Rogers, M., 2008. Self-reported online child pornography behavior: A psychological analysis, *International Journal of Cyber Criminology*, 2(1), pp. 286–97.

Simon, M. and Slay, J., 2009. *Enhancement of Forensic Computing Investigations through Memory Forensic Techniques*. [online] Available at: <http://www-scopus-com.libezproxy.open.ac.uk/citation/export.url?origin=recordpage&sid=&src=s&stateKey=OFD_133815393&eid=2-s2.0-70349687555&sort=&linkClicked=&exportFormat=TEXT&view=FullDocument&selectedCitationInformationItemsAll=on&selectedCitationInformationItems=Author%28s%29&selectedCitationInformationItems=Document+title&selectedCitationInformationItems=Year&selectedCitationInformationItems=Source+title&selectedCitationInformationItems=Volume%2C+Issue%2C+Pages&selectedCitationInformationItems=Citation+count&selectedCitationInformationItems=Source+and+Document+Type> [Accessed 21 January 2011].

Skype, 2013. *Does Skype use encryption?* [online] Available at: <https://support.skype.com/en/faq/FA31/does-skype-use-encryption> [Accessed 25 March 2013].

Smith, B., 2013. *Microsoft Releases 2012 Law Enforcement Requests Report*. [online] Available at: <http://blogs.technet.com/b/microsoft_on_the_issues/archive/2013/03/21/microsoft-releases-2012-law-enforcement-requests-report.aspx> [Accessed 25 March 2013].

Smith, R., 2007. Biometric solutions to identity-related crime. In: Y. Jewkes, ed. 2007. *Crime online*. Cullompton, UK: Willan, pp. 44–59.

Smith, R.E., 2002. *Authentication: From Passwords to Public Keys*. Upper Saddle River, NJ: Addison-Wesley.

Snort, 2013. *Snort*. [online] Available at: <http://www.snort.org>. [Accessed 25 March 2013]

Snow, G., 2011. *Statement Before the Senate Judiciary Committee, Subcommittee on Crime and Terrorism*, [online] Available at: <http://www.fbi.gov/news/testimony/cybersecurity-responding-to-the-threat-of-cyber-crime-and-terrorism> [Accessed 25 March 2013].

Solomon, M.G. and Chapple, M., 2005. *Information Security Illuminated*. Sudbury, MA: Jones & Bartlett Learning.

Sommer, P., 2006. Criminalising hacking tools, *Digital Investigation*, 3(2), pp. 68–72.

Sommer, P., 2010. Forensic science standards in fast-changing environments, *Science & Justice*, 50(1), pp. 12–17.

Sommer, P., 2012. *Written evidence submitted by Professor Peter Sommer [EC 14] Home Affairs Committee: Written evidence e-Crime*. [online] Available at: <http://www.parliament.uk/documents/commons-committees/home-affairs/120828%20eCrime%20evidence.pdf> [Accessed 25 March 2013].

SplashData, 2012. *Worst Passwords of 2012 — and How to Fix Them*. [online] available at: <http://splashdata.com/press/PR121023.htm> [Accessed 25 March 2013].

Squid, 2013. *Squid: Optimising Web Delivery*. [online] Available at: <http://www.squid-cache.org/> [Accessed 25 March 2013].

Squid Cache, 2007. *SquidFaq/SquidLogs – SquidWiki*. [online] Available at: <http://wiki.squid-cache.org/SquidFaq/SquidLogs> [Accessed 14 Nov 2007].

Stallings, W., 2010, *Cryptography and Network Security: Principles and Practice*, 5th edn. Upper Saddle River, NJ: Prentice Hall Press.

Sterling, B., 1992. *The Hacker Crackdown: Law and Disorder on the Electronic Frontier*. New York: Bantam

Strickland, P., 2012. *Insulting Words or Behaviour: Section 5 of the Public Order Act 1986*. London: House of Commons.

Suler, J., 2004. The online Disinhibition Effect, *Cyberpsychology & Behavior*, 7(3), pp. 321-326.

Suler, J., 2012. *The online Disinhibition Effect*. [online] Available at: <http://users.rider.edu/~suler/psycyber/disinhibit.html> [Accessed 25 March 2013]

Sumuri, 2011. *Sumuri - Forensics Simplified*. [online] Available at: <http://sumuri.com/index.php> [Accessed 9 November 2011].

Svantesson, D. and Clarke, R., 2010. *Privacy and consumer risks in cloud computing*, [online] Available at: <http://epublications.bond.edu.au/cgi/viewcontent.cgi?article=1346&context=law_pubs> [Accessed 25 March 2013].

Sykes, G. and Matza, D., 1957. Techniques of neutralization: A theory of delinquency, *American Sociological Review*, 22, pp. 664–70.

Symantec, 2012. *Press Release: 2012 Norton Study: Consumer Cybercrime Estimated at $110 Billion Annually*. [online] Available at: <http://www.symantec.com/about/news/release/article.jsp?prid=20120905_02> [Accessed 25 March 2013]

Tanenbaum, A.S., 2003. *Computer Networks*, 4th edn. Upper Saddle River, NJ: Prentice Hall PTR.

Taylor, M. and Quayle, E., 2003. *Child Pornography: An Internet Crime*. Hove: Brunner-Routledge.

Taylor, M., Haggerty, J., Gresty, D. and Hegarty, R., 2010. digital evidence in cloud computing systems, *Computer Law & Security Review*, 26(3), pp. 304–8.

Taylor, M., Haggerty, J., Gresty, D. and Berry, T., 2011. Digital evidence from peer-to-peer networks, *Computer Law & Security Review*, 27(6), pp. 647–52.

The Herald, 2011. *Pre-paid cards being used for money laundering scam*, [online] Available at: <http://www.heraldscotland.com/news/crime-courts/pre-paid-cards-being-used-for-money-laundering-scam.15608340> [Accessed 25 March 2013].

The Honeynet Project, 2004. *Know Your Enemy: Learning About Security Threats*, 2nd edn. Boston, MA: Addison-Wesley.

The Honeynet Project, 2012. *About The Honeynet Project*. [online] Available at: <http://www.honeynet.org/about> [Accessed 25 March 2013].

The Honeynet Project, 2013. *Projects*. [online] Available at: <http://www.honeynet.org/project> [Accessed 25 March 2013].

The Sunday Telegraph, 2010. *Police chief warns of rise in cyber crime*. [online] Available at: <http://www.telegraph.co.uk/technology/news/8038736/Police-chief-warns-of-rise-in-cyber-crime.html> [Accessed 17 August 2012].

Townsend, P., 2012. *Who I Am*. Glasgow: Harper Collins.

Travis, A., 2012. *Gary McKinnon Extradition Case Reviewed at High Court*. [online] Available at: <http://www.guardian.co.uk/world/2012/jul/24/gary-mckinnon-extradition-review-hacker> [Accessed 25 March 2013].

Treadwell, J., 2012. From the car boot to booting it up? eBay, online counterfeit crime and the transformation of the criminal marketplace, *Criminology and Criminal Justice*, 12(2), pp. 175–91.

TrendMicro, 2012. *The True face of the Android threat*. [online] Available at: <http://www.trendmicro.co.uk/newsroom/pr/the-true-face-of-the-android-threat/> [Accessed 25 March 2013].

Urbas, 2010. Protecting children from online predators: The use of covert investigation techniques by law enforcement, *Journal of Contemporary Criminal Justice*, 26(4), pp. 410–25.

Vacca, J.R., 2009. *Computer and Information Security Handbook*. Waltham, MA: Morgan Kaufmann.

Van Dijk, J., 2012. *The Network Society*, 3rd edn. London: Sage Publications Ltd.

Van Dongen, W.S., 2007. Forensic artefacts left by Windows Live Messenger 8.0, *Digital Investigation*, 4(2), pp. 73–87.

van Tassel, D., 1970. *Computer Crime*, In: Proceedings of the November 17–19, 1970, fall joint computer conference. Houston, Texas, 17–19 November 1970.

van Wilsem, J., 2011. Worlds tied together? Online and non-domestic routine activities and their impact on digital and traditional threat victimization, *European Journal of Criminology*, 8(2), pp. 115–27.

VGT, 2013. *Who we are*. [online] Available at: <http://www.virtualglobaltaskforce.com/who-we-are/> [Accessed 25 March 2013].

Volatile Systems, 2007. *Volatility*. [online] Available at: <https://www.volatilesystems.com/> [Accessed 3 February 2012].

Voss, A., Vander Meer, E. and Fergusson, D., 2009. *Research in a Connected World*. [online] Available at: <http://cnx.org/content/m20834/1.3/> [Accessed 25 March 2013].

Wade, C., Aldridge, J. and Hopper, L., 2011. Hacking into the hacker: Separating fact from fiction. In: T. Holt, ed. *Crime online Correlates, Causes, and Context*, 2nd edn. Durham, NC: Carolina Academic Press.

Wakefield, J., 2005. *Wireless Hijacking under Scrutiny*, [online] Available at: <http://news.bbc.co.uk/1/hi/technology/4721723.stm>.[Accessed 25 March 2013].

Walden, I., 2007. *Computer Crimes and Digital Investigations*. Oxford: Oxford University Press, Inc.

Walker, C., 2009. Data retention in the UK: Pragmatic and proportionate, or a step too far? *Computer Law & Security Review*, 25(4), pp. 325–34.

Walker, S., 2012. Economics and the cyber-challenge, *Information Security Technical Report*, 17, pp. 9–18.

Wall, D., 2001. Cybercrimes and the Internet. In: D. Wall, ed., *Crime and the Internet*. New York: Routledge. pp. 1–17.

Wall, D., 2004. What are cybercrimes? *Criminal Justice Matters*, 58, pp. 20–21.

Wall, D., 2007. *Cybercrime*. Cambridge: Polity Press.

Wall, D., 2010. *Policing Cybercrimes: responding to the transnational challenges of cybercrime* (presentation to Dartmouth College, Institute for Security, Technology and Society) [online] Available at: <http://www.ists.dartmouth.edu/docs/davidwallpresentation.pdf>

Wall, D., 2013. Future Identities: Changing identities in the UK – the next 10 years DR 20: The Future Challenges of Identity Crime in the UK In *Foresight Future Identities, 2013. Future Identities Changing identities in the UK the next 10 years Final Project Report*. London: The Government Office for Science.

Wall, D. and Yar, M., 2009. Intellectual property crime and the Internet: Cyber-piracy and 'stealing' informational intangibles. In: Y. Jewkes and M. Yar, eds. *The Handbook of Internet Crime and Criminal Justice*. Cullompton, UK: Willan.

Wallisch, P., 2009. *Meterpreter: Be Afraid | HBGary. HBGary - Phil's blog.* [online] Available at: <https://www.hbgary.com/phils-blog/meterpreter-be-afraid/ > [Accessed 1 February 2011].

Walters, A.A., 2006. FATKit: detecting malicious library injection and upping the "'anti'." Technicalreport. 4TFResearch Laboratories.

Walters, A. and Petroni Jr, N.L., 2007. *Volatools: Integrating volatile memory forensics into the Digital Investigation process*, [online] Available at: <http://www.blackhat.com/presentations/bh-dc-07/Walters/Paper/bh-dc-07-Walters-WP.pdf> [Accessed 25 March 2013].

Ward, T., and Hudson, S.M., 1998. The construction and development of theory in the sexual offending area: A meta-theoretical framework, *Sexual Abuse: A Journal of Research and Treatment*, 10, pp. 47–63.

Ward, T. and Hudson, S.M., 2000. A Self-regulation model of relapse prevention. In: D.R. Laws, S.M. Hudson and T. Ward, eds. *Remaking Relapse Prevention with Sex Offenders: A Sourcebook*. Thousand Oaks, CA: Sage, pp. 79–101.

Ward, T., Bickley, J., Webster, S.D., Fisher, D., Beech, A. and Eldridge, H., 2004. *The Self-regulation Model of the Offense and Relapse Process: A Manual: Volume I: Assessment*. Victoria, BC: Pacific Psychological Assessment Corporation.

Whiteside, T., 1978. *Computer Capers: Tales of Electronic Thievery, Embezzlement, and Fraud*. New York: Crowell.

Wiles, P. and Costello, A., 2000. *The 'Road to Nowhere': The Evidence for Travelling Criminals*. Home Office Research Study 207. London: Home Office.

Willassen, S., 2008a. *Methods of Enhancement of Timestamp Evidence in Digital Investigations*. Doctoral thesis. Trondheim, January 2008 Norwegian University of Science and Technology, Faculty of Information Technology, Mathematics and Electrical Engineering, Department of Telematics.

Willassen, S., 2008b. Timestamp evidence correlation by model based clock hypothesis testing. In: (Institute for Computer Sciences, Social-Informatics and Telecommunications Engineering), *Proceedings of the 1st international conference on Forensic applications and techniques in telecommunications, information, and multimedia and workshop*. Adelaide, Australia, 21–23 January 2008, p. 15.

Willassen, S.Y., 2003. Forensics and the GSM Mobile Telephone System, *International Journal of Digital Evidence*, 2(1), pp. 1–17.

Wilson, A., 2010. The Law Commission's proposal on expert opinion evidence: An onerous demand upon judges. *Web Journal of Current Legal Issues*, 1, pp. 1–13.

WILSON, A. 2012. *The Law Commission's Recommendation on Expert Opinion Evidence: Sufficient Reliability?* [online] Available at: http://webjcli.ncl. ac.uk/2012/issue3/pdf/wilson3.pdf> [Accessed 25 March 2013].

Wilson, C., 2011. *Digital Evidence Discrepancies – Casey Anthony Trial*. [online] Available at: <http://wordpress.bladeforensics.com/?p=357> [Accessed 25 March 2013].

Witt, P.H., 2010. Assessment of risk in Internet child pornography cases, *Sex Offender Law Report*, 11(1), pp. 1, 4, 13–15.

Wolpe, T., 2010. *Early-adopter criminals embrace cloud computing*. [online] Available at: <http://www.zdnet.com/early-adopter-criminals-embrace-cloud-computing-3040035885/>

World Economic Forum, 2013. Interview with Rob Wainwright, Director of Europol [online] Available at: <http://www.weforum.org/content/what-if-internet-collapsed>

XKCD, 2013. *Password Strength*. [online] Available at: <https://xkcd.com/936/>

Yahoo, 2013. *Yahoo! Messenger for PC*. [online] Available at: <http://info.yahoo. com/privacy/us/yahoo/messenger/pc/details.html>

Yan, J. and El Ahmad, A.S., 2008. A Low-cost Attack on a Microsoft CAPTCHA. In: *Proceedings of the 15th ACM conference on Computer and communications security*, Alexandria, VA, USA – 27–31 October 2008, pp. 543–54.

Yar, M., 2005a. Computer hacking: Just another case of juvenile delinquency? *The Howard Journal*, 44(4), pp. 387–99.

Yar, M., 2005b. The novelty of 'cybercrime': An assessment in light of Routine Activity Theory, *European Journal of Criminology*, 2, pp. 407–27.

Yar, M., 2006. Teenage kicks or virtual villainy? Internet piracy, moral entrepreneurship, and the social construction of a crime problem. In: Y. Jewkes, ed. 2007. *Crime Online*. Collumpton, UK: Willan.

Yip, M. and Webber, C., 2013 (forthcoming). Trust among Cybercriminals? Carding Forums, Uncertainty and Implications for Policing, [in special issue: Policing Cybercrime] *Policing and Society*.

Yusoff, Y., Ismail, R. and Hassan, Z., 2011. Common phases of computer forensics investigation models, *International Journal of Computer Science & Information Technology*, 3(3), p. 17.

Zamoon, S. and Curley, S., 2008. Ripped from the headlines: What can the popular press teach us about software piracy? *Journal of Business Ethics*, 83(3), pp. 515–33.

ZDNet UK, 2002. *RIPA demands push up ISP costs*. [online] Available at: <http://www.zdnet.com/ripa-demands-push-up-isp-costs-3002118813/ > [Accessed 17 August 2012].

Index